New Madrid County, Missouri Marriage Records

1874-1881

Vol. #2

Transcribed & Compiled
by
Mary M. Brown and Fay Hedgepeth

Copyright 2005
By: Southern Historical Press, Inc.

All rights reserved. No part of this publication may be reproduced, stored in a retrieval system, transmitted in any form, posted on to the web in any form or by any means without the prior written permission of the publisher.

Please direct all correspondence and orders to:

www.southernhistoricalpress.com
or
SOUTHERN HISTORICAL PRESS, Inc.
PO BOX 1267
375 West Broad Street
Greenville, SC   29601
southernhistoricalpress@gmail.com

ISBN #0-89308-804-8

Printed in the United States of America

PREFACE

The marriage records in this book have been transcribed from Marriage Records on file in the office of the New Madrid County Recorder, New Madrid, Missouri. These marriages were taken exactly as shown on the record. It would be well to check all variations of the spelling of a name, not only beacuse these records were hard to read, but also because many of the Justices were evidently not too good at spelling

NEW MADRID COUNTY MISSOURI MARRIAGE RECORDS
1874-1881

John A. Mott, Recorder; Wm. W. Waters, Deputy
Page 1
Oct. 15, 1872 Wilson Cary Newsum to Elizabeth Imboden in the presence of R.J.Waters and Wm. Riley by Abel D. Cook, J.P.

Nov. 18, 1874 Arthur F. Eastwood of Caruthersville, Mo. to Mary Harriet Waters of New Madrid in the presence of Louis A. Waters, Jr., and William W. Waters Jr. by P.P.Brady, Catholic Priest.

Nov. 23, 1874 Luke Byrne Howard to Lena Dawson at the Catholic Church in presence of Louis A. Tickell and Henry C. Riley by P.P.Brady, Catholic Priest.

Page 2
Nov. 15, 1874 William L. Hunter to Irene C. Coker by Wm. J. Denhart, J.P.

Nov. 18, 1874 Nelson Davis to Susan A. Morris by Wm. J. Denhart, J.P.

Nov. 22, 1874 William W. Shultz to Mary J. Steed by Wm. J. Denhart, J.P.
Page 3
Nov. 22, 1874
Albert T. Neill to Anna Graham by Wm. J. Denhart, J.P.

Nov. 24, 1874 Jacob Wright to Mary E. Simms by Wm. J. Denhart,J.P.

Dec. 13, 1874 James M. Shanks to Mary F. Gray by Wm. J.Denhart,J.P.

Page 4
Dec. 24, 1874 William Dawson to Miss Ella A. Hunter by William McCarty.

Dec. 8, 1874 William Johnson to Ann Ranels (Reynolds on index) at C.M.E.Church by E.A.McKenney, in presence of John Randolph & Willis Marywether.
Dec. 10, 1874 Alfred Yates to Nallie Miner at house of Joseph McCoy in presence of Joseph McCoy and Anna McCoy by L.B.McDaniels, Minister
Page 5
Nov. 26, 1874 William Y. Harper to Malinda Jane Reed at Big Prairie Township by Wm. Stringfield, J.P.

December 24, 1874 Samuel Allen to Elizabeth Stallcup at Big Prairie Township by Wm. Stringfield, J.P.

Dec. 27, 1874 David Powers to Sarah Francis Ray at Big Prairie Twp. by Wm. Stringfield, J.P.

NEW MADRID COUNTY MISSOURI MARRIAGE RECORDS
1874-1881

Page 6

November 18, 1874 Benj. C. Adkins to Sallie Anne Howe at Lessieur Township by Robert LaFont, Co. Court Justice.

December 17, 1874 William A. Tyrart to Mary Oliver by Ambrose Keith, J.P.

Feb. 25, 1875 Joseph Barnes to Martha Robertson at David Neal's by Daniel N. Neill.

Page 7
March 14, 1875 Elisha Barnes to Sarah E. Jones by Joel Cook, J.P.

Jan. 28, 1875 H. Richey to Mary Kane by Wm. J. Denton, J.P.

March 18, 1875 Robert G. Hodge to Sarah E. Strong by Wm. J. Denhart, J.P.

Page 8
Jan. 6, 1875 George Stewart to Sarah Price by A. Keith, J.P.

Jan. 21, 1875 James Rutherford to Permelia Ann Oliver by A. Keith, J.P.

Jan. 17, 1875 John Sigars to Martha McAlister by Wesley F. Settles, J.P.

Page 9
May 25, 1875 Joseph Weigle to Prude Butler by Hy Willenbrink, C.P.

April 4, 1875 Thomas J. Burns to Elizabeth C. Kew by Wm.J.Denhart,J.P.

April 25, 1875 John Davis to America E. Steiman by Wm.J.Denhart,J.P.

Page 10
April 28, 1875 Daniel Fleming to Mary Donavan by Wm.J.Denhart,J.P.

May 20, 1875 Jacob Wright to Mary S.Q.Combs by Wm. J. Denhart

June 13, 1875 Thomas Knight to Mary Carney by Wm. J. Denhart

Page 11
May 16, 1875 Franklin Llewallyn to Amanda Catheran at John R. Drew's by Daniel N. Neill, J.P.

July 4, 1875 Harry McFarland to Sallie Johnson by Napoleon Frey, Minister G.   W.E.Sherwood, Deputy Clerk

June 27, 1875 Ephrian Scott to Elizabeth Huntsinger by Wm.J. Denhart, J.P.

NEW MADRID COUNTY MISSOURI MARRIAGE RECORDS
1874 - 1881

Page 12
July 7, 1875 George Corbett to Sarah Shultz b y Wm.J.Denhart,J.P.

Aug. 27, 1875 Charles Carlisle to Ada E. Dewen by Wm.J.Denhart,J.P.

May 2, 1875 John E. Mason to Minerva Love at my residence by Robert LaFont, Co. Court Justice.

Page 13
July 2, 1875 John Martin to Matilda Lett by Joseph Wood, Min. of the Gospel.

January 26, 1875 John W. Anderson of Lessieur Twp. to Mary Leferney of Lessieur Twp in the aforesaid twp. by Jas. M.Dockery, J.P. in presence of J.B.Dockery and Mrs. J.M.Dockery

June 18, 1875 Manuel Cutler to Florinda Pasquin by Jas. H. Howard, Justice Co. Court.

Page 14
July 18, 1875 George W. Head of Lessieur Twp. to Mary Lawrence of Lessieur Twp. at the twp. aforesaid by James M. Dockery, J.P. in presence of Newton Griffith and Louis Dark.

April 1, 1875 Rudolf Lamb of Lessieur Twp. to Eliza Louis of Lessieur Twp. in the Twp. aforesaid in presence of James Atkinson, Augustus Crevoisieur by James M. Dockery, J.P.

September 7, 1875 Eugene F. Mahone to Martha J. Williams by Wm. J.Denhart, J.P.

Page 15
July 18, 1875 William J. Ellis to Nancy A. Bascomb at Wm. R. Neill's in presence of Wm. R. Neill & wife, W.A.Anthony & others by David N. Neill, J.P.

July 18, 1875 James H. Cunningham to Rebecca Housele at Joseph Cunningham's in presence of Thomas Ward, Joseph Cunningham, Susan Settles, Sam Settles & others by Daniel N. Neill, J.P.

October 26, 1875 Joseph Christesten to Margaret A. Allison by Wm. J. Denhart,J.P.

Page 16
October 26, 1875 James W. Allison to Roena Smullins by Wm.J. Denhart, J.P.

November 6, 1875 Union Richardson to Amanda Hampton by Wm. J. Denhart, J.P.

August 15, 1875 Andrew Godair of Lessieur Twp. to Mary E. Nicholas of Lessieur Twp at said Twp. by Robert LaFont, Co.Court Justice

NEW MADRID COUNTY MISSOURI MARRIAGE RECORDS
1874-1881

Page 17
Sep. 26, 1875 Freeman L. Mason to Amanda Nanson at my residence by Robert Lafont, Co.Court Justice in presence of Alonzo Elliot, Charity Vanover.

August 31, 1875 Andrew Peevyhouse to Sarah E. Ling by James M. Dockery,J.P.

November 21, 1875 Robert S. McCary to Martha A. Stewart by Wm.J. Denhart,J.P.

Page 18
October 18, 1875 Charles Avery to Dalsey Louis by Joel Cook,J.P.

Sept. 31, 1875 George A. Reeves to Mary C. Carson at Wm. R. Carson's by Robt. Lafont, Co. Court Justice.

December 9, 1875 John Reeves to Sarah Coats at my residence by Robert Lafont, Co. Court Justice.

Page 19
Dec. 1, 1875 William F. Shanks to Vina Gray by Wm. J.Denhart,J.P.

Dec. 12, 1875 James P. Daniels to Mary E. Davis by Wm.J.Denhart,J.P.

December 30,1875 Andrew J. Smullon to Caroline Gross by Joel Cook,J.P.
Page 20
Dec. 27, 1875 Luther B. Delman to Mary Louiza Hatcher b y Henry Hanesworth, Minister

Dec. 30, 1875 John D. Timberman of Dunklin County to Emma Bishop of New Madrid Co. at Point Pleasant by Henry Hanesworth, Minister.

Jan. 3, 1876 William Thomas Brown to Nancy Ann Paxton by Ambrose Keith, J.P.

Page 21
Dec. 1, 1875 John H. Roper to Melissa J. Barnes by John J. Martin, Minister.

Jan. 5, 1876 Silas Knox to Polly Roungee by Wm.J.Denhart, J.P.

Jan. 6, 1876 Warren Bledsoe to Emily Townsend by Wm.J.Denhart,J.P.

Page 22   to
Jan. 11, 1876 Bowman Paxton of Portage Twp./Hellen B. Stewart of New Madrid Co. by A. Keith, J.P.

Feb. 22, 1876 Charles Nelson to Mary Martin by Rev. Hy Wellenbrink

Jan. 30, 1876 James Crawford to Elizabeth Jones at New Madrid Twp. by Wm. J. Denhart, J.P.

NEW MADRID COUNTY MISSOURI MARRIAGE RECORDS

Page 23
Jan. 23, 1876 Isiah Moore to Purcilla Slaws?y Cullin Downing, Min.

Feb. 16, 1876 Jefferson Woods to Bettie Bevins at Portage Twp. by A. Keith, J.P.

Feb. 14, 1876 Mark H. Stallcup to Miss Susan A. Gregory at Big Prairie Twp. in presence of H.A.Smith, Anna Sikes, Judge Handy & others by L.F.Aspley, Minister.

Page 24
March 27, 1876 John M.P. Stacy to Dicey Burks by Wm.J.Denhart,J.P.

March 28, ____ . Charles Forest to Catharine Mitchell by Wm. J. Denhart, J.P. Filed for record April 20, 1876.

Feb. 13, 1876 Raphael Lessieur Jr. to Clairemour Meatte in the presence of Edward Meatte and George Davis by Jas. M. Dockery, J.P.

Page 25
May 11, 1876 Benj. L. Shirkey to Elizabeth Watson by Wm. J. Denhart, J.P.

July 2, 1876 Augustus Godair to Christine Lessieur by Young Young, J.P.

June 14, 1876 Henry Judy to Mollie West by/Young John, J.P.

Page 26
April 23, 1876 J. F. Shelby to Caroline Hendrix by J. J. Presson, Minister.

May 11, 1876 John Ling to Elizabeth A. Swilley by Jas. M.Dockery,J.P.

Aug. 10, 1876 Murray Phillips to Miss Annie Howard by T.J.O. Morrison, J.P. in presence of Robert Parks, Henry C. Riley, L. F. Hunter, and others.

Page 27
April 6, 1876 Edward Crevisieur to Rebecca Dockery by Robt.Lafont, Co. Court Judge

May 12, 1876 William Laygrane to Nancy A. Mason by Robt. Lafont, Co. Court Justice.

July 24, 1876 John King to Margaret Carpenter by Jas. M.Dockery,,J.P.

NEW MADRID COUNTY, MISSOURI MARRIAGE RECORDS

Page 28
Sept. 3, 1876 William A. Willis to Mrs. Mary Jane Myers at the residence of said Willis by Rev. Ervin A. Ewing.

March 5, 1876 Daniel McKinnan to Emma Marshall by Joel Cook, J.P.

March 4, 1876 William S. James to Jennie Mayes by Joel Cook, J.P.

Page 29
Nov. 8, 1870 (clearly shown as 1870) Samuel A. Waters to May R. Watson at the Catholic Church by P.P. Brady, Catholic Priest in the presence of Thomas Henry Digges and Lizzie LaForge.

July 25, 1877 Louis A. Waters Jr. to Ella Phillips at the residence of Mrs. Anna Phillips by T.J.O. Morrison, J.P. in presence of G. W. Dawson, H.C. Latham, Ferg. Hunter and many others.

Dec. 25, 1877 Lewis Hoard to Bettie Dunklin by Raleigh Hayes, Min. of the Gospel

Page 30

April 7, 1877 Thomas F. Rittenhouse to Elizabeth Meatte by Tilford T. Hogan, Min. of the Gospel.

June 17, 1879 George E. Vail of St. Louis, Mo. to Lena A. DeRocher of New Madrid by T.J.O. Morrison, J.P. in presence of Joseph Weigel, Mary McDowell and Sallie Conran.

July 14, 1879 Joseph C. Picket to Mrs. Amanda L. Sheppard by Saml. A. Mason, M.G. M.E. Church S.

Page 31
Jan. 31, 1874 George W. Dunklin to Mary Latimore by Samuel S. Watson, J

Aug. 16, 1874 Asa Riddle to Ellen M. Taylor b y Saml. S. Watson, J.P.

Sept. 15, 1875 Gustavus Warrington to Elizabeth J. Edmondson by Robt. Lafont, Co. Court Justice.

Page 32
Dec. 12, 1877 Richard J. Phillips to Miss Melinda Powell by U. McCluer, Minister

Dec. 20, 1877 George W. Fisher to Mrs. Jennie Dawson by U. McCluer, Minister of Gospel

Dec. 24, 1877 Mr. P. A. Bray to Miss Ann Delia Phillips by U. McCluer, M. G.

NEW MADRID COUNTY, MISSOURI MARRIAGE RECORDS

Page 33
Oct. 17, 1877   Henry Johnson to Sarah Wilson by Joel Cook, J.P.

May 13, 1877   Wm. B. Bounds to Mrs. Sarah A. Hendricks at Big Prairie Twp. by C.H.Harris, J.P.

June 3, 1877   David Downs to Mrs. Julia Dawson at Big Prairie Twp. by C.H.Harris, J.P.

Page 34
May 27, 1877   Columbus DeLisle to Sarah Mitchel by John Young, J.P.

Nov. 22, 1876   Mr. Anson Richardson to Susan LeSieur by Jas. M. Dockery, J.P.

Jan. 22, 1877   Isaac LaValley to Silvia Gay in New Madrid Twp. by Joel Cook, J.P.

Page 35
May 12, 1877   Mr. George Lee to Mrs. Mary Thomas by E.A.McKinney, M.G.

June 17, 1877   Mr. John Long to Miss Vina A. Davis by George W.Clark J.P.

June 24, 1877   William J. Ellis to Miss Elizabeth F. Branscom af St. John Twp. by Geo. W. Clark, J.P.

Page 36
July 5, 1877   Mr. Alford Evans to Miss Mary E. Chatman of St.John Twp. by Geo. W. Clark, J.P.

July 22, 1877   John W. Colson to Miss Samantha M. Roberson at St. John Twp. by Geo. W. Clark, J.P.

July 15, 1877   Jas. Underwood to Miss Elizabeth Alexander by Jas.M. Dockery, J.P.

Page 37
May 23, 1877   Jacob Wynn to Miss Dora Michell by Jas. M. Dockery, J.P.

Sept. 27, 1877   Jeremiah Gulion to Miss Amanda J. Neill at St. Johns Twp. by Geo. W. Clark, J.P.

Oct. 14, 1877   Mr. Samuel D. Bates to Mrs. Minerva J. Sparks; by Joel Cook, J.P.

Page 38
Dec. 21, 1877   James Hatchley to Mary Eliza Thurmon by Jas. M. Dockery, J.P.

Dec. 25, 1877   Thomas Hillis to Harriett Hampton (col'd) by Jas. M. Dockery, J.P.

Jan. 2, 1878   Crocket Dowdy to Mary Ann Julien by Jas.M.Dockery,J.P.

NEW MADRID COUNTY, MISSOURI MARRIAGE RECORDS

Page 39

Dec. 29, 1877 Mr. John Sanders to Miss Mary J. Ewing by U. McCluer, M. G.

Feb. 14, 1878 Martin A. Salt to Marie E. Earles by Joel Cook, J.P.

Jan. 10, 1878 Mathew McDowell to Mollie J. Summers by Joel Cook, J.P.

Page 40
Feb. 14, 1878 Mr. Arthur Matherson to Miss Elizabeth Roth by U. McCluer, M.G.

Feb. 11, 1878 Jas. C. Allen to Miss Annie Caldwell by U.McCluer,M.G.

Feb. 19, 1878 Mr. F. A. Harnisch to Miss Mollie Murphy of Scott County by U. McCluer, M.G.

Page 41
Feb. 26, 1878 George Baldwin to Mary Patrick by Saml S.Watson,J.P.

Feb. 28, 1878 John Taylor to Miss Olivia Reynolds by Saml L.Watson,J.P.

Feb. 27, 1878 John W. Lafoe to Nancy A. Alford by Robt. Lafont, Co. Court Justice'

Page 42
Feb. 25, 1878 John H. Willis to Mary Jane Belcher by T. J. O. Morrison, J.P. in presenee of Thomas Atterbury, Elizabeth Atterbury, and William A. Willis.

March 21, 1878 Thomas Babb to Henrietta Nelson by J.H.Howard, Co. Court Justice

April 7, 1878 John R. Vaughn to Sarah Demint by Robt. Lafont, Co. Court Justice.

Page 43
Sept. 29, 1877 Saml. Hooper at Big Prairie Twp. by C.H.Harris,J.P.

July 21, 1875 (1875 on book) Danie Lewis to Morley Coleman by L.B.McDaniels, Elder.

June 9, 1878 Mr. J. W. Phillips to Plaseldin Gaingne by Joel Cook,J.P.

Page 44
March 12, 1878 James S. Emory to Miss Mary Fletcher at residence of James H. Fletcher b y Wm. Stringfield, J.P.

March 3, 1878 J.J.Coleman to Angeline Midgett at Big Prairie Twp. by Wm. Stringfield, J.P.

May 26, 1878 Benj. Taylor to Lily Williams at Big Prairie Twp. by Wm. Stringfield, J.P.

NEW MADRID COUNTY MISSOURI MARRIAGE RECORDS

Page 45

May 26, 1878 James W. Hodge to Miss Sarah Barnhart at Big Prairie Twp. by Wm. Stringfield, J.P.

Jan. 6, 1878 Mr. Jas. Neill to Miss Susan F. Gulion at St. John Twp. by Geo. W. Clark, J.P.

Feb. 17, 1878 Mr. Thomas A. Bias to Miss Mary A. Cunningham at St. John Twp. by Geo. W. Clark, J.P.

Dec. 8, 1877 Mr. Allen Williams to Miss Rebecca A. Cunningham at St, John Twp. by Geo. W. Clark, J.P.

Jan. 6, 1878 Robert F. Colson to Miss Nancy E. Beard in St. JOhn Twp. by Geo. W. Clark, J.P.

March 28, 1878 Mr. Thos. M. Connor to Miss Selena B. Darnell at St. John Twp. by Geo. W. Clark, J.P.

Page 47
June 6, 1878 Mr. Jas. Gallagher to Mrs. Margaret Paxton at L.R.V. and A.R.R. by U. McCluer, M. G.

Nov. 8, 1877 Mr. W. W. Nunnelly to Miss Nancy K. Glover at Mr. Glover's residence by T. W. Williams, M.G.

April 25, 1878 Mr. J. W. Lewis to D. E. Hopkins at Mr. Glover's residence by T. W. Williams, M.G.

Page 48
March 17, 1878 Adolphus Godair to Laura Deprow at residence of Bride/s Mother by T. W. Williams, M.G.

May 26, 1878 Thomas J. Barry to Laura M. Henson by Robt. Lafont, Co. Court Justice

June 5, 1878 Stephen H. Sharp to Ellen Bandy by Robert Lafont, J.P.

Page 49
July 4, 1878 Mr. Lawrence Everett to Miss Lavenia Baynes by J. N. Hawkins, M.E.C. S.

Oct. 2, 1878 Mr. A. Ruddle Bird of Jackson, Mo. to Miss Sallie M. Hunter of New Madrid, Mo. at New Madrid by T. C. Barret, Min.of Gos.

Oct. 3, 1877 James B. Shields to Louisa Young by Robt. Lafont, J.P.

Page 50
Jan. 30, 1879 John R. Gray to Samantha Sutton by Irvin A. Ewing, M.G.

Nov. 10, 1878 Rivers McCormac to Francis Vanover by Robt Lafont, Co. Court Justice

NEW MADRID COUNTY, MISSOURI MARRIAGE RECORDS

Page 50
Jan. 26, 1879 John R. Johnson to Amanda Bunch by Robt. Lafont, Co. Court Justice

Page 51
Jan. 22, 1879 Henry Heaton to Tillie Poe by M.J. Whitaker

Dec. 11, 1878 John Carey to Nancy Deitmore by Joel Cook, J.P.

Jan. 1, 1879 Charles Allen to Julia Cantrell by Joel Cook, J.P.

Page 52

Jan. 2, 1879 Alexander Jones to Elizabeth Davis by Joel Cook, J.P.

Jan. 28, 1879 Jo Cook to Sarah Underwood by Joel Cook, J.P.

Feb. 12, 1879 John Watt Jackson to Mary L. Dawson in presence of Wm. Pinnell and Hattie LaForge by J. A. Connolly, C.P.

Page 53
Feb. 21, 1879 Thomas G. Wright to Sarah P. Tompkins by J.A. Connolly, C. Priest in presence of Basil Raidt and Lena Raidt.

March 9, 1879 Marcus Floro to Mrs. Tabithe J. Carson by J. W. M. Dockery, J.P.

April 8, 1879 Charles W. Johnston of St. Louis City to Mrs. Mollie H. Klein at residence of the bride by Henry N. Watts, Minister, in presence of Needham Sikes, H. A. Smith and others.

Page 54
March 11, 1879 John Will Brownell to Mrs. Nannie Buford by C. E. DeVinney, M.G.

Feb. 25, 1879 William J. Whitson to Amelia Delisle by Robt. Lafont, Co. Court Justice

Feb. 25, 1879 John Grover to Mrs. Rebecca A. Causly by J. N. Hawkins. M. G.

Page 55
June 23, 1879 Albert B. Hunter to Miss Ella Pack by J.A. Connolly, R. C. Priest in presence of Chilion Riley, Ida Latham and many others.

July 3, 1879 John Clay Hunter to Miss Mary Elizabeth Tickell by J.A. Connolly, R.C.P. in presence of Mr. M.J. Tickell and Mrs. L.A. Tickell.

Aug. 1, 1876 Geo. W. Houston to Louisa Parker by Wm.J. Denhart, J.P. Recorded July 5, 1879.

NEW MADRID COUNTY, MISSOURI MARRIAGE RECORDS

Page 56

Nov. 9, 1876   Atlas Hall to Bettie Toney by Wm.J.Denhart, J.P.

Dec. 4, 1876   John D. Welchance to Eliza Sutton by Wm.J.Denhart,J.P.

Jan. 7, 1877   Jordan Green to Kittey White by Wm. J. Denhart, J.P.

Page 57

Jan. 7, 1877   John Heron to Alice Foster by Wm. J. Denhart, J.P.

March 26, 1877   Richard Connelly to Mary McDonough by Wm.J.Denhart,J.P.

April 1, 1877   Jordon Morris to Melvina Cathrell by Wm.J.Denhart,J.P.

Page 58

April 8, 1877   Alford Clarkson to Phebe Ogden by Wm. J. Denhart, J.P.

June 26, 1877   Israel Manuel to Henrietta Ross by Wm.J.Denhart, J.P.

July 8, 1877   Walker Bledsoe to Jane Daniels by Wm. J.Denhart, J.P.

Page 59

July 10, 1877   James E. Williams to Mary L. Olney by Wm.J.Denhart,J.P.

July 18, 1877   Albert C. Shultz to Antonette Gray by Wm.J.Denhart, J.P.

July 27, 1877   William A. Willis Jr. to Josaphine Lemons by Wm.J. Denhart, J.P.

Page 60

Aug. 15, 1877   Michael Ryan to Pernelia J. Haden by Wm.J.Denhart,J.P.

Sept. 13, 1877   Wm. A. Ferrenburg to Sarah A. Baker by Wm.J.Denhart,J.P.

Oct. 25, 1877   Elisha Burns to Nancy Henry by Wm.J.Denhart, J.P.

Page 61

Nov. 3, 1877   John Manuel to Billi McLean by Wm.J.Denhart, J.P.

Nov. 15, 1877   James M. Foy to Martha J. Demint by Wm.J.Denhart,J.P.

Jan. 13, 1878   John Riggs to Nancy D. Stewart by Wm. J. Denhart,J.P.

Page 62

Jan. 13, 1878   George P. Bush to Elizabeth Ford by Wm.J.Denhart, J.P.

March 6, 1878   Benj. F. Allen to Susan J. Willet by Wm.J.Denhart,J.P.

March 10, 1878   William Kerr to America Potter by Wm.J.Denhart, J.P.

NEW MADRID COUNTY MISSOURI MARRIAGE RECORDS

March 20, 1878 George W. Jackson to Martha W. Morris by Wm. J. Denhart, J.P.

March 20, 1878 Alford H. Skaggs to Laura A. Jones by Wm. J. Denhart, J.P.

March 21, 1878 Rancily Blizzard to Mary E. Shelton by Wm.J.Denhart,J.P

Page 64

April 7, 1878 James R. Bell to Sarah J. Brown by Wm.J.Denhart,J.P.

June 23, 1878 Thomas Shaffer to Mary Sulivan by Wm.J.Denhart,J.P.

June 23, 1878 Frank Dudley to Vina Horton by Wm.J.Denhart, J.P.

Page 65

July 1, 1878 John Cooper to Minerva Moody by Wm.J.Denhart, J.P.

July 3, 1878 Pleasant B. Sions to Mary Packett by Wm.J.Denhart,J.P.

July 3, 1878 Joseph Geeham to Loo Connelly by Wm. J.Denhart, J.P.

Page 66
July 9, 1878 Walter G. Jacobs to AmandaU. Beavers by Wm. J.Denhart,J.P

July 10, 1878 Frank Ward to Druzilla C. Knox by Wm.J.Denhart, J.P.

July 10, 1878 William B. Ward to Mary E. Ford by Wm. J. Denhart, J.P.

Page 67
July 28, 1878 John T. Lane to Alice Shaw by Wm. J. Denhart, J.P.

Aug. 2, 1878 Janus McDaniel to Sarah C. Barns by Wm.J.Denhart, J.P.

Aug. 4, 1878 Henry H. Jones to Mary Wright by Wm.J.Denhart, J.P.

Page 68
Sept. 19, 1878 John B. Denazier to Mary Ash by Wm.J.Denhart, J.P.

Nov. 17, 1878 Mathew H. Pfoff to Louisa Houston by Wm.J.Denhart,J.P.

Jan. 22, 1879 William Wilson to Elizabeth Willis by Wm.J.Denhart,J.P.

page 69
Jan. 30, 1879 Thomas Delury to Ann Allen by Wm.J.Denhart, J.P.

Feb. 9, 1879 Samuel J. Earle to Julia Keaster by Wm.J.Denhart, J.P.

July 22, 1879 Mr. William R. Norris to Mrs. Mary Ann Perminter at Mrs. Shaver's residence by J.D.Stepp, J.P.

Page 70
Sep. 15, 1878 John A. Thomas to Miss Mahala Upton at St.John Twp. by Geo. W. Clark, J.P.

NEW MADRID COUNTY, MISSOURI MARRIAGE RECORDS

Page 70

Elam B. Mills, Deputy Clerk for Recorder

Aug. 3, 1879

Alfred Hill to Mrs. Elizabeth Ross by T.W.Carpenter, M.G.

Aug. 3, 1879 Rich'd. Ratliff to Mrs. Elvatine Porter by Jas. M. Dockery, J.P.

Page 71

Aug. 6, 1879 Henry Percell to Martha J. Bravois by Jas. M. Dockery,J.P

Sept. 18, 1879 Wm. H. Toney to Elizabeth Holland by James M.Dockery "

Sept. 21, 1879 John A. Southern to Jennie Lamb by Jas, M. Dockery, J.P.

Page 72

Oct. 9, 1879 Mr. Adam Schneider to Mrs. Ann Mary Schneider at Barnes' Ridge by J.A. Connolly, R.C.Priest in presence of Thomas Lawfield, and Lena Lawfield.

May 9, 1877 Henry C. Riley to Miss Jennie Howard by Joseph Hunter, Co. Court Justice in presence of E. T. Davis, L. Lewis, Richard J. Phillips, and others.

Sept. 25, 1879 F. M. Binkley to Mary Jane Gibbin by James Stewart,J.P.

Page 73

Aug. 28, 1879 Augustus Lafont to Tereasy Godair by Robert Lafont, Co. Court Justice

Oct. 12, 1879 Peter Datiee to Mary Masonville by Robert Lafont, Co. Court Justice.

March 23, 1879 Walter Harden to Miss Melinda Lay at the Baptist Church by Thomas Johnson, M.G. in presence of Ransom Lay and Toliver Lay.

Page 74

March 27, 1879 Manuel Williams to Miss Caroline Wayde at Manuel Williams' by Thomas Johnson, Minister of Gospel in presence of Patsey Wade and Thomas Johnson.

April 3, 1879 Robert Graham to Mrs. Amelia Walls by Thomas Johnson, Min. Gospel in presence of Mary Lee and Sissy Walls.

Aug. 6, 1879 Pud Henderson to Miss Mary Brown at Sam Hampton's by Thomas Johnson, Min. of Gospel in presence of Sam Hampton & Sally Hampton

NEW MADRID COUNTY MISSOURI MARRIAGE RECORDS

Page 75

Aug. 17, 1879 Charley Smith to Miss Lucy Jane Kurney at Point Baptist Church by Thomas Johnson, Min. of Gospel in presence of Jo White and Martin Cops.

Oct. 31, 1879 James L. Horton to Sallie Cables by Joel Cook, J.P.

Dec. 10, 1879 Arthur Broughton to Nannie Hunter at residence of L. F. Hunter by Thos. J. O. Morrison, J.P. in presence of Lilbourne Lewis, H. C. Latham, et al.

Page 76

Dec. 31, 1879 Alvin Goodin to Miss Jennie Hempstead at Smith Henderson's by Thomas Johnson, Min. of Gospel in the presence of Manuel Williams and Smith Henderson.

Jan. 14, 1880 William W. Pinnell to Miss Hattie Laforge at A.A. Laforge's residence by J.A. Connolly, R.C. Priest in presence of Robert Laforge and Eliza Dawson.

June 3, 1879 Franz Kopp to Miss Sallie C. Morrison at residence of T.J.O. Morrison by J.A. Connolly, R.C. Priest in presence of Joseph Weigle & wife and Phillip Raidt.
(Sallie Morrison was daughter of T.J.O. Morrison)

Page 77
Jan. 1, 1880 William Caldwell to Harriette E. Sumner by Jas. M. Dockery, J.P.

Jan. 8, 1880 Peter Pikey to Martha M. Shepard by Jas. M. Dockery, J.P.

Jan. 15, 1880 Jacob S. Cade to Elizabeth Madray by Joel Cook, J.P.

Page 78
Jan. 19, 1880 John H. Lucas to Jennie Hall by Joel Cook, J.P.

Oct. 14, 1879 Benjamin F. Chaney of Sikeston to Miss Kate Brown of New Madrid Co. at Big Prairie by Henry N. Watt, Minister in the presence of R. G. Applegate, H. Smith and others.

Oct. 17, 1879 Needham Sikes of Scott County to Miss Sallie Wyatt of New Madrid County at Big Prairie by Henry N. Watt, Minister in presence of Noah Handy, his wife, and others.

NEW MADRID COUNTY, MISSOURI MARRIAGE RECORDS

Page 79
May 12, 1880 Shapley R. Hunter to Miss Libbie Broughton by Thos. J. O. Morrison, J.P. in presence of J. M. Broughton, Zenus G. Lewis, and Richard J. Phillips.

March 30, 1880 George T. Price to Miss Sallie E. Broughton by Wm. W. Farmer, J.P. in presence of R. L. Ulott & Chas. Broughton.

June 8, 1880 Winfield S. Williams to Mrs. Francis E. Brown by C. E. Devinney, Min. of Gospel.

Page 80
April 21, 1880 Rev. Jas. V. Worsham to Miss Mary A. Kochtitzky by L. R. Jones, Min. of Gospel.

May 23, 1880 Jacob A. Wynn to Miss Mary Chandler at Portageville by John Young, J.P.

May 11, 1880 Alphonse DeLisle to Miss Modest Meatte at Portageville by Robt. Lafont, Co. Court Justice.

Page 81
June 10, 1880 James Livingston to Leona Depro by G.W. Williams, M.G.

May 20, 1880 William H. Sutton to Emma Adasms at residence of Mr. Adams by Irvin A. Ewing, M.G.

March 22, 1878 Theodore Smith to Miss Elvinia Powell at Big Prairie by C. H. Harris, J.P.

Page 82
Feb. 19, 1879 George A. Matthews to Miss Maggie Bryant at Big Prairie by C.H.Harris, J.P.

May 4, 1879 B.F.Petty to Josaphine Barnett at Big Prairie by C.H.Harris, J.P.

Aug. 10, 1879 Jas L. Gentry to Viola G. Busby at Big Prairie by C.H.Harris, J.P.

Page 83
Dec. 1, 1879 John H. Trollinger to Hannah F. Clayton at Big Prairie by C.H.Harris, J.P.

Dec. 25, 1879 William Smith to Miss Etta Legett at Big Prairie by C.H.Harris, J.P.

Jan. 11, 1880 William Brown of Scott Co. to Annetta Cotton of New Madrid Co. at Big prairie by C.H.Harris, J.P.

Page 84
Jan. 25, 1880 Thomas Ross to Miss Maude Goodin at Big Prairie by C.H.Harris, J.P.

March 7, 1880 Alfred Mayweather to Josaphine Sewell by C.H.Harris, J.P.

NEW MADRID COUNTY, MISSOURI MARRIAGE RECORDS

Page 84
June 18, 1880 Henry Ray to Francis Ann Jane Nally at Big Prairie by C.H.Harris, J.P.

Page 85
July 22, 1880 Daniel Sloas to Miss Laura Willis by T.J.O.MOrrison

June 23, 1880 Olive Delisle to Miss Ida Wood by Robt. Lafont, Co. Court Justice.

July 7, 1878 James Johnson to Mrs. Mary E. Toney by C.H.Harris,J.P.

Page 86
Oct. 20, 1879 C.M.Harris to Nancy M. Busby by C.H.Harris, J.P.

Sept. 8, 1880 Robert P. Rhodes to Mrs. Sarah E. Knox by C. E. Devinney, min. of Gospel.

Sept. 2, 1880 Mr. F. S. P. Swift to Mrs. Theresa Chamberlain by C.E.Devinney, Min of Gospel.

Page 87
Sept. 9, 1880 A. J. Lafont to Paralee Delisle by John Young, J.P.

Sept. 12, 1880 Adolphus M. Brannum to Emma Morland by/John Young, J.P.

Sept. 16, 1880 Mitchell Meatte to Ellen M. Welchance by John Young,J.P.

Page 88
Oct. 10, 1880 Mr. R. H. Markham to Miss A. E. Hancock at Mrs. Ellis' by J.J. Presson, Min. of Gospel

Nov. 25, 1880 Godfrey Albert LeSieur to Miss Clara Waters of New Madrid at the residence of Louis Waters by Rev. J.A.Connolly, R.C. Priest in presence of Felix N. LeSieur and Miss Clara Mott and others.

Dec. 1, 1880 James B. Simmons to Eliza M. Rose by Benton Akin, Judge Co. Court

Page 89
Nov. 25, 1880 John Reaves to Miss Josaphine Night by James M. Dockery, J.P.

Oct. 17, 1880 Simon Nelson to Polina Saint Aubin by Jas. M. Dockery, J.P.

Oct. 10, 1880 John Alfred Alexander to Miss Ina B. Reed at Big Prairie by C.H.Harris, J.P. in presence of Miss Katie Waugh, Miss Katie Emory, Mrs. Hita Harris and others.

NEW MADRID CO. MISSOURI MARRIAGE RECORDS

Page 90

Dec. 12, 1880 Mr. Stephen Hudgens to Miss Margaret C. Jones by Benton Akin, Judge Co. Court.

March 12, 1881 James Jackson (col) to Miss America Williams (col) by Joel Cook, J.P.

May 15, 1881 Mr. Jas. Lawghlin to Mrs. Mary Secoy by James M. Dockery, Co. Court Justice

Page 91
Dec. 25, 1878 Samuel A. Phillips of Pt. Pleasant to Mary E. Watson, of Pt. Pleasant by C.C. Devinney, min. Gospel.

Oct. 12, 1879 James Brunston to Miss Adale Bradshaw at Adale Bradshaw's by Thos. Johnson, M.G. in presence of Jack Dorsey and A Alonz. O'Bannon.

NEW MADRID COUNTY MISSOURI MARRIAGE RECORD
BOOK 1, 1881 - 1889

Page 1
All males over age 21, females over 18 unless shown otherwise.
June 29, 1881 George Wayett (col) to Cristine Blackman (col) by Elder Shirirk Grimus, Min. Gospel.

June 30, 1881 Wilson Bennet to Mrs. Mary Chism by Henry Hunter, Min. Gospel

Page 2

July 1, 1881 License issued to Luke Meatte of Portage Twp. and Miss Clara Crabtree of Portage Twp. with written consent of Father, Samuel Crabtree and mother, Mary Crabtree. Minister's return not completed.

July 4, 1881 John Riggs to Miss Sarah J. Patterson over 18 who was proven to be such by testimony of Alex Ferrenburg at the residence of David Patterson by J. D. Stepp, J.P.

Page 3
July 6, 1881 Nathaniel Wheat to Mrs. Elizabeth Terry by J.D. Stepp, J.P.

July 6, 1881 Valentine Marque to Mary S. Still under 18 with written consent of E. D. Still and MJ.Still, parents at Big Prairie by C.H.Harris, J.P.

May 10, 1861 Loose paper in book. "This is to certify that I an ordained minister of the M.E.Church did on the 28 of April, 1861 in New Madrid County State of Missouri solemnize the rites of matrimony between JAMES E. Waugh and Cyntha A. Sikes both of New Madrid Co. Mo. Signed by Alenn Rucker. Filed May 10, 1861

July 10, 1881 William Crater to Miss Lucinda Davis by Benton Akin, Presiding Judge of County Court.

July 13, 1881 Joseph Meatt of Portage Twp. to Miss Anna K. Welchance by James M. Dockery, Judge Co. Court at residence of Taylor Welchance.

Page 5
July 15, 1881 John Garton, Min. of Gospel married Bowman Paxton to Miss Mary A. Stuart.

July 16, 1881 Marriage license issued to David W. Ward and Janieve G Godair under 18, consent given by Andrew Godair, father , and Mary Godair, Mother. Minister's return not completed.

Page 6
July 17, 1881 H. C. Black to Mary E. Ford at residence of William Knox by Joel Cook, J.P.

July 21, 1881 John Thomas Starr to Miss H. C.Lewis by Wm. J. Denhart, J.P. at residence of H. Davis.

Page 7
July 26, 1881 Solomon Levy to Miss Clara B. Riffle by Benton Akin, Judge Co. Court.

July 28, 1881 Jerry Wilkerson of Cape Girardeau, Mo. to Emma Woods by Joel Cook, J.P.

Page 8
July 31, 1881 William Richardson to Lucy Arbuckle of Portage Twp. at residence of J.W. Arbuckle by Robt. Lafont, J.P.

July 31, 1880? Scott Martin of Lesieur Twp. to Stella Fontain of Lesieur Twp who is over 18 as stated by George Smith under oath by Robt. Lafont, J.P. at residence of J.W. Arbuckle.

Page 9
July 30, 1881 George W. Charter of City of New Madrid to Mrs. Eliza A. Burchell of City of New Madrid by Wm. J. Denhart, J.P.

Aug. 1, 1881 License issued to George Martin of Lesieur Twp. and Mary Hunter of Lesieur Twp, the said Mary Hunter being proven to be over age eighteen by sworn oath of Daniel Johnson and George Martin. No minister's return filed.

Page 10
Aug. 1, 1881 Richard G. West of Big Prairie Twp. to Mary Jane McCloud by Wm. J. Denhart, Judge of County Court.

Aug. 7, 1881 Andrew J. Williams to Lackey J. Barker by Joel Cook, J.P. at residence of Mrs. Barker.

Page 11
Aug. 31, 1881 Jeff D. Adams of LeSieur Twp. under age of 21 and Mary H. Arbuckle of Lesieur Twp. who is over 18, consent of Luella Bell, mother of Jeff Adams being given by Robt. Lafont Justice Peace at J. W. Arbuckle's house.

Sept. 4, 1881 James D. Smith to Miss Alice Gossett by C.H. Harris, J.P. at Big Prairie.

Page 12
Sept. 4, 1881 George W. Banks under 21 to Miss Mary J. Marsh over 18, Mrs. Jennie Gurr, Mother of George Banks, consenting, by Irvin A. Ewing, Min. Gos. at residence of John Gurr.

Sept. 4, 1881 James W. Sawyers of Lesieur Twp. under 21 to Letha E. H. Ragsdale of Lesieur Twp., James W. Sawyers, Sr., giving consent, by Robert Lafont, J.P.

page 13
Sept. 7, 1881 Walker a Bledsoe to Miss Virginia Bolton of Big Prairie Twp. by Joel Cook, J.P. at Mrs. Puckett's.

Sept. 19, 1881 James Moseley of Portage Twp. to Paulina Austin of Portage Twp. by John Young J.P. at residence of James Moseley.

Page 14
Sept. 13, 1881 Charles Blessing to Levina Hayes by J. D. Stepp, J.P. at Mrs. Blessing's.

Sept. 18, 1881 John M. Yates of New Madrid Twp. to Melberry A. Dillard of New Madrid Twp. under 18, James Dillard, father, consenting by Joel Cook, J.P.

Page 15
Sept. 18, 1881 Richard A. Phillips to Leana A. Stewart by Rev. Irvin A. Ewing, at residence of John C. Stewart.

Sept. 20, 1881 Henry F. Moss to Sarah W. Denhart by Joel Cook,J.P.

Page 16
Sept. 21, 1881 Wesley Gregory to Rebecca Gregory by Robt. Lafont,J.P

Sept. 24, 1881 License issued to William Gregory of Sikeston, Mo. and Miss Mollie Reed of Big Prairie Twp. No minister's return filed.

Page 17
Sept. 28, 1881 George Edwin Hess of Iuka Springs, County of Tishimingo, State of Miss. to Miss Mollie E. Reeder by John Gordon, Minister of Gospel at house of Jno. Reeder.

Sept. 28, 1881 Jefferson M. Alexander of Hickman, Fulton Co., Ky. to Miss Mollie Thomas of Lesieur Twp. by E. K. Bransford, Min. M.E.Church S. at Mrs. C.C.Thomas'.

Page 18
Sept. 25, 1881
Rufus B.West to Fanny Sanders,=under 18, Abraham Sanders, father, consenting, by J.D.Stepp, J.P. at Abram Sanders'.

Oct. 2, 1881 John W. Lewis to Miss Fannie Wyne by Benton Akin, Presiding County Court Judge.

Page 19
Oct. 2, 1881 James Watson of Pt. Pleasant under 21 to Beulah B. Jackson of Lesieur Twp. under age 18, the parents of both having given written consent, by James M. Dockery, Co. Court Justice.

Oct. 5, 1881 William T. Poe to Portage Twp. to Miss Ada Vest of Portage Twp. by C.C.Hudspeth, J.P. at residence of G.W.Davis.

Page 20
Oct. 9, 1881 James Adams of Portageville to Miss Mary Ann St. Aubin of Portageville by John Young, J.P.

Oct, 10, 1881 Marriage License issued to Benjamin F. Barnhill of Wolf Island Twp, County of Miss., to Miss Theodocin E. Parker of Wolf Island, county of Miss. No minister's return filed.

Page 21
Oct. ___ 1881 Columbus Basham of East Twp. to Miss Henrietta Carilton of East Twp. by _____ Justice of Peace.

Page 21
Oct. 13, 1881 William H. Edwards of New Madrid Twp. to Miss Mary E. Jones of New Madrid Twp. by W. Faill, Min. Gos.at Mr. E. Jones'.

Page 22
Oct. 14, 1881 License issued to John Seward and Miss Ellen Roach, over, 18, mother having given consent for Ellen. Return not filled out, recorder's note: License returned Dec. 8, 1881, not filled out".

Oct. 15, 1881 George W. Powers to Mrs. Nancy Ann Dorson of Big Prairie Twp. by Wm. J. Denhart, J.P.

Page 23
Nov. 6, 1881 Delisle Lamb to Sidney Godair of Portage Twp. by A.A.Ritterhouse, J.P.

Oct.28, 1881 William Gilbow under age 21 to Victoria Arbuckle of Lewis Twp. over 18. Consent of Napoleon B. Bartholemy, Guardian of said minor, William Gilbow, given, by Robert Lafont at residence of J.W.Arbuckle.

Page 24
Oct. 27, 1881 Joseph Masonville of Lesieur Twp. to Ellen Gossett of Lesieur Twp by James M. Dockery, Co. Justice.

Oct. 27, 1881 Henry S. Lewis of Princeton, Caldwell Co., Ky. to Miss Melissa Brown of New Madrid Twp. at the Harbin House by Wm. J. Denhart, Justice of County Court.

Page 25
Oct. 30, 1881 William A. Gossett to Miss Martha E. Moody (both of Big Prairie Twp.) by J.D.Stepp, J.P.

Nov. 6, 1881 William T. York of East Twp. to Miss Margaret E.Canoy of East Twp (under 18) (parent of minor giving consent) by J.L.York, J.P.

Page 26
Nov. 8, 1881 Jerry L. Dewitt of East Twp. (under 21) to Miss Katie Shelby of East Twp. (over 18) father of Dewitt giving consent, at residence of J.E.Shelby W.B. Richardson, M. G.

Nov. 10, 1881 Robert C. Stonebreaker of Big Prairie Twp to Eliza Ann Eugram by J.D.Stepp, Justice of Peace.

Page 27
Dec. 10, 1882 ? Lafayette Lafont of Lesieur Twp. (under 21) to Miss Mary E. Long of same twp. (under 18), Robert Lafont, father of Lafayette consenting and John Long, father of Mary consenting by John Young, J.P. (License issued Nov. 16, 1881.

Nov. 8, 1881 Hugh Marrs of Portage Twp. to Fanny McElhaney of Portage Twp. at residence of J.E.Shelby by Rev. W. B. Richardson.

Page 28
Nov. 26, 1881 Jas. M. Rust to Martha Blacken of New Madrid Twp. (under 18) father consenting. Rust of Big Prairie Twp, by E.H. McKinney at Jere Blacken's. *McKinney is Min. of Gospel.

Dec. 1, 1881 Frank H. Hill of Lesieur Twp. to Miss Lela Parker of Lesieur Twp by Webster Tull, M.G. at Mrs. Nancy Lazell's.

Page 29
License issued Dec. 12, 1881 to William C. West and Josaphine Allison who is over 18 as shown by affidavit of Wm.C.West. No minister's return filed.

Dec. 8, 1881 Charles W. Benedict of Pt. Pleasant to Miss Alice Sands of Pt. Pleasant (an orphan) by Webster Full, M.G. at John Atwell's.

Page 30
Dec. 22, 1881 Augustus Easle? of New Madrid Twp. to Alice Bradshaw of New Madrid Twp, he over 21, she over 18 (shows parents consenting) by Benton Akin, Presiding Judge of CountyCourt at Stephen St.Mary's

License issued Dec. 22, 1881 to William F. Black and Miss Amanda E. Knuckles. No minister's return.

Page 31
Dec. 25, 1881 Joseph S. Moore of Big Prairie Twp. to Louisa Hill of Big Prairie Twp. Shows both of age but has note "an orphan no parents or guardian" by J.D.Stepp, J.P. at J.F. Mainord's.

Dec. 28, 1881 James A. Williams to Elmina Culbertson about 18 (an orphan, no parents or guardian) at Willaim Nunley's by Thomas Williams, M.G.

Page 32
Dec. 25, 1881 John H. Gordon (col'd) to Vick Waters (col'd) by J.L.Brown, Ord. Minister of CME Church at Gleen Curry's residence.

Dec. 29, 1881 Robert L. LaVallee to Miss Cornelia G. Newsum, an orphan, by Wm. J. Denhart, Judge of County Court.

The following is a license and return loose in the book, is not recorded in proper place so I am entering here.

Dec. 26, 1881 Bill Williams of Pt. Pleasant to Mattie Hamilton of Pt. Pleasant by M.C.Cox at Elic Hamton's residence.

Page 33
Jan. 1, 1882 Benjamin F. Wright of Lesieur Twp. to Mrs. Nannie Lazell (a widow) at Mrs. Nancy Lazell's by Webster Full, M.G.

Jan. 10, 1882 Oscar Dapron to Josaphine Ewing under 18, Emeline Ewing, mother of Josaphine, having consented, by Benton Akin, Presiding Judge of Co. Court.

Page 34

Jan. 8, 1882 William Brunson to Anny Graham by Henry Hunter.

Dec. 4, 1881 John E. Poe of Portage Twp, under 21, to Miss Della Lou Allen of Lesieur Twp. over 18. Father of Minor giving consent. Married at residence of Herbert Week by W. G. Henson, Elder of the Baptist Church.

Page 35
Dec.18, 1881

Caleb R. Rasson to Elizabeth Ranson by Webster Full, M. G.

Feb. 5, 1882 Louis F. Harvey to Rosana Rileford by James Stewart,J.P. at Lake Como.

Page 36
Feb. __ 1882 George W. Shields to Emma Mote by J. D. Stepp, J.P.

Feb. 3, 1882 Charles Lunyow? to Martha Martin by John A. Mott, J.P. at John Martin's.

Page 37
Feb. 5, 1882 Joseph B. Pace of Lesieur Twp. over 21 to Jenny Bohannon of Lesieur Twp, under 18, A.J. Bohannon, father, giving consent, by Robt. Lafont, J.P.

Dec. 26, 1881 William T. Black to Amanda E. Kunckels by James Stewart, J.P. at Amos Paxton's.

Page 38
Jan. 26, 1882 Joseph N. Atterbury under 21 to Martha M. Darnall, over 18, consent of father being given for minor, by Jas. A. Workman, Min. of Gospel, at Mrs. Helms'.

Jan. 19, 1882 James C. Sutton? of City of New Madrid to Jenny Tomy? by Wm. J. Denhart, J.P. at residence of Wm. Roth.

Page 39
Feb. 9, 1822 Nehemeah Harland of Big Prairie Twp. to Mrs. Rebecca Brooks of Big Prairie Twp by a Judge of County Court at office of Clerk of Circuit Court (signed by John A. Mott, Recorder)

Feb. 12, 1882 Charles N. Mainord of Big Prairie Twp to Mary E. Mize of Big Prairie Twp. by J. D. Stepp, J.P. at J.F.Brown's.

Page 40
Feb. 11, 1882 Joseph J. Cunningham to Nelly Ann Cartee of Portage Twp. by Joel Cook, J.P. in New Madrid.

Dec. 4, 1881 (License issued Dec. 3, 1881) William D. Sackett to Polly Ann C. Braden by J. D. Stepp, J.P. at William Wilson's.

Page 41
James Massey to Emeline Rodis, a widow, on Jan. 1, 1882 at residence of the bride by J.D. Stepp, J.P.

James R. Lee to Lelia P. Crawford on Feb. 15, 1882 by J.D. Stepp, J.P.

Page 42
Feb. 14, 1882. James G. Kelly to Mary McGrew of Malden, in city of New Madrid, by Joel Cook, J.P.

2-16-1882 Jefferson Burnett of LeSieur Twp. to Mary Sanville of LeSieur Twp. at residence of bride by J.P. (name not shown).

Page 43
James Williams to Hester Ross, on Feb. 16, 1882, both of Big Prairie Twp. At T. Ross residence by a min. of gospel (name not shown).

2-13-1882 George Compton to Julia McGowan in City of New Madrid by Joel Cook, J.P.

Page 44
License issued Feb. 18, 1882 to John W. Colson to Mary Farmer, both of St. John Twp. Cert. not filled out.

1-22-1882 David Richards to Susy Davis by H. Hunter.

Page 45
2-26-1882 Jefferson Patterson to Sally Johnson at residence of E.T. Riley by Thomas Johnson, Min. of Gospel.

2-28-1882 George H. Seal to Miss Sykes of Stoddard County on 2-28-1882 at New Madrid by James Stewart, J.P.

Page 46
3-4-1882 Phillip M. Trammel of Stoddard County and Isabel Herolde of New Madrid Twp. by James Steward, J.P.

License issued on 3-4-1882 to Newton Davis, New Madrid Twp. and Harriet Mudd, New Madrid Twp. No return made.

Page 47
3-4-1882 Anthony Sikes of New Madrid Twp. and Betty Morgan of New Madrid Twp.

12-23-1881 Bill Williams, Town of Pt. Pleasant & Mattie Hamilton of Pt. Pleasant at Alex Hamilton's residence.

Page 48
License issued to William Gilbert of New Madrid & Jennie Ralston of New Madrid on 3-23-1882. No return made.

Goodwin Treadwell of LeSieur Twp. (under 21) and Susan Portel of LeSieur (under 21). Adaline Treadwell, mother and only surviving parent and -daline Portel only surviving parent of Susan having given consent on May 6, 1882. No return made.

Page 49
James Hendricks of East Twp. & Meleny Robbins of East
Twp., written consent of Joseph Robbins & Ellen Robbins,
parents of said minor, Meleny, New Madrid office on 26 of
April, 1882 at residence of Joseph Robbins by J.L.York,J.P.

Benjamin Ramsey of N.M.Twp. & Melinda Gray, N.M.Twp with
the consent of Seth W. Gray, father of said minor, Melinda,
On May 5, 1882 married at Seth Gray's by Rev. W.W.Lewis

Page 50
William C. Carter of N.M.twp. and Esther Woods of N.M.Twp.
as represented by Matt Wood, her father, May 7, 1882 at
the residence of Mott Wood by Henry Hunter.

James R. Brown of Big Prairie Twp. & Sarah A. A. Grovis of
Big Prairie Twp. July 9, 1882 married at Wm. Smith's b y
J.D.Stepp, J.P.

Page 51
Henry Jackson of New Madrid Twp. and Jane Bryant of New Madrid
Twp., Jane under age, given consent by parents married on
April 1, 1882 at residence of Peggy Davis b y Johnson.

George W. Brooks of City of New Madrid and Martha E. Dunn of
New Madrid by Joseph A. Gravis July 11, 1882

Page 52
Joseph J. Carr of County of Mississippi in State of Arkansas
and Susie L. Phillips of LeSieur Twp. May 31, 1882 (no return)

Andrew Sumner of New Madrid and Septima Ward of New Madrid
Twp. on June 5, 1882 (no return)

Page 53
Jonah Howard of New Madrid and Alice Campbell of New Madrid
June 10, 1882 by Joseph S. Brown, J.P. at the colored
Methodist Church.

James C. Williams, Big Prairie Twp. & Miss Milkey A. Stonebracker
of Big Prairie Twp. in New Madrid, Mo. on June 11, 1882 at
Robert Stonebracker by J.D.Stepp, J.P.

Page 54
John Q. Stephens of Big Prairie Twp. & Miss Maud Huff of Big
Prairie Twp. on June 15, 1882 at Baymasville by J.D.Stepp, J.P.

Robert Alexander of Big Prairie and Mrs. Mary Stringfield
of Big Prairie on June 15, 1882 by Joel Cook, J.P. at New Madrid

Page 55
Hardan Basham and Miss Letha Nelson of New Madrid with consent
of Francis Nelson, father of said Letha on June 15, 1882 .
(No return)

John Murphy of New Madrid & Fannie Riley   of New Madrid on
June 19, 1882 at residence of B. Akins, Justice of Co. Court.

Page 56

Siah D. Hill of Big Prairie and Mary A. Vaughn of New Madrid Twp. on July 11, 1882. (No return).

John A. Booton of New Madrid and Jerusha Rankin of New Madrid on July 12, 1882 at the residence of Judge of County Court by Wm. J. Denhart.

Page 57

Alvin Moore of New Madrid and Mrs. M. L. Stone on 4-11-1882 at residence of F. Kopp by Benton Akins, Co. Judge. (Mrs. M. L. Stone is daughter of T.J.O.Morrison)

Greer Dixon of New Madrid and Martha A. Trigned of New Madrid July 13, 1882 by John Cooke, J.P.

Page 58

Ansclem Russell of Portage Twp. and Miss Emma Foust of Portage Twp. on July 14, 1882 by A.A.Rittenhouse, J.P. at LeSieur Twp.

J.C.Stuckney of New Madrid and Mary Vickers of New Madrid June 25 by John Mott, J.P. at Mr. J. C. Stuckney.

Page 59

William Carlisle of New Ma drid and Betty Underwood on July 5, 1882 by Irwin Ewing on July 5 at Powell Ford.

Frank Pasquin of New Madrid and Margaret Pasquin of New Madrid married at James Waatshins on July 1882 by Benton Akins, Judge of Co. Court.

Page 60

Henry C. Rummels of Big Prairie and Mrs. Decilla Reddick of Big Prairie on 7-25-1882 at Wesley Yarbroughs by J.D. Stepp, J.P.

Alexander Lattremon of LeSieur Twp and Mrs. Eliza O. Cobb of New Madrid on 8-4-1882 by James M. Docking, Co. Judge.

Page 61

Wm. Noel of Gaynesville of Green Co., Ark. and Catherine Love of Gaynesville of Green Co. Ark. on 8-11-1882 by Joel Cook, J.P. at New Madrid, Mo.

Page 61

David McConnell of New Madrid and Miss Mary Pinley
of New Madrid shown by testimony of Henry Sutton Esq.
of county of New Madrid Aug. 18, 1882 by Denhart J.C.C.
at residence of the Judge of County Court.

Page 62

Amos Burnett of LeSieur Twp. and Lucy Cuningham of
LeSieur Twp. 8-24-1882 at New Madrid by W. Full M.G.

Dan C. Pollicke of Portageville and Bettie Gilmore
of Portage Twp. on 8-24-1882 (no returns).

Page 63

Richard Allen of LeSieur Twp and Mrs. Hannah Bratton of
LeSieur Twp. 25th of Aug. at Ruddle's Point by M. C.
Cox Sep. 3, 1882,

Page 63

Oubjbet Autry of New Madrid and Miss Martha (M.E.)
Evans of Big Prairie by testimony of John D. Westerman
on April 13, 1882 at office of J.D.Stepp, J.P.

Jacob Peine of LeSieur Twp. and Mrs. Alsey Johnson of
LeSieur Twp. on 8-26-1882. (no return)

Charles Beavors of Big Prairie and Katy Missouri Bell
of Big Prairie Twp. Samuel Bell the father of Katy
Missouri Bell having signified his consent in writing
to the marriage on 9-13-1882 (no return)

Page 65

Charles A. Simpson of Johnson Co. Ill. and Nancy A. Hood
of Johnson Ill on 9-18-1882 by Joel Cook J.P. in New
Madrid.

Napoleon LeSieur of LeSieur Twp. and Sally E. Stone of
LeSieur Twp. on 9-27-1882 (no return).

Page 66

Dewitt C. Phillips of New Madrid and Martha V. Newsum of
New Madrid on 10-9-1882 by Judge of County Court at his
residence on Oct. 11 by Benton Akins Judge of Co. Court.

Page 66

Francis Paxton of New Madrid Twp. and Mrs. Jane Pinkley of New Madrid Twp. on 10-11-1882 at F. M. Paxton's by James Stewart, J.P.

Page 67

James Sutton and Bettie Williams both of New Madrid on 9-30-1882 at home of Judge Wm. J. Denhart, J. Co. Court.

Newt Lovingoode of Town of Pt.Pleasant and Flonna Allen of Pt. Pleasant Sept. 1882 (no return)

Page 68

Hureleus Coe and Minnie Cunngingham on 10-20-1882 both in County of New Madrid.

Isaac What of Big Prairie & Saundra Burkinson of Big Prairie Twp. on Oct. 20, 1882 at James Bloomfields by J.D.Stepp, J.P.

Page 69

John W. Wilson of New Madrid Twp and Mary J. Walker of N.M. Twp. Nancy Walker mother of Mary J. Walker being personally present & consenting on 10-29-1882 at residence of Judge of County Court,Benton Akin.

John W. Sauls of N.M.Twp. and Francis O. Baker of New Madrid Twp. Peter Baker father of Fannie O. Baker being present and consenting in person on 8-29-1882 at residence of bride's parents by Rev. W. W. Lewis.

Page 70

Thomas Mulligan of New Madrid and Mary Brunson of New Madrid. Catharine Babteste, Guardian of the said Mary F. Brunson, attended and gave consent on 11-9-1882 by W. J. Denbow. M.G.

Charles Broodshacker of Long Prairie Twp. Co. of Mississippi and Barbara Elizabeth Robbins of East Twp. of New Madrid County with consent of parents by John L. York, J.P. at home of Joseph Robbins on 12-8-1881.

Page 71

Thomas Alexander Branham of New Madrid Twp. and Clarrisa C. Williams of New Madrid Twp. on 11-10-1882 (no return)

Levi J. Everhart of New Madrid Twp. and Miss Mary E.Horn of New Madrid Twp. Mrs. L. J. Garned, mother of said Mary E. and only living parent having consented in writing to said marriage on 11-15-1882 by James Stewart, J.P. at

Page 72

Charles W. Holmes of New Madrid Co. and Ella Minerva Yates of Co. of New Madrid. Samuel Yates, father of said Ella Minerva consented in writing on 11-30-1882 at Samuel Yates' home by Joseph L. Brown, M. G.

David Richards of Co. of N. M. and Lucy Davis of Co. of N. M. 1-22-1882 by Henry Hunter.

Page 73

Andrew J. Morlary Kelly of New Madrid and Caroline Worley (Curley) of New Madrid at Mason Mill 12-31-1882 by James Stewart.

Nathan Tarven and Levena Furlong of New Madrid Co. on 12-18-1882 (no return)

Page 74

Joseph H. Story of New Madrid Twp. and Nancy Hampton of New Madrid 12-18-1882 (no return)

Albert Johnson of Co. of N. M. and Minta Huston of New Madrid Co. at Riley's School House 6-1-1884.

Page 75

George Ellis of New Madrid Twp. and Martha Ellis of N. M. Twp. as shown by statement of her father Talbot Ross on Dec. 21 (no return)

Robert H. Nicholas of Portage Twp and Mollie S. Marcus of LeSieur Twp by Robert LaFont (Co. Clerk Justice) at Robert Frazier's Residence Jan. 11, 1883.

Page 76

Henry Nicholas of New Madrid Twp. and Julia Henderson of New Madrid Twp. on 6-30-1887 (no return)

George Jackson of New Madrid and Mary Harrell of New Madrid on 2-17-1889 by Chsel Reed, M.G.

Page 77

George M. Doyle of St. James Co. of Mississippi and Katy E. Maulsby of New Madrid on 1-11-1883 by Oscar K. Justin C. Court.

William Atterberry of LeSieur Twp. and Susan Blue of LeSieur Twp. at William Atterberry's 11-5-1882 by C. C. Hudspeth, J.P.

Page 78

William B. LaBow of Pt. Pleasant and Ida L. Piggott of Pt. Pleasant on 1-17-1883 (no return)

Douglas Richardson of LESieur Twp. and Eliza Sawyers of LeSieur Twp at E. Sawyers' by Joseph O'Bannon J.P. on 1-21-1882.

Page 79

John K. Ingram of Trenton Co. of Giburn, Tenn. and Nellie S. Standford of Brinkley in Co. of Morrow in Arkansas with written consent of William Sandford father of said Nellie Sandford on 1-21-1883 by Joel Cook, J.P.

John Trammel of New Madrid Twp and Dania Cochran of New Madrid Twp at James Stuart on 1-23-1883 by James Stewart J.P.

Page 80

Robert W. Wynne, Portage Twp. and Miss May R. Howard of Portage Twp. by Robt. LaFont J.P. at John Howard's residence on 1-25-1886.

Joseph Myers of New Madrid and Mrs. Alice Caldwell of Big Prairie in Big Prairie at residence of Mrs. Caldwell on 1-28-1883 by John M. Mills, J.P.

Page 81

Charles M. Sawyers of Pt. Pleasant and Julia A. Lewis of New Madrid, James W. Sawyers, father of Charles M. and M. M. Sawyers, mother of Julia A. consenting in writing at Mrs. Sawyers' 2-1-1883 by Robert LaFont J.P.

Edward Pritchett of New Madrid Co. and Harriet L. Dazan? co. of New Madrid at Fritches Duyson on 3-11-1883 by James Winders, J.P.

Page 82

Robert Mitchell of New Madrid Twp. and Mattie Grimes of New Madrid on 2-3-1883 (no return)

Duke Evans of LeSieur Twp and Martha Treadwell of LeSieur Twp. 2-2-1883 (no return)

Page 83

Larkin Caldwell of Portage Twp. and Amanda E. Moore of Portage Twp. on 2-3-1883 (no return)

Richard Basken of New Madrid Twp. and Lizzie Merlen of New Madrid Co. on 2-13-1883 (no return).

Page 84

Henry S. Bartlett of LeSieur Twp. and Dora Wilson of LeSieur Twp. at Sam Maulsby's on 2-18-1883 by Joseph O'Bannon J.P.

Samuel Suttles of St. John Twp. and Margaret Jones of St. John Twp. at Henderson Mounds on 3-5-1883 by James Winders J.P.

Page 85

Marcus Shumaker of New Madrid Twp. and Mrs. Lizzie Mars of New Madrid Twp. at home of bride by J. D. Stepp, J. P. on 3-21-1883.

Alford Parker of St. John Twp. and Louisa Terry of st. John Twp. at residence of Mrs. R. Millan on 3-25-1883 by Joseph O'Bannon, J.P.

Page 86

John J. Fisher of Pemiscot Co. and Miss Fanny Lewis with written consent of John F. Fisher, father of John J. and of Rev. N. Lewis, father of said Fanny on 3-6-1883 (no return)

Jeff D. Keger of New Madrid Co. and Mattie Cooley of N.M. Co. on 4-1-1883 (no return)

Page 87
Emmund T.
Riley of New Madrid and Eliza Dawson of New Madrid by Catholic Priest, P. J. McNamee 4-5-1883

Andrew Miller of Portage Twp. and Amanda Price of Portage Twp. by Zilford Hogan on 4-3-1883

Page 88

William Wyatt of Big Prairie Twp and Miss Mary Parker of Big Prairie with written consent of John Parker, father of Mary at the residence of the bride by J.N.Miller,J.P. on 4-22-1833

George Miller to Ann Coleman on 4-29-1883 by Henry Hunter 4-30-1883 at Albert Lee's farm.

Page 89

F.H.Curley of LeSieur Twp. and Elizabeth Thompson of
LeSieur Twp. on statement of B.F.Wright on 3-14- (no return)

Elijah Abbott of New Madrid and Mary Elizabeth Stallings
by Joel Cook, J.P. on 4-29-1883.

Page 90

J.A.Cornall (indexed Hudgens(of Jackson Co, Cape Girardeau,
Mo. and Miss Lucy Riley of New Madrid at Judge Riley's on
8 day of May 1888 by J.W.Rose Borough, M.G.

George W. Dawson of New Madrid and Mariah Howard by J.McNaruman
M.G. at church of Immaculate Conception on 5-10-1883

Page 91

Wm. Jones of New Madrid Co. & Alice Johnson of N.M. on
May 8-1883 at LeSieur Twp. by M.C.Cox

John S. Waters (col) of New Madrid and Elizabeth Williams
(col) on 5-21-1883 by Charles Reed.

Page 92

William B. Purdy and Zula Randsburg b y William S. Smith
on 5-24-1883 at New Madrid, both of New Madrid

Z. T. Garden of Big Prairie and S. C. Hogwood of Big P. by
William s. Smith, J. P. on 5-31-1883.

Page 93

John Tinsley of Fulton Ky. and Anna Evans of Fulton, Ky.
by Wm. S. Smith, J.P. 6-4-1883.

G.W.McClellan of Fulton Ky. and Emma Tompkins of Fulton Ky.
in New Madrid by ____Bymune, M. G. 6-21-1883 at home of
Mrs. Tompkins in St. John Township.

Page 94

C. M. Parkison of Fulton Ky. to Nancy Talley of Tulton Ky.
by Wm. Smith J.P. on 7-6-1883

George W. Willson of Co. of N.M. and Sarah E. Lane of N.M.
Co. by Elder W. G. Henson on 7-1-1883.

Page 95

Joseph Johnson of Co. of New Madrid and Mollie Clemons of Co.
of New Madrid by J.L.Brown M. G. at residence on 7-1-1883

Page 95

Edward Sikes of Co. of N.M. and Manurvey McCoy of Co. of N.M. on July 8, 1883 by Rev. W. J. Deboe, M.G.

Page 96

Frank Gibson of West Twp. and Mary Ida Landers of West Twp. by written consent of A. Landers, father of said Mary by John A. Mills, J.P. on July 1, 1883.

James Gibson of West Twp. to Mary M. Petty of West Twp. with written consent of Rufus West, Guardian of Mary M. Petty & Annie Smith, mother of said James whose father is not living by John N. Mills J.P. on July 1, 1883.

Page 97

J. H. Lang of Farmington of St. Francois Co. and Mrs. Mollie Kline of New Madrid by Webster Full, M.G. on March 8, 1883.

James Aesterman of LeSieur Twp. and Martha E. Cancell of LeSieur by C. C. Hudspeth, J.P. on July 15, 1883

Page 98

Charles W. McElhaney of Portage Twp. and Johanah Jones of Portage Twp. by J.A.Workman, M.G. on 9-4-1883.

Bias Dunklin (col) LeSieur Twp. and Mattie Williams (col) LeSieur Twp. 7-26-1883, (no return)

Page 99

William Hawkins of New Madrid Co. and Maggie J. Hay by Rev. Cullin Downing, M.G. on 9-10-1883.

E. J. Hadson (Cadson) of New Madrid and Mrs. Ancie D. Hall (Call) of New Madrid by Geo. W. Clark, J.P. on 3-4-1883

Page 100

W.B.Sturgill of Pikeston, Co. of Pike State of Ky. and S. Francis Blackburn, Clay Co. Ark. by Webster Full, M.G. on 4-16-1882

Joseph A. Riddle of New Madrid and Miss Josephine Bailey of Co. Of New Madrid by C.C.Hudspeth, J.P. on 4-5-1882

Page 101

Jeff Fox of Co. of N.M. and Lena Shelton consent of grandparents as she has no parents by J.W.Mills J.P. on 4-29-1883

John Hayes, Co. of N.M. and Catherine Johnson by J.W.Mills, J.P on 4-16-1883 at Hayes house

Page 102

Note: Elizabeth Lewis married Richard Phillips Feb. 20, 1820 Deed Book 11, page 282

Em. C. Moore of Co. of New Madrid and Ed Gartney of New Madrid by Frank D. Kimes, J.P. in his office on May 26, 1882

MR. A. Haas city of New Madrid and Miss Ella A. Slayton of New Madrid by Wm. J. Denhart, J.P. at his residence on 5-23-1882

Page 103

James R. Lenon of Co. of New Madrid and Alice Farrenb urg, Co. of New Madrid, she is her own guardian and James Lenon, consent of his parent, Nancy Lenon by Rev. W. H. Lewis at his residence on May 20, 1882.

Jonathen Lair of Portage Twp. and Fanny Hany of LeSieur Twp by John Young, J.P. on May 21, 1882 in LeSieur Twp.

Page 104

Dabney M. Daughtery of Big Prairie and Samantha C. Gray of Big Prairie on 7-28-1883

Henry Williams of Big Prairie and Miss Maggie J. Carrol of Big Prairie Andrew Carrol, father of Maggie J, gave consent (no return)

Page 105

David C. Pollack of Portageville and Betty Gilmore of Portageville by John Young, J.P. on 8-27-1882

James C. Hufstetter of LeSieur Twp. and Nancy Hurley of LeSieur by Frank D. Kimes J.P. on 9-18-1882

Page 106

Charles M. Smith of Big Prairie and Miss Margie E. Hatchel in Scott Co. on 8-15-1883 (no return)

Elliot Sloas of New Madrid Co. and Etta Willis with consent of Texana Willis, parent of Etta, by Joe Cook, J.P. 3-4-1883

Page 107

Wm. H. Andrews of Big Prairie and Emma Ingram of Sikeston, Scott Co. by T. A. Bowman, M. G. at residence of J. Simmons on 11-5-1883

Robert Davis of New Madrid & Eliza Davis by J.D.Stepp, J.P. at James Bloomfields 1-3-1883

Page 108

R.W.Rolends of New Madrid Co. and R. C. Moody by John N. Mills, J.P. 2-18-1883

Andy Waters of Co. of New Madrid and Mollie Gibson of Co. of New Madrid by C. C. Crowder, M.G. 5-19-1883

Page 109

Henry Williams of Big Prairie and Miss Maggie J. Carroll of Big Prairie, Andrew Carroll father of Maggie consents by J.N.Mills J.P. 8-12-1883 at the residence of the bride

Lawson Hunt and Verry Young by Adolph Reed on 3-10-1882

Page 110

Chester Trammell of New Madrid and Mary Paxton consent given by Joseph Paxton father of Mary J. by James Stewart, J.P. on 5-11-1882 at Amos Paxton's.

Green Tucker of New Madrid and Dinah Booker by Henry Hunter, M.G. on 8-26-1882

Page 111

John Batiste Henry Jaspar of New Orleans, Parish of Orleans, State of La. to Mrs. Laura Kate Davis of New Madrid by Roman Catholic Priest of New Madrid, R.J.McNamee, M.R. on 10-20-1882

Henry M. Phillips of New Madrid to Miss Ada F. Barnes of Co. of N.M. by Judge of Co. Court at their home on 11-19-1882 by Judge Benton Akins

Page 112

James Sander of New Madrid Co. and Mrs. Amanda Townsend of New Madrid Co. by J.D.Stepp, J.P. on 11-29-1882

Wade Hampton of New Madrid Co. and Lorena Allen of New Madrid Co. by Joseph O'Bannon 1-16-1882 (of LeSieur Twp.)

Page 113

Mary English of New Madrid Co. to Harison Mineweather of New Madrid Co. by Wm. Smith J.P. on 2-1-1883

James M. Alley of New Madrid Co. and Jane Black of New Madrid Co. by Joseph O'Bannon, J.P. 3-15-1883

Page 114

James Irvin of Portage Twp. and Sarah Lie Flore of New Madrid Co. Portage Twp. with written consent of Mark Flare, father of Sarah L. Flare by Joseph O'Bannon at residence of P. Pikey on 3-6-1883

Page 114

W. A. Roberts, Co. of New Madrid and Mollie Tibbs by A. J. Winbry, J.P. at residence of Wm. Robbins on 4-25-1883

Page 115

John Tinsley of Fulton, Ky. and Anna Evans of Fulton, Ky. by Wm. L. Smith, J.P. on 6-4-1883 at New Madrid

A. J. Dement of New Madrid Co. to Mrs. Anna Josephine Hill of New Madrid Co. by John N. Mills J.P. at residence of Bride on 6-12-1883

Page 116

Robert Godair of Portageville to Lucy Godair of Portage Twp. at W. Evansurlle on July 1, 1883

S. J. Campbell Co. of Miss. to Mary Jane Riach of Mississippi Co., Mo. by James Winders J.P. on 7-5-1883 at his office

Page 117

William Johnson of New Madrid Co. to Florence Gray of New Madrid by Rev. M. C. Cox, M.G. at Pt. Pleasant

Bias Dunklin, LeSieur Twp. of New Madrid Co. to Mattie Williams LeSieur Twp at Pt. Pleasant on 7-29-1883

Page 118

Webster Bunting of New Madrid Co. to Elizabeth Manuel of New Madrid Co. by C. C. Hudspeth J.P. 7-7-1883 at residence of Bride

Thomas J. Fontaine of New Madrid Co. to Matty E. Hall of county b y Robert LaFont, county court justice on 7-19-1883

Page 119

Bourb on Bellon of City of New Madrid and Ruth McGarin of City of New Madrid by Benton Akin Judge of County Court at residence of J.R.Parks on 11-2-1883

Samuel Pikey LeSieur Twp. and Mrs. Etta Babb of New Madrid Twp. by Robert LaFont, County Court Judge at Edward LeGrands residence on 11-6-1883

Martin T. Dunklin of New Madrid Co. to Mrs. Anna Keeler of State of New York by J. A. Workman M. G. on 5-18-1883

Page 120

James M. Clayton of Big Prairie twp. to Katy Minner with consent of William Murmed by F. M. Holclen J.P. on 9-19-1883

Page 121

Charles T. Jarvis of LeSieur Twp. and Mattie Mays of Martin Station in Weakley Co., Tenn. by B. F. Boyce at LeSieur Twp. on 9-9-1883

Hume H. Marshall of LeSieur Twp. and Theodore Maxey of LeSieur twp. by Elder W. G. Henson at his residence

Page 122

James L. West of West Twp. and Ellen Lander of West Twp. by consent of Abraham Landers, father of Ellen, by John N. Mills, J.P. at residence of bride.

Shadrack Henderson of Co. of New Madrid and Ida Neill of Co. of New Madrid by Joe Cook, J.P. on 9-25-1883

Page 123

Robert Adams of New Madrid Co. and Mollie McElhany of New Madrid Co. b y Rev. Cullen Downing, M.G. at residence of Mrs. McElhany on 10-16-1883

William Harris of New Madrid Co. and Ellen Case of New Madrid Co. C. L. Williams guardian of said Ellen Case had written consent (note: returned not executed 11-10-1883 John A. Mott)

Page 124

Auby Dunklin of City of New Madrid and Patsey Harris of New Madrid by Henry Hunter at the Baptist Church on 10-14-1883

Walt Taylor of Co. of N.M. and Henerietta Hughes of Co. of New Madrid by Charles Rude, M.G. at New Madrid on 10-27-1883

Page 125

George W. Knott of New Madrid City and Eliza J. Massey of New Madrid by Joel Cook, M.G. on 10-11-1883

John Haniphan of New Madrid and Arlee Willis of New Madrid with Cerero Willis, father of Arlee present and giving consent, by W. T. Puler J.P. on 10-14-1883

Page 126

Charles Ates of New Madrid and Lucinda Dorsey by E.A.McKenney M.G. on 10-17-1883 in New Madrid Twp.

C. A. Shelby of East Twp. and Mrs. N. E. Stringer of Scott Co. by F. M. Holden, J.P. in office on Oct 24, 1883.

Page 127

Edward Nicholas of City of New Madrid and Eliza Williams of City of New Madrid by T. W. Clemon, M. G. on 10-27-1883

William A. Pikey of LeSieur Twp. and Susan A. McLemore by C.c.Hudspeth, J.P. at residence of Mrs. McLemore on 11-4-1883

Page 128

Mattison Mulligan (col) of New Madrid and Florence A. Say (col) by W. L. Smith, J.P. on 10-31-1883

Robert A. Fisher of Portage Twp. and Sidney Frazer of Portageville with consent of Robert Frazer, father of Sidney, byCullen Downing M.G. at residence of R.B.Frazier on 11-4-1883

Page 129

Jerry Lemm of New Madrid Twp. and Mary Banks of New Madrid Twp. consent of Allen Lemm, father of Jerry, by Henry Hunter at Samuel McCoys on 11-2-1883

Alphonse Wimp of St. John Twp. and Jerry Baines of St. John Twp. by W. G. Peeler, J.P. on 11-25-1883

Page 130

Joseph Morros (col) of LeSieur Twp. and Margaret Smith (col) LeSieur Twp. by Jos.O'Bannon J.P. on 11-3-1883

Page 131

Lemuel Cupp of New Madrid C ity and Mary Orrall of Big Prairie Twp., John Orrall father of Mary gave consent, by F. M. Holden, J.P. at residence of Mrs. Orrall on 11-17-1883

Charles Rice of New Madrid Twp. and Mary E. Masterson of New Madrid twp by William L. Smith, J.P. on 11-15-1883

Page 132

Isaac Graves of LeSieur Twp. and Leverna Porter of LeSieur Twp. Isaac Porter and Archy Dunklin testified, by Jos. O'Bannon J.P. on 1-15-1884

Page 133

Allen Winston Mainard of Brush Prairie and Laura B. Hill of Brush Prairie by John N. Mills, J.P. at residence of Wm. Graham on 11-21-1883

Page 133

William Daniels of East Twp. of New Madrid to S. A. Lucy Cade
of East Twp., Jacob Cade, father of S.A.Lucy Cade gave consent,
by James Winder, J.P. at home of bride on 12-2-1883

Page 134

Martin Pasquin of New Madrid Co. to Terase LeGrand of
Portage Twp. at Mrs. Elizabeth LeGrands on 11-22-1883 by
Robert LaFont, Co. Court Judge

James Devers of Co. of New Madrid and Rebecca Harney of
Co. of New Madrid, consent of Nancy Harner, mother of Rebecca,
by John N. Mill J.P. at Big Prairie on 7-17-1884

Page 135

William H. Crow of New Madrid Co. and Elizabeth Crockett of
New Madrid Co. by James Stewart J.P. at Como Twp. 11-22-1883

Washington D. Smith of City of New Madrid and Mary Ellis of
City of New Madrid by Wm. L. Smith, J.P. on 11-27-1883

Page 136

John Keinghaw of New Madrid Twp. and Rosa Meleck of New Madrid
Twp by Wm. L. Smith, J.P. at New Madrid on 11-24-1883

Rubin Troter of New Madrid Twp. and Margaret Sinnerill by
Wm. L. Smith, J.P. at New Madrid on 11-25-1883

Page 137

Henry F. Henson and Hattie Toney of New Madrid Co. (no return)

Joseph Daughtry of Co. of N.M. and Sarah Fletcher of Co. of
New Madrid by Charles Rude, M. G. Dec. 30, 1883

Page 138

James H. Hill of Lake Co., Tenn and Betty Allsup of Lake Co.
Tenn. by Joel Cook, J.P. 12-4-1883

William R. Poe of LeSieur Twp. and Mrs. Deshey Wells of LeSieur
Twp. by C. C. Hudspeth J.P. at Mrs. Wells residence on 12-6-1883

Page 139

Milas Mainard of Co. of New Madrid and Mary Patterson of Co.
of New Madrid by John N. Mills, J.P. on 12-3-1883

Lemuel Minner of Big Prairie and Dora Graves of Big Prairie
at residence of William Minner by F. M. Holden on 12-9-1883

Page 140

Joe M. Halery of Louisana Parish, Co. of Pike and Lucinda T. Crow (Chrou?) of Henderson Mounds of New Madrid Co. by James Winders J.P. on 12-9-1883

Jesse Shy of Co. of New Madrid and Mary Kemerothy by Junior? A. Ewing, M. G. at residence of Charles Pike on 12-16-1883

Page 141

George Dunlap of New Madrid and Anna Lee of Co. of New Madrid on testimony of Frank Smith by C.C.Hudspeth, J.P. on 12-3-1883

William Adams of LeSieur Twp . and Josephine Riddle of LeSieur Twp. by C.C.Hudspeth J.P. on Dec. 15, 1883

Page 142

John Townsend of St. John Twp. and Mary Beasy (Bracy?) of St. John Twp. by W. T. Peeler, J.P. on 12-29-1883

Shelby Sheeks of Co. of Mississippi and Francis K. Ellis of County of New Madrid by W.T.Peiler, J.P. on 30 of Dec.

Page 143

John Thomas A. Ward of county of Miss., Mo. and Georgia Wimp of Co. of N.M. by W. T. Peeler, J.P. on 1-26-1884

John A. Leftmueh and Josephine Brown of New Madrid Co. with consent of J. D. Smith, her guardian, by J. N. Mills, J.P. on 12-25-1883

Page 144

John Dunklin of New Madrid Co. and Martha Woods of New Madrid County by Martin Cox, M.G. at residence of Nat. Woods on 1-26-1883.

William H. Farmer of St. Johns Twp. and Alice Neal of St. Johns Twp., Arthur Neal Gdn. of Alice consented, by W. T. Peeler, J.P. Dec. 26, 1883.

Page 145

Fernando C. Stewart of New Madrid Twp. and Ella Mawdy of New Madrid Co. by Joel Cook, J.P. on 12-26-1883

Samuel F. Moore of Big Prairie and Florne E. Morte of Big Prairie by J.A.Mills, J.P. at residence of Chas. Mote

Page 146

Levy Hill of Big Prairie and Margaret L. Rainwater of
Big Prairie by J.A.Mills, J.P. at Samuel J. Moore's
Dec. 13, 1883

John H. Binkley of Rufner Ridge, New Madrid Co. and Mrs.
Nannie Jackson of Rufners Ridge, father consented for Nannie,
by James Stewart, J.P. on 1-1-1884

Page 147 Rank Barnes (col) of New Madrid Co. and Mattie
LaFont of New Madrid Co. by Mury Holmes on 1-3-1884

James Minner of Big Prairie and Martha Sewell of Big Prairie
by F. M. Holden J.P. on 1-13-1884

Page 148

Kane Crowder of Ruddle Point of New Madrid Co. and Alsy
Johnsonof New Madrid by W. M. Brooks, M. G. on 1-24-1884
at Ruddles Point

William H. Dillard of Portage Twp. and Amanda Hogan of
Portage Twp. Tilford Hogan, father of bride, gave consent,
b y John Young, J.P. at residence of Tilford Hogan 1-20-1884

Page 149

Henry F. Henson of New Madrid and Hattie Giny at Alice Hall's
by Irwin Ewing 11-21-1883

Joseph Wimp of St. Johns Twp. and Molly Hayes of New Madrid
by Geo. W. Clark, J.P. at Groom's residence on 2-20-1884

Page 150

Louis Newbauer of New Madrid and Miss Barbara Raidt of
New Madrid by Catholic Priest, P. J. McNamee on 1-30-1884.

Henry Harris (col) of New Madrid and Eliza Merrett (col) of
New Madrid by C. C. Cander on 2-8-1884

Page 151

Marshall Thomas (col) of New Madrid and Caroline Snider (col)
by Henry Holman, M. G. on 2-9-1884

William Singleton of Big Prairie and Annie Swan of Big
Prairie , Thomas Swan, father, gave consent by J. N. Mills, J.P
on Feb. 10, 1884

Page 152

James Merrell of New Madrid and Jane Castleberry of New Madrid Co., John Hart, gdn. of Jane consented, by Joel Cook J.P. on 2-11-1884

William D. Humburger of New Madrid Co. and Elvaline Holden of N.M.Co., William Holden, father of Elvaline, consenting. Married by F. M. Holden, J.P. 2-17-1884

Page 153

Isac P. England of St. John Twp. and Nannie Clark of St. John by W. T. Peeler, J.P. on 2-17-1884

William T. Smitten of Cairo, Alexandria Co., Ill. and L. Josey Riffle of New Madrid by Webster Tull, M. G. on 2-19-1884 at Sol. Levy's house

Page 154

Davis B. Riley of New Madrid Twp. and Hatty Reeder of New Madrid at John Reeder's by Rev. Jas C. Buchanan on 2-20-1884

William W. Hunter of Portage twp. and Ellen Gilmore of Portage Twp., John Young's testimony, by John Young, J.P. on 3-2-1885

Page 155

George T. Hunter, Portage Twp. and Anna Bird of New Madrid by testimony of John Young, J.P. on 3-2-1884

Adolph LeSieur of New Madrid Co. and Terase Phillips of New Madrid Co. by John Young, J.P. at LeSieur Twp. on 2-13-1884

Page 156

Ranson Scott of New Madrid and Missouri Suggs of New Madrid by Joel Cook, J.P. on 3-8-1884

Andy Seas of New Madrid and Amanda Carr of New Madrid by Henry Hunter, M. G. on Mar. 9, 1884

Page 157

Robert Tarteton (col) of New Madrid to Margaret Gitton (col) by Wm. L. Smith, J.P. on 3-13-1884

Page 157

William McGlothlin and Erivn Busby of Co. of N.M. (no return)

Page 158

Tom Harris (col) of New Madrid and Mattie Henderson (col) by Henry Hunter, M.G. on 4-5-1884

John W. Gray of New Madrid Twp. and Lizzie Davis (W.J.Gray, uncle of John proved aged) by Webster Tull, M.G. on 4-10-1884

Page 159

James D. Brinkley of Portageville and Mary E. Hay of Portage Twp, by John Young, J.P. on 4-13-1884

George Alexander (col) of Fulton, KY. and Judy Ward of Fulton, Ky. by Joseph Piggs, M. G. on 4-18-1884

Page 160

John Alexander (col) of New Madrid Twp. and July Ann Watson, (col) of New Madrid on 4-20-1884 by T. M. Clemons, M.G.

Abraham B. Adams of St. John Twp. and Mrs. Mollie Hayes of St. Johns by W. T. Peeler, J.P. on 4-20-1884

Page 161

Samuel Henderson (col) of New Madrid Twp. and Amanda Bennett(col) (no return)

John Jones of New Madrid Twp. and Elizabeth Carter of New Madrid Twp. by Joel Cook, J.P. on 5-15-1884

Page 162

George Dibbrel and Mrs. Jane Carter of New Madrid, Mo. by Joel Cook J.P. on 5-26-1884

Page 163

George S. Jones of New Madrid and Laura Paul of New Madrid Co. by Peter Hoehn, J.P. on 5-26-1884

James Edward Broughton, New Madrid Twp. and Mrs. Jessie Dorch Toney of New Madrid Twp. by Rev. H.H.Riley, Catholic Pastor at Mr. Eakins on May 28, 1884

Page 164

William H. Goldon of Ruffners Ridge and Susan Everhart of Ruffners Ridge in New Madrid Co. by James Stewart J.P. on May 31, 1884

Scott Alexander (col) of LeSieur Twp. to Lula McFarland (col) by Charles Reed, M.G. on 6-11-1884

Page 165

Thomas Martin of West Twp. and Mrs. Ella Westerman of West Twp. by J. N. Mills, J.P. on 6-8-1884

Amos Barnes of New Madrid Twp and Mrs. Mary Ann Harden of New Madrid Twp. by Peter Hoehn, J.P. on 6-17-1884

Page 166

Miller Mukes of New Madrid Twp. and Sarah Hall of New Madrid Twp. by T. W. Clemons on 6-22-1884

James A. Gold and Mrs. Druzila Ward of New Madrid Twp. by Joel Cook, J.P. on 7-8-1884

Page 167

William Hall of Brush Prairie and Mollie Carroll of Brush Prairie by John Mills, J.P. on 7-10-1884

Samuel Yates (col) New Madrid Twp. and Mary King (col) of New Madrid Twp. (no return)

Page 168

James P. Higgs of Big Prairie Twp. and SallieCaldwell of Big Prairie Twp. by John N. Mill J.P. on 7-25-1884

Earnest Robison (col) of New Madrid and Mrs. Jane Johnson (col) of New Madrid by T. W. Clemons, M.G. on 7-30-1884

Page 169

Richard Jones (col) of Big Prairie and Mary Caral (col) of Big Prairie by C. C. Harlan, M. G. on 8-4-1884

James Robinson (col) of New Madrid and Amelia Smith (col) LeSieur Twp. by Henry Hunter M.G. on 8-8-1884 on Brownell's farm.

Page 170

Bishop Purcell of LeSieur Twp. and Atlanta G. Stewart of LeSieur Twp. by Joel Cook, J.P. on 8-3-1884

John Logan Roper of Little River and Nancy Catharine Buckhart of Little River by L. D. Sibley, Judge of 1st Dist. of Scott Co. at Sikeston, Mo. on 8-6-1884

Page 171

Junior Scott Harrison of Mississippi Co., Mo. to Katie Francis Brady of Miss. Co. by W. Z. Peeler J.P. on 8-7-1884 at David Hopkins.

George W. Williams of Como Twp. and Emily Bradshaw of Como Twp. , Simeon Golden, gdn. gave consent for Emily, by C. B. Jackson, Jr. J.P. on 8-11-1884

Page 172

Charles Grant of Big Prairie and Mrs. Sarah Snider of Big Prairie by John Mills, J.P. on 8-10-1884

William C. Hendrix of Pemiscot Co. and Nancy J. Meadors of Pemiscot Co. by B. F. Boyce, J.P. on 8-14-1884

Page 173

Nathan Carter of New Madrid Co. and Amanda Ross of New Madrid Co. by John Mills, J.P. at residence of William Lee on 8-14-1884

James Preston of Garret Co. Ky. and Nancy Gibson of St. John Twp. Mo. by Joel Cook J.P. at residence of William Lee of New Madrid on 8-20-1884

Page 174

George W. Williams of Como Twp. and Emily Bradshaw of Como Twp., Simeon Goldon, Gdn. gave consent for Emily by C.B,Jackson Jr. J.P. on 8-11-1884

Hoza Hornberger of Big Prairie and Mrs. Catharine Jones of Big Prairie by W. W. Ellis M.G. at residence of Catharine Jones on 8-21-1884

Page 175

Winston P. Ellington of Green Co. Ark. and Martha E. McMillan of Green Co. Ark by Peter Hoen J.P. on 9-1-1885

Alonza O'Bannon of New Madrid and Melissa Walker of New Madrid by Henry Hunter on 9-15-1884 at Robert Lee's farm.

Page 176

William Brunson of New Madrid Twp. and Eva Davis, Morris Davis, father of Eva, consenting by Henry Holman, M.G. (methodist) on 9-12-1884

Ples Young (col) of Pt. Pleasant and Lula Bowens (col) of Pt. Pleasant by Jas. O'Bannon, J.P. on 9-16-1884

Page 177

William J. Caldwell of Big Prairie of New Madrid and Mrs. Margarett Presley of New Madrid (Big Prairie) on 9-23-1884 by James Winders, J.P.

Joseph Wellman of Sikeston and Mrs. Mary Witt of Sikeston by Rev. H. H. Reilly, Catholic Priest on 9-23-1884

Page 178

William Spencer of Brush Prairie and Mrs. Lavada McCloud by John N. Mills J.P. on 10-16-1884

John McKinney of Big Prairie and Mrs. Amanda Davis of Big Prairie by John N. Mills, J.P. on 9-29-1884

Page 179

Edward A. Wright of New Madrid City and Miss Cora Groves of New Madrid City by John A. Davis, J.P. on 10-1-1884

Weston Shirkey of Co. of New Madrid and Fannie Barron of City of New Madrid, consent of W. J. Barron, father of Fannie, by H.H. Rielly, Catholic Priest on 10-1-1884

Page 180

Augustus LeSieur of New Madrid City and Miss Ella Davis of New Madrid City by Webster Tull, M.G. at Mary A. Newton's on 10-9-1884

Peter Miller (col) of Big Prairie and Jane Ogden (col) of Big Prairie by M. C. Cox, M.G. at Mark Stallcup's

Page 181

Daniel Johnson of LeSieur Twp. and Carry Harrison of LeSieur Twp. by consent of Squire Harrison, father of Carry, by John A. Davis, Judge of Co. Court

Thomas Woods of New Madrid Twp. and Tishy Cherry of New Madrid City by Henry Hunter at F.W. Baptist Church on 10-18-1884

Page 182

Albert D. Fortest of Brush Prairie and Sarah A. Mote of Brush Prairie with consent of M. Mote, father of Alsie? Mote by Webster Tull, M. G. on 10-23-1884

Charles W. Heath of East Twp. and Miss Eliza Settles of East Twp. M. G. Settles, brother of Eliza says Mother is willing & father deceased, by James Winders, J.P. on 10-26-1885

Page 183

James Young (col) of New Madrid Twp. and Sarah Carson (col) of N.M. Twp. by Elder Charles Reed, M.G. on 10-11-1884

Jacob L. Shelby of East Twp. and Mrs. Sarah Cerne of Scott Co. Mo. by F. M. Holden, J.P. in East Twp on 11-2-1884

Page 184

Warren R. Tolbett of St. Johns Twp. and Mrs. Lizzie Ellis of St. Johns Twp. by W. Z. Peeler J.P. on 11-9-1884

Page 184

James Eackus of New Madrid Co. and Elizabeth Allison of New Madrid Co. by John N. Mills J.P. on 11-12-1884

Page 185

Marcus Shumaker of New Madrid Co. and Paushy Bearde by George W. Clark, J.P. of St. John Twp. on 11-15-1884

James Williams of New Madrid City and Lou Nash of New Madrid Co. by M. C. Cox M.G. on 12-6-1884

Page 186

Daniel S. Cooper of New Madrid Twp. and Mrs. Elizabeth Shumaker of N.M. Twp by John N. Mills J.P. at Big Prairie on 11-30-1884

Gayle L. Darnell of City of New Madrid and Sally Connor of City of New Madrid by Joel Cook, J.P. on 12-15-1884

Page 187

Samuel H. Martin of Brush Prairie and Miss Martha Keester by John N. Mills, J.P. on 12-22-1884

Bart Hackney of LeSieur Twp . and Cornelia Wilson of LeSieur consent of Robert Wilson, father of Cornelia, by C. C. Hudspeth, J.P. on 1-4-1885

Page 188

Daniel Weatherspoon (col) of N.M.twp. and Jane Ogden (col) of N.M.twp. by Rev. J.P.Pigg, M.G. on 12-26-1884

George W. Wray of Big Prairie Twp. and Mrs. Sarah E. Choat of Big Prairie Twp. by Webster Tull, M.G. on Dec 24, 1884

Page 189

Samuel Thomas (col) of N.M.Twp. and Amanda Watson (col) of N.M.Twp. by Charles Reed, M.G. on 12-25-1884

Gaines Pearce of City of New Madrid and Theresa Fuller of City of New Madrid by Joel Cook, J.P. on 12-23-1884

Page 190

Stephen A. Davis (col) of N.M.Twp. and Mary Ann Waters (col) N.M.Twp. with Thomas & Sallie Waters, parents of Mary Anne consenting, by E.A.McKinney, M.G. on 12-31-1884

Page 190

Henry McFarland (col) of N.M. Twp. and Ida Lafont of N.M.Twp. by Henry Hunter, M.G. on 12-30-1884

Page 191

Henry Murphy of West Twp. and Elizabeth Leeke of West Twp. with Joseph F. Leake ,father of Elizabeth consenting, by John N. Mills, J.P. on 1-20-1885

Albert Thompson of LeSieur Twp. and Emma Richy of LeSieur Twp. by Jas. A. Workman, M. G. on 1-11-1885

Page 192

Richard Laster of East Twp. and Julia H. Earles of East Twp. by F. M. Holden, J.P. on 1-22-1885

William McGlothen of City of New Madrid and Erion Busby of Co. of New Madrid by A. C. Wyatt, J.P. on 4-2-1884

Page 193

Joseph A. Cresap of Sikeston, Mo. and Bell Newton of City of New Madrid by Webster Tull M.G. on 11-12-1884 at Mary Newton's in New Madrid

W.J.Dodson of Lake Co. Tenn and Elizabeth Hart of Lake Co. Tenn by Peter Hoehn J.P. on 6-3-1884

Page 194

Rapheal LeSieur Jr. of LeSieur Twp. and Tearce Adams of Portage Twp. Robert LaFont, County Court Judge at residence of Frank Meatt on 1-18-1885

Joseph Adda of City of New Madrid and Cora Davis with Alonzo O'Bannon verifying age of Joseph Adda (cert. ret. but not filled out)

Page 195

Hesekiah Dennis of City of New Madrid and Betty Buchanan of City of New Madrid by written consent of V.V.Waters, Gdn of said Betty, b y H.H.Riley, Catholic Priest on 1-18-1885

Robert Hatcher Allen of City of New Madrid and Frances Julia Waters of City of New Madrid with consent of W.B. Allen, father of said Robert, by H.H.Riley, Catholic Priest on 1-20-1885

Page 196

Thomas Hick and Della O. Brine of New Madrid Twp. by C. P. Jackson J.P. on 1-28-1883

Frans W. Morrison of Brush Prairie and Mary Miller of Stewart's Station of New Madrid Co. by James Stewart J.P. on 2-2-1885

Page 197

Jessie F. McIntire of Como Twp. and Nancy E. Dowdy of Como Twp. by James Stewart J.P. on 2-4-1885

Benjamin Williams of LeSieur Twp. and Amanda Dunklin of City of New Madrid by Henry Hunter, M.G. at Daniel Dunklin on 2-6-1885

Page 198

Benjamin Heron of LeSieur Twp. and Mrs. Lue Parker of LeSieur Twp. by Elder W. G. Henson, M.G. at residence of Betty Sine

William A. Rice of LeSieur Twp. and Miss Bettie McConnel of LeSieur Twp by Joseph O'Bannon J.P. on 2-13-1885

Page 199

George W. Manuel of LeSieur Twp. and Equilee Lenier of LeSieur Twp. by Elder W.G.Henson, M.G. on 2-15-1885

Upton B. Foxe of City of New Madrid and Nelly Smith at Thomas Smiths, father of Nelly, by Webster Tull, M. G. on 2-17-1885

Page 200

William Harmon Laster of East Twp. and Olive Jane Johnson of East Twp. with consent of Frances Floro, only living parent of Olive Jane, by James Winders, J.P. on 2-22-1885

Andrew DeLisle of Pt. Pleasant and Mary DeLisle of Portage Twp. by J. A. Wynn, J.P. on 2-26-1885

Page 201

Albert S. Davis of Kansas City, County of Jackson, Mo. and Carrie Dawson of City of N.M. by H.H.Riley, Catholic Priest on 3-2-1885

A., J, Pillow and Mary Shafer of Co. of New Madrid by John N. Mills, J.P. at residence in Big Prairie on 3-7-1885

Page 202

WilliamHiggerson and Miss Mollie Pickett of New Madrid Co. by D. Q. Sanders on 3-8-1885 at James Bayou of Miss. Co., Mo.

James E. Finn of New Madrid Co. and Eliza Ann Finn. Eliza Ann Brooks, mother of Eliza Ann Finn consetns, by John N. Mills on 3-12-1885

Page 203

Thomas K. Sims of Big Prairie and Pamela A. Winchester of Big Prairie with consent of Mandy Brown, mother of Pamela, by John N. Mills, J.P. on 3-18-1885

Aft Penders of Brush Prairie and Emeline Ketterman of Brush Prairie, consent of David Ketterman, father of Emeline, by R. C. V inson, J.P. at Malden, Mo. on 5-24-1885

Page 204

Jaike M. McClane of New Madrid and Elizabeth Davis on Mar. 29, 1885 by Rev. J.A. Ewing
Page 205
Robert Mays of Big Prairie and Laura Hodges of Big Prairie with consent of J.H.Pherris, her guardian, on 4-5-1885 by John N. Mills

Page 204

Newton Lovengood of LeSieur Twp. and Adelia Miflen of Lesieur Twp. of LeSieur Twp by C.C.Hudspeth,J.P. on 4-5-1885

Page 205

Charles Green of City of New Madrid to Mrs. Sarah Blizzard of St. John Twp. by W. T. Peeler, J.P. on 2-11-1885

Page 206

Elias Porter of New Madrid Twp. and Sylvia Daughtery of New Madrid Twp. on 4-5-1885 at Robert Branssuces by Joseph Pigus, M.G.

Samuel C. Jones of New Madrid City and Anny P. Mahar of New Madrid City by Irwin A. Ewing, M.G. on 4-19-1885 at residence of Wm. T Mahar

Page 207

James McCoy of New Madrid Twp. and Carry Dow of New Madrid Twp by Henry Hunter M.G. on 4-19-1885

Nathaniel White of LeSieur Twp. and Ann Small by Joel Cooke,J. on May 12, 1885

Page 208

James B. Clayton of Big Prairie Twp. and Jenny Ligon of Big Prairie by John N. Mills J.P. on 4-26-1885

William May of East Twp. and Norma Caroline Jout of East Twp. as by testimony of James Winder Esq. by James Winders, J.P. on 5-6-1885

Page 209

William Thorn of Brush Prairie and Lou Wheat of Brush Prairie b y Walton McDenough M. G. on 4-22-1885

Page 210

Marshall Spaulding of New Madrid Twp. and Mary E. Tompkins of New Madrid Twp. by Henry Hunter J.P. on 5-13-1885

Thomas Jackson of New Madrid City and Mary LaForge by Joseph Piggers, M. G. on May 22, 1885

Page 211

Luke Douglass of City of New Madrid to Press Brown of City of New Madrid by Henry Hunter, J.P. on 5-14-1885

Apelles C. Yelleman of Paducah, Ky. county of McCrackin and Mary E. Simmon of New Madrid with consent of Catharine James, Guardian of said Mary by C. B. Jackson on 6-12-1885

Page 212

Andrew Carroll of Big Prairie and Mrs. M. I. Helm of Big Prairie by J. D. Stepp, J.P. on 6-21-1885

John A. Hutchenson of Anna, Ill. Union County, and Cyntha A. Vowell of Anna by Joel Cooke on 6-25-1885

Page 213

Henry Hall of New Madrid Twp. and Betty Beavers of New Madrid Twp by Joel Cooke, J.P. on 6-25-1885

David F. Bruckman of Big Prairie and Mrs. Martha E. Gilbert of Big Prairie on 7-20-1885 by James Winders, J.P.

Page 214

John A. Lefturch of Big Prairie and Miss Katy Yarber of Big Prairie by J. D. Stepp, J.P. on 7-5-1885

Emerson D. Jackson of New Madrid and Miss Nanny Adams of LeSieur Twp. by C. C. Hudspeth, J.P. on 7-5-1885

Page 215

James N. Campbell of New Madrid Co. and Eliza Forde of New Madrid Co. with consent of James N. Campbell, father of said James N. Jr. and Eliza Bush mother of said Eliza on July 9, 1885 by J.P. (name not given)

Isaac Franklin Caldwell of Big Prairie and Margaret C. Flannery of Big Prairie with Geo. W. Ray, stepfather of said Margaret consenting by John A Mott, J.P.

Page 216

William A. Wright of West Twp. and Jennett Landers of West Twp. by John N. Mills J.P. on July 19, 1885.

James C. Massey of Big Prairie Twp. and Mrs. Polley Westerman of Big Prairie by James Stepp, J.P. on 7-21-1885

Page 217

John Hix of Big Prairie Twp. and Mary Moody of New Madrid by J. N. Mills, J.P. on 7-26-1885

Alford Dorsey of New Madrid Twp. and Nettie Clark of New Madrid Twp. by E. A. McKinney M.G. on 7-23-1884

Page 218

Jerome Worth of LeSieur and Mrs. Deby E. Strong of LeSieur by C. B. Jackson J.P. on 7-25-1885

William Jackson of LeSieur Twp. and Mattie Brown of LeSieur Twp. by E. A. McKinney, M. G. on 7-25-1885

Page 219

Jessie Lewis of Pt. Pleasant and Elizabeth Earington of Pt. Pleasant by C. C. Hudspeth on July 28, 1885

Francis M. Reed of Big Prairie and Polly Lany, testimony of J.T. Swan as to ages, by John Mills, J.P. on 8-9-1885

Page 220

James C. Price of LeSieur Twp. and Naomia Dillard of LeSieur Twp. , testimony by John Young as to ages, by John Young, J.P on 8-4-1885

Robert Adams of Portage Twp. and Bell White of Portage Twp. on testimony of Young as to age of Bell White by John Young, J.P. on 8-9-1885

Page 221

Vallee Godiar and Maggie Burny of Portage Twp. with consent of M.C.Burney, mother of Maggie, by W. G. Henson, M.G. on 8-16-1885

Benson W. Peples of Big Prairie and Eliaza A. Whitworth of Big Prairie Twp. by J.N.Mills, J.P. on 8-10-1885

Page 222

Charles Wilson of St. John Twp. and Mrs. Hester E. Goins of St. John Twp. by W. T. Peeler, J.P. on 8-9-1885

James Champion of St. John Twp. and Bell Parker of St. John Twp. , consent of Sarah Parker, mother of said Bell, b y G. W. Clark J.P. on 8-8-1885

Page 223

Samuel Dickerson of Donaldson Pt. New Madrid Co. and Pamela Willis of Donaldson Point by C. B. Jackson, J.P. on 8-9-1885
(Murray Webster)
Murry W. Phillips of New Madrid and Mary Hardin of Jefferson Co., Ky. on 8-13-1885 by J. Webster Tull, 8-13-1885

Page 224

Ike Lowry of New Madrid and Martha Lynch of New Madrid by C. B. Jackson J.P. on 8-14-1885

Page 225

Albert Young and Emeline Walker of LeSieur Twp. by Charles Reed, M. G. on 8-19-1885

George M. Talbot and Adaline Noble of New Madrid Twp. with consent of Mary J. Noble, Mother of Bride, by C. B. Jackson, J.P. on 8-18-1885

Page 226

John L. Connor of St. John Twp. and Miss Minerva Sloas of St. John Twp. by C. B. Jackson, J.P. on 9-1-1885

Wm. Henry Newman of Big Prairie and Miss Hester Branham (index says Brown). Thomas Newman, father of Henry and Guardian of Hester Brown gives consent, by John Mott on 9-4-1885

Page 227

Jefferson D. Stepp of Brush Prairie and Miss Cora L. Ross of Brush Prairie by John Mills J.P. on 9-3-1885

Page 227

William Alexander Gray of New Madrid and Eliza Bell Foster of New Madrid by C. B. Jackson, J.P. on 7-7-1885

Page 228

John H. Reed of Big Prairie and Lueritia Weaver of Big Prairie by G. P. Boggan, guardian of Lueretia giving consent, by James F. Bishop, M.G. on 9-17-1885

Charles Reed of Lewis Prairie and Susan Fletcher of New Madrid b y Joseph Piggus, M.G.

Page 229

James Freeman and Harriet Mudd of City of New Madrid by H.Hunter, M.G. on 9-15-1885

William Hayes and Penese Mayes of Big Prairie twp. on 9-23-1885 at Big Prairie by John Mills, J.P.

Page 230

C.A.Barley of County and Annie E. Hedge of County of N.M. on 9-27-1885 by James Winders, J.P.

James F. Jewell of New Madrid Twp. and Laura J. Jackson of New Madrid Twp. by Joel Cooke,J.P. at Sarah Jackson's residence on Oct. 7, 1885

Page 231

John Brown of St. Francis, Clay Co., Ark. and Mrs. Mary Stolder of St. Francis, Clay Co., Ark. by Joel Cook, J.P. on 10-20-1885

Napoleon Williams of Co. of N.M. and Sarah E. Blair of County of N.M. on 8-16-1885 by Joseph O'Bannon, J.P.

Page 232

William Smithman of Ruddles Point and Jennie Parker of Ruddles Point consent of guardian of said Jennie Parker by Irvin A. Ewing, M.G. at Mrs. J. LaZell's on 10-25-1885

Irvin A. Ewing, M.G. of Lewis Prairie and Anna Bell Shields of Brush Prairie by Webster Tull, M.G. at Joseph Shields on 10-28-1885

Page 233

Willie H. Herbert of Sikeston of Scott Co. and Miss Mamie Reade of New Madrid by W. H. Reade, Minister of Presbyterian Church on 10-29-1885

Page 233

Jordan Wilson of New Madrid and Laura Rhodes of LeSieur Twp. with consent of Edward Rhodes, father of Laura, on Nov. 1, 1885 by M. Bass, M.G.

Page 234

Frank Harbold of New Madrid Twp. and Lelia Reeder of New Madrid Twp. at Mrs. Harriet Evans by Webster Tull M.G. on 11-4-1885

Natt Wood and Martha Bennett of New Madrid by H.Hunter,M.G. on 11-1-1885

Page 235

John Workman of Brush Prairie and Cynthia Workman of Brush Prairie by L.F.Bishop M.G. on 11-8-1885

John A. Hummel of New Madrid and Bell Sherwood of New Madrid by Wesel Beall Minister of the Presbyterian Church at Joseph Hunter's residence.

Page 236

Henry P. Wilson of New Madrid and Ella Conley of New Madrid at residence of Ella Conley by Ephraim A. McKinney, M.G. on 11-13-1885

Everett Reed of East twp. and Julia M. Gutdridge of East Twp. by affiant of George Thompson as to age of Julia M. Guthridge at residence of John Thompson by F. M. Holden, J.P. on 11-15-1885

Page 237

George Atcheson of LeSieur Twp. and Lucy Henson of LeSieur Twp. at residence of G. W. Henson by Elder Cullen Downing,M.G. on 11-17-1885

William H. Sowders of Portage Twp. and Sarah Wintz of Portage Twp. by Rofert LaFont county judge on 11-17-1885

Page 238

Lafayette Gibson of Portageville and Sarah O. Wyatt of Portageville by G.W.Boon, Elder on 11-17-1885

John L. Priddy of Big Prairie and Miss Eliza Brown of Big Prairie by John N. Mills J.P. on 11-29-1886

Page 239

Eli Jones of New Madrid County and Sylva Guy of New
Madrid Twp. by Scott Alexander, M.G. on 11-22-1885.

Robert M. Black of LeSieur and Mrs. Emma E. Parkerson of
LeSieur by John H. Workman, M.G. at James Huffsteder's on
11-28-1886.

Page 240

George H. Shank of St. John Twp. and Martha E. Simmons
of St. John Twp. by George W. Clark, J.P. on 12-9-1885

George W. Gray of N.M. County and Lucy E. Fiske of N.M.
Co. by James F. Bishop, M.G. at James Fisks on 2-7-1886.

Page 243

William H. Till of LeSieur Twp. and Mrs. Ellen Bullock of
LeSieur Twp. by Joseph O'Bannon, J.P. on 12-9-1886

Samuel Ates of New Madrid Twp. and Josephine Branson
(Index shows Bunson) alias Louise Brunner consenting
by Hamilton Hott, M.G. at Louise Low? (See page 245)

Page 244

Mathew Vaughen of Big Prairie and Katy Lincke of Big
Prairie by John N. Mills, J.P. on 10-7-1885

Thomas B. Crow of Brush Prairie and Sarah J. Martin of
New Madrid At. B. B. Crow's residence by James Stepp,J.P.
on Dec. 8, 1885

Page 241

Louis W. Wade of New Madrid Twp. and Eda Hunter of New
Madrid Twp. by Epraim McKinney, M.G. on 12-27-1888 at
Neal Hunter's residence.

Ambrose Lumi of New Madrid Twp. and Presulla Isabel of
New Madrid Twp. by W. G. Henson, M.G. on 12-6-1885

Page 242

George W. Shank of St. John Twp. and Martha E.
Simmons of St. John Twp. by George W. Clark, J.P. on
Dec. 9, 1885.

Page 245

Albert W. LaFont of New Madrid Twp. and Carrie Waters,
John B. LaFont, father of said Albert and Elizah Waters,
father of said Carrie, consenting. by Henry Hunter, M.G.
on 12-23-1885

Page 245

Samuel Ate of New Madrid Twp. and Josephine Hampton of New Madrid Twp. Louise Love (alias Hampton) guardian of said Josephine consenting, by Madison Hale, M. G. on Dec. 23, 1885 at Louise Love.

Page 246

Charles Nash of LeSieur and Lena V. Fore of LeSieur (License returned not filled out)

Page 247

George W. Clark of St. John Twp. & Sarah S. Parker of St. John Twp. by W. T. Peeler, J.P. on 12-31-1885

Makinzy Minner of Big Prairie Twp. and Catherine Beavers of Big Prairie Twp. by Joel Cook, J.P. on 12-30-1885

Page 248

Hosey Horneburger of Big Prairie Twp. and Mrs. Nancy Furlong of Big Prairie Twp. by W. S. Boyd, M.G. on Jan. 11, 1886

Page 249

Samuel Mainord of Big Prairie and Miss Perlie Stone of Big Prairie, consent of Josephine Felps, mother of Pearlie at Josephine Phillips by James A. Biship, M.G. on 1-12-1886

Henry E. Broughton of City of New Madrid and Miss Clara Mott of City of New Madrid by Henry G. Hobs, M.G. on 1-12-1886

Page 250

Wm. Howard (other use Wm. Dunn) and Mary Wesley with consent of Ritta Wesly only parent of said ward and John Howard, father of William, at John Howard's residence by Henry Hunter, M.G. on 1-20-1886

John Jardin of New Madrid Twp. and Rozetta Tapp of New Madrid Mo., Frank Davis, stepfather of Rozetta consents by John N. Mills, J.P. on 1-27-1886

Page 251

James Chapman of New Madrid Twp. and Nanney R. Ellis of New Madrid Twp. by Irwin H. Ewing, M.G. on 1-27-1886 at Louis Lee's.

Page 251

Haron Laster of East Twp. and Adele Boon with consent of Mary Boon, only living parent of Adele (no return)

Page 252

George W. Conrad of Portage and Tearesa A. Howard of Portage on 2-9-1886 by John Young, J.P.

Page 252

Charles W. Lonyou of Big Prairie to Fanny Long of Big Prairie with Sally Dean, guardian of Fanny Long consenting, by John N. Mills, J.P. on 2-9-1886

Page 253

Jeff D. Carroll of Big Prairie and Caroline Shelby of Big Prairie on 2-17-1886 by James F. Bishop, M.G.

Aaron Laster of New Madrid Co. and Adell Brown of East Twp. with consent of Mary Brown, Mother & only living parent, on 1-31-1886 by F. M. Holden, J.P.

Page 254

George E. Millard of Big Prairie and Mrs. Addie Long of Big Prairie with consent of J.H. Trollenged having care and custody of Addie Long, by John N. Mills, J.P. on 2-14-1886

Archibald Bush of Portage Twp. and Mary F. McWilliams by John Young, J.P. on 2-14-1886

Page 255

James Holloway of East Twp. and Alsa Powell of East Twp. with consent of John Long, guardian of James, by A. M. Holden, J.P. on 2-24-1886

Joseph Richard Wilburn of East Twp. and Emma Winters East Twp, Sarah Wilburn, mother & only living parent of Joseph and Caroline Shelby, gdn. of Emma Winters consenting, by F. M. Holden, J.P. on 2-25-1886

Page 256

Berry Downs of St. John Twp. and Asalee Morris with Robert Morris, father of Asalee consenting, by F. M. Holden, J.P. on 2-25-1886.

Page 257

William J. Farrell of New Madrid and Mary Clark by Joel Cook J.P. on 3-1-1886

Benjamin Pasquin of Portage Twp. and Martha LeGrand of Portage Twp. at residence of Edie LeGrande by Robert Lafont, county judge, on 3-25-1886.

Page 258

Joseph Howard of LeSieur Twp. and Lotty Porter of LeSieur Twp. (return not filled out)

William McGintry of Brush Prairie and Jenny C. Alexander of Big Prairie, Robert Alexander, father of Jenny, consenting, by James F. Biship M.G. on 3-7-1886 at Robert Alexander's.

Page 259

Wm. A. Green of St. John Twp. and Cornelia Kelly of St. John Twp. by W. T. Peeler J.P. on 3-14-1886.

Charles Richards of New Madrid and Mary Ashby of New Madrid by Joseph Pigg J.P. on 3-14-1886

Page 260

William J. Edmondson of New Madrid Twp. and Anna Henson with consent of John Edmondston, father of William J. & W. G. Henson, father of Anna, on 12-5-1885 by Irwin A. Ewing, M.G.

James B. Jones of New Madrid Twp. and Henrietta Gilbert of New Madrid Twp. by John Young, J.P. on March 17, 1886

Page 261

James Wesley of New Madrid and Nanny Olsby of New Madrid with consent of Molly Johnson, gdn. of Nanny, by Henry Hunter, M.G. on 3-21-1886 at Joseph Johnson's.

Christopher M. Harris of Lake Co. Tenn. and Francis E. Early of New Madrid by Webster Tull, M.G. of ME Church S. at New Madrid, Mo.

Page 262

Charles M. Parkerson of Madrid Bend, Fulton Co., Ky. and Mary E. Woods of Madrid Bend, Fulton Co., Ky. by Joel Cook, J.P.

Page 262

David E. Jones and Miss Sallie Ransburgh of Co. of New Madrid by Webster Tull, M.G. of M.E.Church South on 3-24-1886.

Page 263

Robert L. Godard of Portage and Emma Ward of Portage at D. W. Wards March 25 by Telford T. Hogan, M.G.

Millard F. Jinen or St. John Twp. and Bell Connor of St. John Twp. on 6-23-1885 by W. T. Peeler, J.P.

Page 264

William Warren of New Madrid Twp and Emma Martin of New Madrid Twp. by Henry Hunter, M.G. on March 29, 1886.

Riley Leadbetter of New Madrid Co. and Georgia A. Ray of Mississippi Co., Mo. with consent of Polk Ray, father of said Georgia, on March 28, 1886.

Page 265

Josiah Patterson of Brush Prairie and Mary E. B urns of Brush Prairie by James F. Bishop , M.G. at Milas Mainords.

Charles Nash of Co. of New Madrid and Emaline Marsden of New Madrid Co. by Joseph O'Bannon, J.P. on 4-18-1886.

Page 266

Lavalle DeLisle of Portageville and Mary Carson of Portageville by James Workman, M.G. at residence of J.Workman.

John Milligan of LeSieur Twp. and Adale Dunklin of Lewis Twp. by C. C. Hudspeth, J.P. at LeSieur Twp on 4-7-1886.

Page 267

Columbus B. DeLisle of Portage Twp. and Anna Tomisson of Portage Twp. by J. A. Wynn, J.P. on 4-10-1886.

Charles Robinson of LeSieur Twp. and Elizah Godaird of LeSieur Twp. by Joseph O'Bannon, J.P. at L. LaFerney on 4-22-1886.

Page 268

Felix N. LeSieur of City of New Madrid and Miss Nannie Miller of City of N.M. by Webster Full, M.G. at J.R. Parks in New Madrid on 4-21-1886

Page 268

Clein J. Benton of New Madrid and Ellen Murphy by Webster Full, M.G. on April 21, 1886

Page 269

John H. Hodge of New Madrid Twp. and Mrs. Mary J. Shultz of New Madrid Twp. by James F. Bishop, M. G. on 5-13-1886

William Hereford, New Madrid Twp. and Lena F. Oaitain of New Madrid Twp. by Henry Hunter, M.G. on 5-29-1886

Page 270

John Beavers of Big Prairie Twp. and Martha Dillard of Big Prairie, consent of James Dillard, father of Martha, b y J. N. Mills, J.P. on 5-23-1886.

James R. Divinny and Miss Eliza Stonebraker of Big Prairie by John A. Bishop, M.G. on May 8, 1886

Page 271

Andrew W. Babb of New Madrid Twp. and Miss Mary Etta Cravens of New Madrid Twp. by Irvin A. Ewing, M. G. on 6-6-1886

Benjamin Smith of New Madrid Twp. and Melissa Adkins of New Madrid Twp. by Ephraim A. McKinney on 6-6-1886

Page 272

J. H. Sutherland of LeSieur Twp. and Addie Herron of LeSieur Twp., Mrs. Sallie Herron, mother of said Addie consents, by John O'Bannon, J.P. on 6-16-1886

George W. Crafton of Como Twp. and Mary Susan Stratton of Como Twp. by James Stewart, J.P. on 6-27-1886

Page 273

John W. Lewis of New Madrid City and Mary Bell King of New Madrid City at Christ Church by J.R. Parks on 6-6-1886

John W. Sauls of New Madrid Twp. and Ellen Pacquett of New Madrid Twp., Jenneth Pacquett, Mother of Ellen, gives consent, by James Bishop, M. G. on 6-26-1886

Page 274

Samuel Lynch of Co. of New Madrid and Ellen Lee of New Madrid by Joseph Piggus, M. G. on May 29, 1886

Joseph Toney of New Madrid Twp. and Dora Butler of New Madrid Twp. by Ephraim A. McKinney, M. G. on 7-4-1886

Page 275

Albert Scott and Eliza Harris of Pt. Pleasant (no return)

William J. Hudgins of New Madrid and Josephine Oakes, consent of Elizabeth Dassett, guardian of said Josephine, by T. J. O. Morrison, J.P. on 7-22-1886

Page 276

John M. Powell of New Madrid and Mrs. Angeline Coleman of New Madrid by Joseph Piggus, M. G. at Crow School House on 8-11-1886

Isaac Minneweather of New Madrid and Mary Hunter of New Madrid by Joseph Piggus, M.G. on 8-4-1886

Page 277

Albert Miller of Pt. Pleasant and Lena Shelby of Riddles Point, Louis Douglas testifies as to age of Lena Shelby, by Rev. T. W. Clements on 8-15-1886

Joseph F. Roberts of Big Prairie and Anna L. Carpenter of Big Prairie at James Stubblefields by James F. Bishop, M.G. on 8-17-1886

Page 278

J. W. Simes of LeSieur Twp. and Ida Conrad of Portage Twp. by John Young, J.P. at Portage Twp. on 8-19-1886

William Akers of LeSieur Twp. and Miss Betty Baker of LeSieur Twp. by Jas. A. Workman, M.G. on 8-19-1886

Page 279

Isaac C. Cooper of East Twp. and Virginia L. Hancock of East Twp. with consent of Louise Hancock, mother of said Virginia, by James Winders, J.P. on 8-6-1886

Joseph L. Allen of New Madrid and Jenny Hogan of New Madrid, consent of Mary Campbell, only living parent of Jenny, by T. J.O.Morrison, J.P. on Aug. 23, 1886

Page 280

Bob Nevils and Maude Booker of New Madrid by E. A. McKinney M.G. on 8-24-1886.

Joseph Thompson of New Madrid and Mariah A. Davis of Readels Point by W. G. Henson, M. G. at Ruddles Pt. Church on 8-29-1886.

Page 281

Rankin Barnes of Lewis Prairie and Dixie Powell of Lewis Prairie by Henry Hunter, M. G. on 9-6-1886

James McGinty of Big Prairie and Sarah Jane Duffy of Big Prairie by James F. Bishop M. G. on 9-9-1886

Page 282

James Shanks of New Madrid Twp. and Molly Ross of Big Prairie by John N. Mills, J.P. on 9-12-1886

William E. Evans of Point Pleasant and Mattie E. Watson of Jefferson City, Cole Co., Mo. by R. J. Carroll on 9-8-1886 in Roman Catholic Church

Page 283

James Gentry of Big Prairie and Rillie Pearie of Big Prairie, consent of Mary Bishop, mother & only living parent of Rittie Pearus, by John N. Mills, J.P. on 9-19-1886

Robert Hamburger of New Madrid and Mattie Holmes of New Madrid Co. Father, Hosia Hamburger, father of said Robert, consent, by John N. Mills, J.P. on 6-26-1886

Page 284

Thomas W. Sauls of New Madrid Twp. and Ella Gray of New Madrid Twp. by Webster Full M.G. on 9-22-1886

Jessie A. Tellefro of East Prairie (Miss. Co.) and Lena A. Raidt of New Madrid by Ph. J. Carroll on 9-20-1886 (Roman Catholic Priest)

Page 285

William Butler and Lena Waters of Lewis Prairie by E. A. McKinney at Caroline Jacksons on 9-22-1886

Page 286

Robert Belson of Pemiscot Co., Mo. and Matty A. Bettis of Pemiscot Co., Mo. by Joel Cook, J.P. on 11-22-1886

Leroy R. Buckner of Big Prairie and Leala Fox of Big Prairie by J. N. Mills, J.P. on 10-1-1886

Page 287

Girumb Crump of Pemiscot Co., Mo. and Benita Downing, testimony of William Fisher & Jennie Crump for Benita. (returned not executed)

William Folks of LeSieur Twp. and Susan Baker of LeSieur Twp. by James A. Workman, M.G. on Oct 4, 1886 at Wm. Akers

Page 288

Greenup J. Hedges of LeSieur and Miss H. E. Johnson by W. G. Henson, M.G. on Oct. 3, 1886.

William H. West of West Twp. and Maggie A. Ford by John N. Mills, J.P. on Oct 5, 1886

Page 289

William Wade of New Madrid Twp. and Henrietta Ross of New Madrid Twp. John Ross, father of Henrietta consents, by Thomas Johnson

J. M. Higgin botham of Como Station and Mary Jane Wood of Como Station by Joel Cook, J.P. on Oct 12, 1886

Page 290

Joseph DeProw of New Madrid Twp. and Mary Sturgeon of New Madrid Twp. by Joel Cook, J.P. on Oct 12, 1886

Wm. M. Brodhaeker of East Twp. and Mrs. Adele Lassler of East Twp. by J. M. Holden, J.P. on Oct 17, 1886

Page 291

Alfred DeLisle of Portage Twp. and Lizzie Stone of LeSieur Twp. by J. A. Wynn, J.P. on Oct. 21, 1886

George Wilson of West Twp. and Amanda Leeke of West Twp. Jasper Leek, father of Amanda, consents by John N. Mills, J.P. On Oct 17, 1886

Page 292

Ben F. Sear of New Madrid and Minerva Cooper of New Madrid by James D. Stepp, J.P. on Oct 24, 1886

Simon Long of New Madrid Co. and Emily Kouner of New Madrid Co. by Jas. O'Bannon, J.P. on Oct 26, 1886

Page 293

John W McElmurray of Scott Co., Mo. and Matty Clemens by T.J.O.Morrison, J.P. on Oct 27, 1886

John Manning of New Madrid Co. and Mary E. Murphy of New Madrid Co. by John N. Mills, J.P. on Oct 31, 1886

Page 294

George A. Thompson of East Twp. and Camelia Florence Robins with consent of Ellen Robins, only living parent of Camelia Florence, by James Windeers, J.P. on Oct. 31, 1886

James E. Bolin of East Twp. and Barbary Brodhacker of East Twp. by James Winders, J.P. on Oct 31, 1886

Page 295

James B. Bearde of N.M. Twp. and Amanda Hutchens of New Madrid Twp. by H. G. Horton, M.G. on Oct 31, 1886

Louis LaFerney of LeSieur Twp. and Julia A. Simeor (or Sinko) of LeSieur Twp., consent of Charles A. Sinko, father of said Julia, on Oct 31, 1886 by Joseph O'Bannon J.P.

Page 296

Robert Lee LaPlant of Barnes Ridge and Annie Miller Porter of Miss. Co. with consent of Mrs. Porter for Annie, on Nov. 7, 1886 by W. H. Morgan, M.G.

Berl Cooper of Miss. Co. and Mary E. Settle of East Twp. At George Settles on Nov. 7, 1886 by James Bishop, M.C.
Page 297
Joseph Surard (Seward) and Sarah Riley of Brush Prairie at M. H. Stallcups on Nov. 7, 1886 by W. C. Cox, M.G.

Charles Tompkins of Lewis Prairie and Mrs. Jenny O'Bannon of Lewis Prairie by Henry Hunter, M.G. at Stephen St. Mary's on Nov. 7, 1886

Page 298

Mr. Charles L. Mitchell, City of New Madrid and Miss Jenny Watson of City of New Madrid by V. J. Millis, M.G. on Nov. 9, 1886

Andrew J. Higgerson of Miss. Co. and Dora LaPlant of Barnes Ridge by W. H. Morgan, M.G. on 11-11-1886

Page 299

James Autry of Portage Twp. and Margaret Campbell of Portage Twp., Luther Gilbow, guardian of Margaret, consenting, by James Workman M.G. on 11-12-1886

Sterling P. Hunter of Brush Prairie and Lilly Gibony of New Madrid Twp by Wasel Beall, M.G. at Lilbourn Phillips on 11-16-1886

Page 300

John T. Douglas of N.M. Twp. and Mary Ann Weaver of N.M Twp. by T. J. O. Morrison, J.P. on 11-18-1886

Lafayette T. Riney of Big Prairie and Mollie C. Lester of Big Prairie Conrad Lester, father of Mollie, consents, by Thomas F. Bishop on 11-27-1886

Page 301

Thomas J. Henlon of Big Prairie and Mrs. Eliza Laury of Big Prairie at John F. Mainords by James F. Bishop, M. G.

Alex Harris of New Madrid Co. and Harriet Cook of New Madrid Co. by Henry Hunter, M.G. at Henry Barkleys on 11-27-1886

Page 302

Henry C. Haney of Portage Twp. and Modest Masonville of Portage Twp. by Jas. O'Bannon J.P. on 11-23-1886

Ling Young of Brush Prairie and Amanda Watson of Brush Prairie by Charles Reed, M.G. on 11-28-1886

Page 303

Samuel Heulett of City of New Madrid and Letitia Cravens of City of New Madrid by T. J.O.Morrison, J.P. on 11-28-1886

Frank Masenville and Edith E. Reese of Portage Twp. by D. W. Gideon, M.G. on 11-28-1886

Page 304

Richard Barbour of City of New Madrid and Hannah Mott of City of New Madrid by Chas. Reed M.G. on 11-29-1886

John H. Gurtey of Big Prairie and Isabel Robberts of Big Prairie by M. Hart, M.G. on 12-5-1886 at A.J.Simmons

Page 305

Miles L. Biship of Brush Prairie and Nellie Hall of Brush Prairie by James D. Stepp, J.P. on 12-8-1886

John Crockett of Riddles Point and Mollie Walker of Riddles Point by B. F. Boyce, Judge of Probate on 12-12-1886.

Page 306

John Wilkerson of New Madrid Twp. and Azalee Allen of New Madrid Twp. by Wm. B. Phillips J.P. on 12-12-1886

B.F.Davis of City of New Madrid and Martha Enlow of City of New Madrid by Chas. Reed, M.G. on 12-11-1886

Page 307

Walter B. Higgerson of St. John Twp. and Parielee Jones of St. John Twp. by Geo. W Clark J.P. on 12-19-1886

George W. Simpson of New Madrid and Nora J. Rice of New Madrid Twp. by W. B. Phillips, J.P. on 12-18-1886

Page 308

Thomas Barr of LeSieur Twp. and Francis Graham of LeSieur Twp. at Saul Jacksons by Henry Hunter, M.G. on 12-26-1886

James Gray of LeSieur Twp. and Lotty Porter of LeSieur Twp. by B. F. Boyce, Judge of Probate Court on 12-25-1886

Page 309

Henry Rhodes of LeSieur Twp and Ella Hampton of LeSieur Twp. by Henry Hunter M.G. on 12-29-1886

Alsa R. Adams of LeSieur Twp . and Mrs. A. M. Inman of LeSieur Twp by Albert G. Horton at residence of Mrs. Adams on 12-19-1886

Page 310

William J. Dodson of Riddles Pt. and Mary F. Poe of Riddles Pt. with consent of W.R.Poe, father and only parent of Mary F. by Albert G. Horton, M.G. on 12-19-1886

E. A. Barnett of Paw Paw Landing to Rosa L. Mitchell of Como Station by James Stewart, J.P. 12-23-1886

Page 311

William LaFerney of LeSieur Twp. and Amelia Bertholison, father N. B. Bertholinn consents, by Jas. O'Bannon, J.P. on 12-23-1886

Page 311

Joseph Martens of New Madrid Co. and Mary Kulumis of New Madrid Co. by Ph..J. Carroll, Catholic Priest on 12-25-1886

Page 312

Charles Jeffrys of Barnes Ridge and Amanda England of Barnes Ridge by George W. Clark, J.P.

James Stubblefield of Big Prairie and Mary E. Jones of Big Prairie by Martin Hart, M.G. on 12-23-1886

Page 313

George W. Ruhey of St. John Twp. and Alice B. Wiseman of St. John Twp. at residence of Wm. Graham on 12-29-1886 by T.J.O.Morrison, J.P.

Charles H. Broughton of New Madrid Twp. and Sallie E. Stewart of New Madrid by Elder Cullen Downing, M. G. on 12-28-1886

Page 314

Shirley Scott of Riddle Point and Mary E. Harris of Ruddles Pt. by B. F. Boyce, Judge of Probate Court on 12-30-1886

Elijah Bird of New Madrid City and Patsy Cherry by Thomas Johnson, M.G. at colored M.E.Church on 12-30-1886

Page 315

Richard McCary and Sally O'Bryan of New Madrid twp. by T.J.O.Morrison, J.P. on 1-5-1887

Sidney Drake of St. John Twp. and Katy Logan of St. John Twp., written consent of Martha Woods, mother of Katy, on July 31, 1887 by T.M.O.Morrison, J.P. (July probably mean Jan.)

Page 316

Lee Phillips of City of New Madrid and Neelie Waters of City of New Madrid by Ph. J. Carroll, Roman Catholic Priest on Jan. 5, 1887

George W. Coleman of Donaldson Pt. and Tennessee Maxey of New Madrid by T. J. O. Morrison, J. P. on 12-6-1886

Page 317

Albert Adams of Portage Twp. and Alemen Conrad of PORTAGE Twp, Jefferson Conrad, father of Alemen consents, by John Young, J.P. on 1-16-1887

Page 317

Washington Wilburn of New Madrid and Deek Ashby of New
Madrid consent by. Fanny Ashby, guardian of Dub Ashby, on
Jan. 27, 1888 by Charles Reed at Dick Ashby

Page 318

Thomas N. Berthotomy of LeSieur Twp. and Jenny LaFont
of Portage, N. B. Berthlomy, father of Thomas, consenting
(no return)

John T. Brown of Brush Prairie and Maggie Witter of Brush
Prairie A. M. Patterson, gdn. of Maggie consenting, by
James D. Stepp, J.P. on 1-30-1887

Page 319

James Allen of Brush Prairie and Mary Baker of Brush Prairie
by James D Stepp, J.P. at David Pattersons on 1-23-1887.

Woodson Butler of New Madrid Twp. and Mary Minneweather of
New Madrid Twp. by E. A. McKinney, M.G. on 1-30-1887

Page 320

Sam C. Jones of New Madrid Twp. and Martha Lawson of Lewis
Twp. by Irvin A. Ewing, M. G. at residence of George Knott
on 2-13-1887

Wm. H. S ouers of New Madrid Twp. and Columbia McCary of
New Madrid by James F. Bishop M.G. at Mr. Riggs on 2-13-1887

Page 321

Joseph Palmier and Jenny Moore of Paw Paw , Josephine Moore
mother and only living parent of Jenny consents by James
Stewart, J.P. at Nathan Carters on 2-24-1887

William Spencer of Brush Prairie and Sophia Martin of New
Madrid by James F. Bishop, M.G. on 2-15-1887

Page 322

John E. Poe of Ruddles Point and Mary E. Edwards by Weisel
Beale, M.G. on 2-15-1887

James F. Bishop of Big Prairie and Narcissus J. Graw of
Big Prairie, Mrs. C. J. Graw mother and only living parent of
Narcissus consenting, by James D. Stepp, J.P. on 2-20-1887

Page 323

Harrison Minneweather of New Madrid Twp. and Caroline Wade of New Madrid Twp. by W. D. Gillman, M.G. on 2-27-1887

Natt Clark of Lewis Prairie and Florence Osburn of New Madrid, Charles Hopel, gdn. of Florence consenting, by Henry Hunter, M.G. on 4-27-1887

Page 324

Louis Hubbard of New Madrid Twp. and Mary Martin of New Madrid Twp. by Henry Hunter M.G. on 4-5-1887

Charles Green of New Madrid Co. and Pettie Snow of New Madrid Co. by Thomas Johnson, M.G. at Andrew Lawsons.

Page 325

William W. Pinnell of New Madrid and Gusta C. Newbauer of New Madrid by Ph. J. Carroll, Catholic Priest on 3-4-1886

Henry Shrader of City of New Madrid and Susan Montgomery of Brush Prairie by Henry Hunter, M. G. on 1-5-1887

Page 326

E. Z. Wyatt of City of New Madrid and Lucille Wise of City of New Madrid by W. B. Phillips, J.P. on 2-2-1887

Jesse DeLisle of Pt. Pleasant and Emma LeSieur of Pt. Pleasant by John McGeugh C.S.S.R. on 2-8-1887

Page 327

Jas. O. Myers of Big Prairie and Mrs. Louisa E. Fry of Big Prairie on 2-8-1887 by A.C. Myatt, J.P.

Page 328

Louis R. Tidwell of Marshall Station and Narcissus Rattliffe of Marshall Station by James Stewart J.P. on 2-27-1887

D. J. Keller of Barnes Ridge and Elizabeth Cook of Sandy Ridge by T. O. Peeler, J.P. on 2-6-   at A. J. Farmers

Page 329

Wm. H. Hurley of Ruddles Pt. and Metilda Baldwin of Riddles Point with Consent of Hendison Wiley, gdn. of Matilda by A. G. Horton, M. G.

James H. Stephens of West Twp. and Sarah R. Jackson by James Stewart J.P. on 4-1-1887 at Mrs. S. R. Jackson

Robert Glisson of LeSieur Twp. and MRS. Mela McLennon of LeSieur by Jas. O. O'Bannon, J.P. on 4-20-1887 at Pt. Pleasant.

James Wyatt of Big Prairie Twp. and Minnie Stubblefield of Big Prairie, James Stubblefield, father of Minnie, consent, by J.F.Bishop, M.G.

Page 331

Henry Grimes of New Madrid Twp. and Alfred Gilbow of New Madrid Twp., Carolina Jackson, mother of said Alfred consents, on 4-24-1887 by James Wesley, M.G.

H.H.Duke of New Madrid Twp. and Emma Johnson of New Madrid Twp. by Henry Hunter at Col. Baptist Church on April 24, 1887

Page 332

Fred Williams of LeSieur Twp. and Angeline Wilson of LeSieur Twp. by Jas. O. O'Bannon, J.P. on 5-8-1887

Christopher C. Shaver of Brush Prairie and Julia Ann Laster of Brush Prairie at Mr. Pillows on 5-11-1887 by Wm. B. Phillips, J.P.

Page 333

George W. Pleasant of Lewis Prairie and Mary Shockonay of Lewis at residence of James Henry by Irvin A. Ewing, M.G. on 5-15-1887.

William Ware of Pt. Pleasant and Gabrella Parrott of Pt. Pleasant by Henry Hunter, M.G. at Alonza O'Bannon's on May 16, 1887.

Page 334

Dennis C. Henry of New Madrid Twp. and Alice M. Ewing of New Madrid Twp. by V. J. Millis, M. G. on 5-19-1887.

Basil B. Crow of New Madrid Co. and Permince J. Simmons at A.B.Crow's by James F. Bishop, M.G.

Page 335

Cave Thompson of LeSieur Twp. and Mary Meatte of LeSieur Edward Meatte, guardian of Mary, consents, on 6-5-1887 by J. M. Dockery, County Judge.

Page 335

Wm. E. Chamberlin of New Madrid Twp. and Alley D. Jacobs of New Madrid Twp., Berdin Chapman, guardian of said Alley consents, by Irvin A. Ewing, M.G. on 6-5-1887.

Page 336

John Ellis of City of New Madrid and Mary Newbauer of New Madrid Twp. by V. J. Millis, M. G. on 6-6-1887.

William H. Gilbert of City of New Madrid and Lizzie Prewitt of New Madrid Twp. on 6-9-1887 by T.J.O.Morrison, J.P.

Page 337

John Harden of Big Prairie and Mary Jane Clack of Big Prairie by M. Hast, M.G. on 6-19-1887.

Mack Thomas of City of New Madrid and Cally Mudd of City of New Madrid by E.A.McKinney, M.G. on 7-17-1887.

Page 338

Samuel Smith of New Madrid County and Sally Henderson of New Madrid County at Randolph Watson by Thomas Johnson, M.G. on 6-19-1887.

William Walls of County of New Madrid and Lydia Ross of Co. of new Madrid, Mariah Ross, only living parent (mother) consents, by Thomas Johnson, M.G. on 5-23-1886.

Page 339

Ed A. Blackman of New Madrid Co. and Mary Guiton of N.M. Co. by Henry Hunter, M.G. at Freewill Baptist Church on Oct 17, 1886.

James R. Fauless of Butler Co. and Sarah Hodge of New Madrid Co. by S. S. Mohler on Nov. 8, 1886.

Page 340

Manuel Williams of New Madrid and Lula Bell Lafont of New Madrid Twp. with consent of John B. Lafont, father of Lula Bell by Charles Reed at Bausll Lafont's on 2-2-1887.

Richard E. Ray of Marshall Co. and Arsenia Vetetoe of Marshall with consent of Wm. Vetetoe, father of said Arsenia, by James Stewart, J.P. on 6-2-1887

Page 341

Oma B. Pickett of New Madrid City and Nancy Abbott of City of N,M. by V. J. Willis, M.G. on 6-19-1887.

Chas. H. Beard of Co. of New Madrid and Josephine McEhavey on 7-1-1887 by W.B.Phillips, J.P.

Page 342

James Young of Portage and Laura Long, Ellen Young consents, Mother of Laura, by John Young, J.P. on 7-3-1887.

William Figue of City of New Madrid and Eva Alexander of New Madrid by W.B.Phillips, J.P. on 7-12-1887.

Page 343

J.A.Brown of Brush PRAIRIE and Rosa Lee Engle of Brush Prairie by James D. Stepp, J.P. at J.A.Burrus residence on 7-13-1887.

John L. Ransburgh of Lewis Prairie and Mollie O. Rodgers of New Madrid Co. by Irvin A. Ewing, M.G. on 8-4-1887.

Page 344

W.M.Gallant of Dunklin Co., Malden, Mo. and Minnie Farmer of Marshall by James Stewart,J.P. on 7-24-1887.

Nathaniel Ingold of LeSieur Twp. and Adrian Dees of LeSieur Twp. by J.M.Dockery, county judge, on 8-7-1887.

Page 345

Daniel Dunklin of New Madrid, Mo. and Francis Bowers of New Madrid by Jas. O. O'Bannon, J.P. on 2-5-1887.

Moses Thorp of Pulaski, Ill. and Birdie Long of Pulaski, Ill. at W.W.Henrys on 8-15-1887 by Ephraim A. McKinney.

Page 346

Charles Mitchell of Portage Twp. and Julia A. Densory of Portage Twp. by John Young, J.P. on 8-11-1887.

Alexander L. Barnes of Mississippi Co. and Linda A. Friske of New Madrid County at A. L. Wimps by W. P. Peeler, J.P. on 8-7-1887

Page 347

James F. Ligon of Marshall of New Madrid and Sarah West of same place by James Stewart, J.P. on 8-16-1887.

John W. Hunter of New Madrid and Fannie Fitzpatrick of New Madrid, Maurie Fitzpatrick, father of Fannie consents, by W.B.Phillips J.P. on 8-27-1887.

Page 348

James H. Dowdy of New Madrid Co. and Ida Pettie, Wm. Pharris guardian of Jas. H. Dowdy consenting, by J.L.Shelby, J.P. on 9-4-1887.

John G. Rice of New Madrid Twp. and Jimmy Dean of New Madrid Twp. J.H.Bishop, Guardian of Jimmy Dean, consents, by W.B.Phillips J.P. on 8-31-1887.

Page 349

John Smith of LeSieur Twp. and Emeline Martin of New Madrid Co. by Henry Hunter on 9-5-1887.

Page 350

John G. Wiley of East Twp. and Martha Shelby of East Twp. , Jerry L. Pruett, guardian of Martha consents, by J. L. Shelby, J.P. on 9-15-1887.

Berdine Chapman of New Madrid Twp. and Mary A. Hunott of New Madrid Twp. by W.G.Peeler, J.P. at John LaPlant's on 9-21-1887.

Page 351

Alphonso P. Herron of Oakland, Miss. Co., and Miss Kate Scott of South Ridge, New Madrid Co.   (no return)

Burrell W. Stewart of New Madrid City and Eula W. Hunter of City of New Madrid by T.J.O.Morrison, J.P. on Oct.5,1887

Page 352

John Bridgeman of Big Prairie and Amelia A. Winchester of Big Prairie b y M. Hart, M.G. on 9-28-1887.

Robert Mitchell of Lewis Prairie and Ella Martin (no return)

Page 353

Wm. McElhany of Portage Twp. and Josephine Cosby of Portage Twp., Wm. F. Mott, guardian of said Josephine, and Sarah McElaney's Mother consents by John Young, J.P. on 10-18-1887.

M.J.Halliburton of Portage Twp. and MRS. Lecretia Keith (no return filed)

Page 354

James B. Simmons of Como and Francis E. Paxton of New Madrid Co. by James Stewart J.P. on 10-9-1887 at Como.

James G. Strong of East Twp. and Martha L. Robbins of East Twp., Ellen Robbins only surviving parent of Martha consents, by J.L.Shelby, J.P. on 10-30-1887.

Page 355

Eliza Duckett of City of New Madrid and Mary Linson of Dunklin Co. by Rev. E. F. Senter, M.E.South on 11-20-1887.

Page 356

John R. Harris of New Madrid and Ada Dees of Scrub Ridge by James O.O'Bannon ,J.P. on 11-23-1887.

W.E.Cochran of Como and Mary E.Orr, Reford ORR, FATHER OF Mary consents, by James Stewart, J.P. on 11-20-1887.

Page 357

Chris Glueck of New Madrid and Mary M. Earley by E.F. Sender, M.G. at the jail on 10-30-1887.

William Henderson of Brush Prairie and Sylvia Watson of Brush Prairie by Thomas Johnson M.G. on 10-30-1887 at A. Watson's.

Page 358

Joseph Edwards of New Madrid Twp. and Lena Palmer of New Madrid Twp. at Fred Palmer's on 10-28-1887 by Henry Hunter,M.G.

James Oglin of Big Prairie and Mattie Terrel of Scott County (no return)

Page 359

A. J. thompson of Curry's Ridge and Mary R. Strong of same place B. M. Strong, father of Mary, consents by J.L.Shelby,J.P. on 11-14-1887.

Page 365

W. C. Newsum of City of New Madrid and Cqrrie Brownell of City of New Madrid b y T. J. O. Morrison, J.P. on 9-7-1887

Page 366

Henry Franklin of City of New Madrid and Missouri A. Scott of City of New Madrid by Charles Reed, M. G. on Dec. 15, 1887.

Alfred Godair of Portage. Twp. and Rosetta McWilliams of Portage Twp. with consent of G. W. McWilliams b y R.L.Lafont, J.P. on 3-4-1888

Page 367

Albert Rochell of New Madrid County and Annie Secoy of New Madrid County on testimony of Joseph O'Bannon as to age of Annie by Joseph O'Bannon, J.P. on 12-29-1887 at home of C. Pikey.

Page 368

Irenius Renes of Big Prairie and Hattie Foley of Big Prairie by Conrad Lissler, J.P. on 12-25-1887.

William R. Poe of Ruddles point and Rosa L. Basset of Reeds Point by J.M.Dockery, Judge of County Court, on 12-30-1887'

Page 369

Jasper N. Tidwell of Como and Dora Johnson of Arkansas by James Stewart,J.P. on 1-1-1889

James Oglin of Big Prairie and Matty Ferrel of Scott Co., Mo. by V. J. Willis, M.G. on 11-6-1887.

Page 370

Burney M. Watson of LeSieur Twp. and Hattie Day of LeSieur Twp, Ida Dees, guardian of Hatty consenting, by Jas. A. Workman, M.G. on 1-5-1888.

James Edmondson of East Twp. and Ellen Potter of East by M. Hart, J.P. on Dec. 8, 1888.

Page 359

James J. Via of Brush Prairie and Georgia Willis, W. C. Willis, father of Georgia, consents, by James Bishop, M.G. on Dec. 1, 1887.

Page 360

Henry W. Ervill of Scrub Ridge and Louisa Jane Garrett of Scrub Ridge by Jos. O'Bannon, J.P. on Dec. 1, 1887.

Thomas McGaray of LeSieur Twp. and Mary Hampton of LeSieur by Henry Hunter, J.P. on Dec. 7, 1887 at Isaac Hamptons.

Page 361

James W. Merrill of Sandy Ridge and Nancy J. Hornbeck of Sandy Ridge by G. W. Clark, J.P. on 12-7-1887.

Thomas Castleberry of Buffington, Scott Co., Mo. and Laura Jones of New Madrid on 12-8-1887 by Rev. E. F. Senter, M.G. of M.E. Church South.

Page 362

John L. Steward of New Madrid and Serena Johnson of New Madrid Twp. by W. W. Ellis, M.G. at residence of J. Johnson on Dec. 14, 1887.

D. Y. Stewart of St. John Twp. and Miss Laura Branham of St. John Twp. by E. F. Senter, M.G. on Dec. 11, 1887.

Page 363

Thomas T. Smith of Pittsburg, Pa. and Amanda May Merrill of St. Paul, Minn., A. C. Merrill, father of Amanda, consents by B. F. Bryce, J.P. at Pt. Pleasant on 12-7-1887.

Dan Nicholis of New Madrid Twp. and Malinda Martin of New Madrid Twp. by Henry Hunter, M.G. at Hill Martins on 12-22-1887.

Page 364

A. W. Chappel of Brush Prairie and Noah Brannum of Brush Prairie by T. J. O. Morrison, J.P. on 12-22-1887.

Andrew Lawson of City of New Madrid and Anna Woods of City of New Madrid at residence of Penn Woods by E. A. McKinney, M.G. on 8-28-1887.

Page 365

George Jackson of Laforge and Ellen Jackson of Lewis Prairie b y Henry Hunter, M.G. on 12-29-1887 at F. Jacksons.

Page 371

Cris Ray of East Twp. and Catherine Evans of East Twp. by M. Hart, M.G. on 12-10-1888.

F.B.Wiseman and Stella St. Liger of New Madrid, Mo. by James A. Workman, M.G. at Wm. Grahams on 1-7-1888

Page 372

James Hayes of New Madrid Twp. and Alice Boggs of New Madrid Twp. by James F. Bishop, M.G. on 1-18-1888.

V. J. Miller of Sikeston, Scott Co. and Mattie J. Williams of Pt. Pleasant by A. G. Horton, M.G. on 1-11-1888

Page 373

Chas. Early of Co. of New Madrid and Harriet Bishop, of Co. of New Madrid, by Conrad Leissler, J.P. on 1-24-1888

James Melrun of City of New Madrid and Cola Davis of City of New Madrid by Elois F. Senter, M.G. on 1-29-1888

Page 374

John Smith of Lewis Prairie and Caroline Mahan of Lewis Prairie at Charles Thompsons by Jones Bishop, M. G.

W.C.Parker of New Madrid Co. and Rebecca Smith of New Madrid Co. of _____ Brandon, only living parent of Rebecca, on 1-25-1888 by W.B.Phillips, J.P.

Page 375

Thomas Patterson of Mississippi Co., Mo. and Anna Lamar of Miss. Co., Mo. by W. B. Phillips, J.P. on 1-24-1888.

William McGill of LeSieur Twp. and Lou Jackson of LeSieur Twp., James Watson, guardian of Lou, consents, by Jas. O'Bannon J.P. on 2-8-1888

Page 376

John Patterson of New Madrid Twp. and Fanny Todd of New Madrid Twp. by James D. Stepp; J.P. on 1-29-1888

Page 376

Conrad Leissler of Big Prairie and Nancy E. Brown of Big Prairie (no return)

Page 377

James T. Underwood of LeSieur Twp. and Emily McLemore of LeSieur Twp. by A. G. Morton, P.C. at Scrub Ridge on Feb. 5, 1888.

Conrad LEISSLER OF Big Prairie and Nancy E. Brown by J.D.Stepp, J.P. on 2-2-1888

Page 378

Chas. Westerman of Big Prairie and Agnes Royers of B ig Prairie, Saloney Seby, mother and only living parent of said Agnes gives consent, by M. Hart,M.G. on 2-12-1888

John Sikes of Big Prairie and Mary Hunter of Brush Prairie, Neal Hunter, father of Mary consents, by Thos. Johnson on 2-12-1888

Page 379

William Hunter of Brush Prairie and Kitty Hampton at Ike Hamptons by Thos. Johnson on 2-12-1888

Henry Cline of New Madrid Co. and Lena Klein of City of New Madrid, Ann Klein only living parent of Lena consents, by E. F. Senter, M.G. on 2-12-1888.

Page 380

Wm. Tanksley of Barnes Ridge and Sarah E. Peeler of Barnes Ridge, William Peeler father of Sarah consents, by Geo. W. Clark, J.P. on 2-21-1888.

John F. Robinson of Laforge and Mary F.A.Thorn, Wm. Thorn, father of Mary consents, by S. A. Hornberger, M.G. on 2-18-1888

Page 381

C.B.Hathwick of Laforge and Martha Burgess of Laforge Henry Burgess, father of Martha, consents, by J.F.Bishop, M/G. at residence of Wm. Spencer on 2-19-1888

Thomas D. Chatman of City of New Madrid and Lucy A. Sullivan of Ristine by James D. Stepp, J.P. at residence of J. Chatman on 2-22?-1888

Page 382

John W. Colson of St. JohnTwp. and Mrs. Caroline
Johnson of St. John Twp. by W. T. Peeler, J.P. on
3-11-1888

Page 383

John J. Williams of Pt. Pleasant and Hatty E. Bristol
of Pt. Pleasant by A. G. Horton,P.C. Feb. 22, 1888.

Olly B. Williams of PT. Pleasant and Allie Robinson
of Pt. Pleasant by Jas. A. Workman, M. G. at residence
of J. W. Williams on 2-28-1888

Page 384

Homar Spiva of Alabama and Miss E. A. Phillips by
J. F. Curtis, pastor of Presbyterian Church at
residence of Lilbourn Phillips on 2-25-1888

Major Green of New Madrid Co. and Everliner Waters of
New Madrid Co. at Harrison Henderson by James L. Bishop,M.G.

Page 385

Cornealius Palhanus of New Madrid and Mary Pope of
New Madrid by E. Franklin Senter, M.E.South on
3-1-1888

Robert Sutton of New Madrid Twp. and Mary Rayburn of
New Madrid Twp. by Irvin A. Ewing, M.G. at residence
of Dr. Starks on 3-4-1888

Page 386

Henry Heckle and J. Henderson of Co. of New Madrid at
Randolph Watsons on 3-4-1888 by Thomas Johnson, P.C.

Charles Wilsonof St. John Twp. and Cinda Robinson of
St. John Twp. ,Charles Wilson testifying as to ages,
by Geo. W. Clark, J.P. on 3-11-1888

Page 387

William B. Phillips of City of New Madrid and Miss Mollie
Phillips by J.F.Curtis presbyterian minister of New
Madrid on 3-14-1888

William Shaw of Como and Zenia Hunter of Como by James
Stewart,J.P. on 3-25-1888

Page 388

Simon F. Catt of Big Prairie and Mary A. Rucketts of Big Prairie by Conrad Leissler, J.P. on 3-30-1888

Martin Dow of City of New Madrid and Jennie Wilson by Rene Jones (Bishop) on 4-3-1888

Page 389
'John Hessling of City of New Madrid and Lee Willie Baehr of City of New Madrid by Edw. Smith, R.C.P. on 4-10-1888

James M. Hill of Brush Prairie and Pauline Ross of Brush Prairie by Conrad Lissler, J.P. on 4-12-1888

Page 390

J.H.Doods and Margat Ratliff (not executed)

James Carr and Madary Willis of New Madrid Co. by T.J.O.Morrison, J.P. on 4-17-1888

Page 391

GeorgeShields of Lewis Twp. and Lilley L. Lavallee of New Madrid Co. by E. F. Senter, M.G. on 4-18-1888

Jess Peelers of Barnes Ridge and Malessa Cunningham of Barnes Ridge by consent of Josephine Cunningham, mother of Malessa, by Geo. Clark, J.P. on 4-29-1888

Page 392

Willie Riley of Laforge of New Madrid County and Laura Jackson, of Laforge by Chas. Reed, M.G. on 5-6-1888

Saml Hicks of Riddle Pt. and Lou Davis of Riddle PT. B Y T. J.O.Morrison on 5-12-1888

Page 393

Willard Sikes of City of New Madrid and Sarah McGloflin of City, consent of Abraham Sikes, father of Willard, by T.J.O.Morrison, J.P. on 5-25-1888

George Y. Hunter of Portage and Amanda McWilliams of Portage consent of her parent, Y.V.McWilliams and Nancy McWilliams, by John Young, J.P. on 6-9-1888

Page 394

D. J. Keller of Kansas City, Mo. and Adene E. Cook of New Madrid by Philip Brady, Roman Catholic Priest on June 13, 1888

W.P.Watson of Scrub Ridge and C. J. Auctine (Indexed as Austine) by John Young, J.P. 6-24-1888

Page 395

J. G. Girvin of Riddles Point and Florence Morrison of Riddles Point, James Morrison and Adaline Morrison, parents, consent, by B. J. Boyce, J.P. on 6-24-1888

Page 396

R.G.Marshal of LeSieur Twp. and Lizzie Brooks of LeSieur Twp., Annie Aldredge, mother of Lizzie, consents and her stepfather, P.H.Aldredge, by W. Henson, M.G. of Baptist Church on 7-1-1888.

S.S.Thompson of Little River Twp of Pemiscot County and Mary Jane Crabtree, Jesse & M.A.Thompson, mother of S.S. and Samuel Crabtree, father of Mary Jane, consent, by John Young, J.P. on 7-1-1888

William Tison of Scrub Ridge and Exer Blot of Scrub Ridge, consent of Mother ,Mary E. Grubs and William Tison, by John Young, J.P. on 7-5-1888

Page 397

Louis W. Sandefur of Como and Lee Ann Hufstutter of Como with consent of Lee Ann's parents, Thomas and Frances Tate,

Riley Magently and Lulesher Husk with consent of John Gasset, father of Lulesher,by Conrad Leissler,J.P. on 7-18-1888

Page 398

T. Stafford of Barnes Ridge and C. Williams of Barnes Ridge by J.F.Bishop, M.G. on 7-13-1888

William Phillips of Portage Twp. and Amelia Meatt of Portage Twp. consent of Sam and Flora Meatt, parents of Amelia by John Young, J.P. on 7-15-1888

Page 399

Wiley J. Well of LeSieur Twp. and Della Wiles of LeSieur, Mrs. Elizabeth Wiles, only living parent of Della consents, by Jas. O'Bannon on 7-8-1888

D.P.Scott of Hickman, Ky, Fulton Co. and Miss Katie Beaclles ? of Hickman, Fulton Co, Ky., by T.J.O.Morrison J.P. on 7-14-1888 at Hickson Hotel

Page 400

William Evins of Big Prairie and Calhony Francis Hornes, William Hornes father of Calhony, gives consent, by F. C. Corsky, M.G. on 7-18-1888

Shap G. Phillips of LeSieur Twp. and Linda C. Phillips of LeSieur Twp. by J.F.Curtis, M.G on 7-25-1888

Page 401

David Matthews of LeSieur Twp. and Ellen Taylor of LeSieur Twp. b y Jas O'Bannon J.P. on 7-29-1888

W.H.Rikard of West Swamp and Alie Southard of West Swamp by H. Chapman, M.G. on 7-4-1888

Page 402

George Smith of LeSieur Twp. and Rosa Goodman of LeSieur Twp. with consent of Rosa Goodman, guardian by W. G. Henson, M.G. on 8-13-1888

Page 402

Edward Jarrett Trammel of Como and Sarah Elizabeth Norman (no return)

Page 403

Elijah Hicks of New Madrid and Lottie Davis of New Madrid Aleck Hicks, father of Elijah, consents by T. J. O. Morrison, J.P. on 8-13-1888

Franklin Pierce Courtney of LeSieur Twp. and Eliza C. Waldrop of LeSieur by Jas. O'Bannon on 8-16-1888

Page 404

George E. Childers of Big Prairie Twp. and Mary E. Mainord of Big Prairie by Jas. D. Stepp, J.P. on 8-16-1888

David Bellant of New Madrid Twp. and Katie Franso of Malden of Dunklin Co. with Mollie Bellant, mother of David, consenting, by T. J.O.Morrison,J.P. on 8-15-1888 at Paw Paw Junction

Page 405

William Byows of LeSieur Twp. and Missouri Dowdy of LeSieur by B. F. Boyce, J.P. on 9-2-1888 at Pt. Pleasant.

Charles T. Murphy of Big Ridge and Mary E. Ray of Big Ridge with Martha J. Ray, mother of Mary, consenting by T.J.O.Morrison J.P. on Aug. 28, 1888

Page 406

William F. Swan of Big Prairie and Elizabeth McGenthy of Big Prairie on 9-11-1888 by E. P. McKinney, M.G.

William A. Marney of Brush Prairie and Terry A. Walls of Scott Co. by James Stepp,J.P. on 9-9-1888

Page 407

John Jenkins of Big Prairie and Annie Hunter of Big Prairie by Conrad Leissler, J.P. at residence of Jacob Goodlin on 9-10-1888

C. F. Carter of New Madrid and Althia Jackson, Mrs. S. R. Stevens, mother of Althia Jackson consents, by James Stewart, J.P. on 6-28-1888

Page 408

George Mass of Big Prairie and Jessey Kaysinger of Big Prairie by Conrad Leesher, J.P. on 8-1-1888

Don Williams of Obion, Tenn and Bell Chaney of Ruthford, Tenn. by T. J.O. MOrrison, J.P. on 7-14-1887

Page 409

Walter Hardin of New Madrid Co. and Emmaline Davis of New Madrid Co. by Ephrain A. McKinney, M.G. on 7-24-1887

Owen Damon of LeSieur Twp. and Clementine Ramatter of LeSieur Twp, Angeline Damon, mother of Owen, consents. (cert. not filled out)

Page 410

John Dotie of New Madrid and Georgia Munson of New Madrid Co. by J.F.Curtis, M.G. on 8-29-1888

Mitchell Meatte of LeSieur Twp. and Cinda LeSieur of LeSieur Twp. by J.M.Dockery, Judge of Co. Court on 9-28-1887

Page 411

Sylvannis Brown of New Madrid and Annie Tucker of New Madrid, consent of James Brown for Sylvernis by Wm. B. Phillips, J.P. on 10-6-1887

Page 411

Abraham Landers of New Madrid and Sarah J. Westerman of New Madrid by M. Hart, M.G. on 12-18-1887

Page 412

Benjamine Pass of New Madrid and Cindy Woods of New Madrid at Thomas Woods on 12-25-1887 by E. A. McKenney, M.G.

John Comer of Fulton, Ky, and Barberry Fuller of Fulton, Ky. by W. B. Phillips, J.P. on 4-20-1888

Page 413

Adolph M. Smith of LeSieur Twp. and Tena Vaughn of New Madrid by Jas. O'Bannon J.P. on 5-13-1888

Keullen Cousins of New Madrid and Florence George of New Madrid by T.J.O. Morrison J.P. on 5-12-1888

Page 414

Talbot E. Bellon of New Madrid and Amelia E. Toney of New Madrid by Rev. Irvin A. Ewing, M.G.

Page 415

Edward Swing of Pharis Ridge and Frances Dawson of Pharis Ridge of Scott Co.(Nancy and Wash Dawson, parents of Frances, consent) Rev. T. C. Cooksy on 7-15-1888

Charles E. Dawson of LeSieur Twp. and Nancy Mizell of LeSieur Twp. by W. King on 9-22-1888

Page 416

Ben Williams of Paw Paw and Mary Sherkey of New Madrid Twp. at Wash Sherkey's by W. King on 9-23-1888

Joe Hoard of LeSieur Twp. and Lena Lafoe of LeSieur (no return)

Page 417

Charles Ates of Lewis Prairie and Catharine Babtest b y James Wesley, M.G. at Lucy Brown's on 9-17-1888

John S. Frowhalk of Big Prairie and Missouri G. Edwards of Big Prairie by Conrad Lessler J.P. on 9-20-1888

Page 418

William Dudley Carter of Como and Sarah Norman of Como
Benjamin Norman, father of Sarah, consents, by James
Stewart,J.P. on 9-30-1888

Richard Morgan of New Madrid Twp. and Maggie Lafoe of
LeSieur Twp. (no return)

Page 419

Meller Mukes of New Madrid and Dicy King of New Madrid
by Henry Hunter, M.G. on 10-7-1888

Gennis Green of New MadridTwp. and Missie Renfoe of
New Madrid by James Wesley, M.G. on 10-7-1888

Page 420

Eblen Barry of LeSieur Twp. and Nannie Wathen by
E.J. Rinkle, M.G. on 9-10-1888

Charles Hopel of New Madrid Twp. and Mollie Waters of
New Madrid Twp. by Henry Hunter, M.G. on 10-12-1888

Page 421

Charlie Prat of Hickman Twp, of Fulton, Ky. and Isa
Cooper of New Madrid Twp. (no return)

John Sever of Portageville and Easter Crownshaw of
Portage Twp., Mrs. Mary J. Crowshaw, mother of Easter,
consenting by John Young, J.P. on 10-21-1888

Page 422

Hamilton Renfro of New madrid Twp. and Lucy Brown of
N.M.Twp. b y James Wesley M.G. on 10-27-1888

James A. Frazier of Pine Bluff Jefferson Co, Ark. and
Carrie Stewart of New Madrid Co. by T.J.O.Morrison
on Oct. 17, 1888.

Page 423

Mack Banks of New Madrid hwp. and Ellen McCarrie of New
Madrid Twp. by Charles Reed M.G. on 10-21-1888

John W. Clement of Big Prairie and Nancy McCormic of
Big Prairie by V. J. Millis, M.G. on 10-21-1888

Page 424

John Barton of Malden, Dunklin Co. and Anie Gamble of
Como by Matt J.A.Conran, Mayor of New Madrid, on 10-25-1888

M.N.Alley of Scrub Ridge and Ida Deas of Scrub Ridge,
Newton Griffen, guardian of said Ida Deas, consents, by
John Young, J.P. on 10-28-1888

Page 425

William W. Alexander of New Madrid and Ida E. Latham by
Frances Branci, M.G. on 10-30-1888

James L. Gentry of Ogden, Co. of New Madrid and Amy A.
Caldwell of Ogden, Co. of New Madrid, Margrett Caldwell,
mother of Amy, consents, by E. P. McKinney, M.G. on
Nov. 5, 1888

Page 426

Dick Laferney of LeSieur Twp. and Laura Pikey of LeSieur
Twp. with Girard Pikey, father of Laura, consenting by
Jas. O'Bannon, J.P. on Nov. 8, 1888

John S. Branch of Kennett, Dunklin Co., and Nancy Nicholas
of Portageville, W. Nicholas, guardian, consent, by Loyd
Hogan, M.G. on 11-11-1888

Page 427

Isack Garrison of LeSieur Twp. and Chincy Harrison of
LeSieur Twp. by Elder W. G. Henson, M.G. on 11-15-1888

Charles D. Sharp of Tiptonville, Tenn. (Lake Co.) and
Mary C. Dean of Tiptonville by B. F. Boyce, Judge of
Probate on 11-14-1888

Page 428

Wilson Kendall of Marshal, New Madrid Co. and Margrett
Copeland of Marshal, New Madrid Co. by James Stewart, J.P.
on 11-16-1888

Matthew Vaughn of New Madrid County and Bettie Price of
New Madrid Co., Mary Bishop, mother of Bettie, consents,
by E.P.McKinney, M.G. on 11-20-1888

Page 429

Douglas Trammel of Como Twp. and Mahaley Stratton of
Como by James Stewart, J.P. at John Stratton's on 11-25-1888.

John A. Butler of Laforge and Jane Robinson of Laforge
by Charles Reed, M.G. on 11-26-1888

Page 430

H. Lee Jasper of New Madrid and Mary H. Boyce of New
Madrid by F. Brand on 11-26-1888

Rufes Cupp of East Twp. and Sarah C. Holloway of East Twp.
James Wilburn, guardian of Sarah, consents, by J.L.Shelby,
J.P. at James Wilburn's residence on 11-4-1888

Page 431

John W. W. Enslow of New Madrid Twp. and Helena McMann of New Madrid Twp. by T.J.O.Morrison on 12-7-1888

Jacob Baehr of LeSieur Twp. and Reny Maxey of LeSieur Twp. by W.W.Ellis, M.G. on 12-4-1888

Page 432

Charles Lee of Laforge and Philleser Maulsby of Laforge by W.T.Johnson, M.G. on 12-7-1889 at W.T. Johnsons.

N. Williams of Barnes Ridge and Sallie Settles of Barnes Ridge by George W. Clark J.P. on 12-16-1888

Page 433

John Fugate of Big Prairie and Miss Carrie Gibson of Big Prairie by T. C. Cooksy M.G. on 12-13-1888

Thomas Alsup of Laforge and Annie Hoefman of Laforge with consent of Sarah Hoefman, mother of Annie, by James D. Stepp, J.P. on 12-16-1888

Page 434

Isaac Taylor of New Madrid Twp. and Mattie Fowler of New Madrid Twp. by W. T. Peeler J.P. on 12-16-1888

Frank Harns of New Madrid and Melie Jones of Lewis Prairie by James Westley,J.P. on 12-16-1888

Page 435

Robert Carson of Scrub Ridge and Emma Workman of Scrub Ridge (rec'd Mar 2, 1889 not filled out)

James C. Hudspeth of LeSieur Twp. and Miss Nora Bayne of LeSieur (no return)
Page 436
John Stratton of Como and Sarah R. Jackson of Como by James Stewart J.P. on 1-1-1889

John Bowlin of Sandy Ridge and Rosalee McDaniel of Scrub Ridge by W.T.Peeler, J.P. on 12-26-1888

Page 437

Chester Trammell of Como Twp. and Laura McGee of Como Twp. James Stewart, guardian of said Laura consents, by Matt J.A.Conran, Mayor of City on 12-25-1888

Page 437

Richard Cherry of Tick Ridge of New Madrid and Careline
Ross of Tick Ridge with John Ross, father of Careline,
consenting on Dec. 25, 1888 by James Bishop, M.G.

Page 438

Mager Petty of New Madrid Twp. and Emma Hampton of New
Madrid Twp., Alfred Petty, father of Mager and Isaac
Hampton, father of Emma, consent, by James H. Bishop,M.G.
on 12-25-1888

Edward Graham of New Madrid Twp. and Jenny Jordin of New
Madrid by Joseph Piggee, M.G. at residence of Warren
Jordin

Page 439

Jim Williams of Brush Prairie and Nellie Petty of Brush
Prairie, Alfred Petty, father of Nellie, consents, by
W.T.Johnson, M.G. at Alfred Petty's residence on 12-28-1888
          Cruchon
David J. C-Quishen of Cape Girardeau and Miss Lizzie
Henze of Cape Girardeau by J.M.Dockery, Judge of County
Court on 12-30-1888

Page 440

Alfred Gamble of Marshal of New Madrid and Mary J. Griffy
Nathan Carter, guardian of Mary, consents, by James
Stewart,J.P. on 1-17-1889

Sidney Ruggles of Paw Paw and Rody Tucker of Paw Paw by
W.B.Phillips J.P. on 1-20-1889

Page 441

H.Y.DeWitt of East Twp. and M.L.McDowell of East Twp.,
J.W.Denbow, step-father of M.L.McDowell and E.J.Denbow,
mother of M.L.McDowell, consent, by J.L.Shelby,J.P. on
1-20-1889

Geo. W. Ward of Portage and Ellen F. Crevoisier of Portage,
Andrew Godair, gdn. of Ellen, consents, b y John Young,J.P.
on 1-20-1889

Page 444

Levi Dunham of Big Prairie and Mrs. Delelah Watson of Big
Prairie by R.J.Simmons, J.P. on 12-23-1889

Henry Thomas of New Madrid Twp. and Mary J. Griffy of
New Madrid Twp. by Matt J.A.Conran, Mayor, on 1-24-1889

Page 445

Albert Shelby of Pt. Pleasant and Beatrice Herndon of
Stewart's Landing by Rev. W. G. Henson, M.G. 2-3-1889

Richard Lovingood of Pt.Pleasant and Roxana Herndon of
Stewart's Landing on testimony of James Summers of
Riddles Point by W. G. Henson, M.G. on 2-3-1889

Page 446
James Wesley of New Madrid Twp. and Mary A. Randolph of
New Madrid Twp., John Randolph, father of Mary, consents,
by James H. Bishop, M.G. on 2-3-1889

George Henderson of New Madrid Twp. and Carrie Randolph
of New Madrid Twp. by James Wesley, M.G. on 2-3-1887

Page 447
J. A. Brown of Big Prairie and Mary Barnes of Paw Paw on
2-9-1889 by A. J. Simmons, J.P.

Frank Jone and Emma Lucy of New Madrid Twp. 2-6-1889
by J. R. Morris

Page 448
Robert Hale of Big Prairie and Emmer Bledsoe of Big
Prairie by E. P. McKinney, M.G. on 2-6-1889

John R. Kasinger of Big Prairie and Mary F. Peepers of
Big Prairie by Conrad Lusler, J.P. on 2-9-1889

Page 449
Harvey Coleman of New Madrid and Louisa Mitchell of New
Madrid by Joseph Piggie, M.G. on 12-23-1888

Sam Auldrich of Riddles Pt. and Emma Girvin of Riddles Pt.
by C. C. Hudspeth, on 2-10-1889

Page 450
Wm. J. Chamberlain of New Madrid and Willie Ann Wilburn of
New Madrid by J.F. Curtis on 2-13-1889

James C. Hudspeth of LeSieur Twp. and Miss Nora Bayne of
LeSieur Twp. on 12-25-1889 by J.M.Dockery, County Judge

Page 451
Archy Wimp of St. John Twp. and Mary Doss of St. John
Twp. on 3-13-1889 by W. T. Peeler, J.P.

Page 451

James M. Sawyers of Portage Twp. and Martha Merrett of Portage Twp. by Jas. D. Stine, J.P. on 2-21-1889

Page 452
William Brown of Big Prairie and Margaret B. Ratliff of Big Prairie in Hudson House of New Madrid by Conrad Lisler, J.P. on 2-16-1889

Gruen Nipper of Portageville and Martha Robertson of Portageville by John Young, J.P. on 10-18-1889

Page 453
Chas. W. Fisher of Haywood of Pemiscot County and Maggie Roan of Haywood, Pemiscot Co. on 2-17-1889 by Matt J.A. Conran, Mayor

Emmett G. Porter of Miss. County and Ms. S. A. Presson of East Twp. with J.M.Presson consenting by J.J.Presson, M.G. on 2-24-1889

Page 454
Charles McAdoo of Big Prairie and Katie Mainord of Big Prairie on 2-27-1889 by J.F.Bishop, M.G.

William T. Bruh of Portageville and Laura Young of Portage Twp. on 2-28-1889 by John Young, J.P.

Page 455
Thos. J. Lair of Portageville and Mrs. Amelia Forsythe on 2-27-1889 by E. J. Rinkle, M.G.

Thomas Fox of Cottonwood Pt. and Amanda Jackson of New Madrid (Returned 3-15th not filled out)

Page 456
Jas H. Dodd of East Twp. and Mary McConnell of East Twp. on 3-3-1889 by J. L. Shelby, J.P.

Robert Harris of Big Prairie and Minty Botton of Big Prairie at W. Bledsoe's by E. P.McKinney, M.G. 3-6-1889

Page 457
Daniel W. Raidt of New Madrid Twp. and Mary P. Mason of New Madrid Twp. by F. Brand, M.G. on 3-4-1889

William Wintz of Portage and Anna J. Irvin of Portage Twp. Mollie Cunningham, mother of Anna consents, by Robert L. LaFont,J.P. on 3-7-1889

Page 458
William Angel of Scrubb Ridge and Sallie Watson of Scrubb Ridge by Jas. D. Stine,J.P. on Mar. 10, 1889

Frank McClister of West Twp. and Rachel Thompson of West Twp., F.F.Thompson and Bettie Thompson, father and mother of Rachel consent, by W. M. Holland, M.G. on 2-10-1889

Page 459

Henry Gills of New Madrid Twp. and Peggy Davis of New Madrid Twp. by W. T. Johnson, M.G. on 3-20-1889.

Ransom Scott of LaForge and Maggie Duw of New Madrid Twp. (no return)

Page 460
J. D. Malody, Fulton Co. Ky. and Mary C. Russell of Fulton Co., Ky. by Geo. W. Clark, J.P. on 8-14-1888

C. F. Wallace of Como and Lula Sherbut of Como, John W. Shubit, father of Lula consents, Oct 24, 1888 by James Stewart, J.P.

Page 461
Robert A. Beshears of New Madrid Twp. and Maggie Wallace of New Madrid, Sarah E. Wallace, mother of Maggie, consents, by Joel Cook, J.P. on 3-11-1889

James Graham of New Madrid and Susie Crowder of New Madrid by Chas. Reid, M.G. on 10-16-1888

Page 462
Barney Bennett of Lewis Prairie and Melinda Hardin of Lewis Prairie by Chas. Reed M.G. on 7-8-1887

Ben Dockery of New Madrid Co. and Rosa LeGrand with consent of Elizabeth LeGrand, mother of Rosa, by Jas. O'Bannon, J.P. on 7-10-1889

Page 463
John Akers of Scrub Ridge and Lou Herring by Jas. A. Workman, M.G. on 9-5-1888

Lemund Lewis and Sarah E. Willis on 9-21-1888 by James Stewart, J.P.

Page 464
Hampton Hunot of New Madrid Twp. and Rebecca A. Sears of New Madrid Twp. at John Sales by James Stepp, J.P. on 10-28-1888

Frank Mitchell and Fanny Orsic of New Madrid Co. at Fernand Stewarts by Henry Hunter, M.G. on 9-3-1888

Page 465
Levi Mohan of Lewis Prairie and Purly McCoy of Lewis Prairie on 11-29-1888 by James H. Bishop, M.G.

Thomas Key of LeSieur Twp. and Nancy Randolph of LeSieur Twp. by B. F. Boyce, Judge of Probate, on 1-7-1889

Page 466

John Randolph of LeSieur Twp. and Sallie Key of LeSieur Twp. by B. F. Boyce Judge of Probate Court on 1-1-1889

John F. Nolen of Paw Paw and Susan Craig of Paw Paw on 1-7-1889 by J. R. Morris, M.G.

Page 467

Isaac Maerley of East Twp. and Louisa Holinsworth of East Twp. by J. H. Michael, J.P. on 1-1-1889

Louis Meatte of Portage Twp. and Ida Gunn of Portage Twp. Saml Meatte, father of Louis and Wm. J. Gunn, father of Ida, consent, by John Young, J.P. on 2-14-1889

Page 468

Henry Mears of LeSieur Twp. and Nellie Bozark of LeSieur Twp. on 3-20-1889 by W. G. Henson, Baptist Minister

Henry H. Ford of LeSieur Twp. and Lewanda Moorehead of LeSieur Twp. by J. O'Bannon J.P. on 3-14-1889

Page 469

Richard J. Seals of Big Prairie and Celinda Whitestore of Big Prairie on 3-16-1889 by Wm. King, D. M.

Willie Nicholas of New Madrid and Ida Lee of New Madrid on 3-17-1889 by Joseph Piggie, M.G.

Page 470

Ned Jackson of New Madrid and Patsy Harris of New Madrid by Henry Hunter, M.G. on 3-26-1889

Amelson Harris of Riddles Point and Linda Bratton of Riddles Point, Hanner Allen gives consent for daughter, Linda, by W.G.Henson, M.G. on 3-28-1889

Page 471

Henry Clay of New Madrid Twp. and Mattie Grimes of New Madrid Twp. by James Wesley, M.G. on 3-20-1889

Andrew J. Cupp of Brush Prairie and Ellen Helms of Brush Prairie on 3-14-1889 by J.F.Bishop, M.G.

Page 472

Robert Wright of Morley, Scott Co. and Emna R. Summers of New Madrid by E. J. Rinkel, M.G. on 3-27-1889

William H. Carter of New Madrid Twp. and Luvene Simpson of New Madrid Twp. on 4-2-1889 by Joel Cook, J.P.

Page 473

Joseph G. St. Mary of New Madrid Twp. and Ola R. Akin of New Madrid Twp. Joseph St. Mary, father of Joseph consents, April 3, 1889 by E. J. Rinkel, pastor of M.E.G.S.

Lee Weed of Cairo, Ill, county of Alexander, and Kate Ellis of New Madrid City on 4-9-1889 by J.A.Curtis, M.G.

Page 474

Sylvester F. Reed of LaForge and MRS. Annie Dow of LaForge by E.P.McKinney, M.G. on 4-21-1889

Richard M. Banks of East Twp. and Lancy Taylor of East Twp. by W. Peeler, J.P. on 4-25-1889

Page 475

Charles W. Hayney of New Madrid Twp. and Mary L. Happy of New Madrid Twp by Jas. D. Stine, J.P. on 4-29-1889

James Minner of Big Prairie and Mary E. Mainord of Big Prairie by James F. Bishop, M.G. on 5-1-1889

Page 476

James Smith of New Madrid Twp. and July Ann Sikes of New Madrid Twp. by James Wesley, M.G. on 5-5-1889

Josiah McDaniel of Sandy Ridge and Lula Stephens of Sandy Ridge by W. Peeler, J.P. on 5-5-1889

Page 477

Gid Thomas England of St. John Twp. and Corriney C. Morris with R. Morris and M.M.Morris father and mother of Corriney consenting, by John M. Presson, M.G. on 5-9-1889

Albert Shimefut of Scrub Ridge and Susan Carrs of Scrub Ridge, Mary Stafford only living parent of Susan consenting, by W.W.Ellis, M.G. on 5-16-1889

Page 478

Dolph Brown of New Madrid and Polly Morgan of New Madrid by Henry Hunter, M.G. at Frank Mitchells on 1-15-1889

Thomas J. Leun of New Madrid Twp. and Arsula Cramon of New Madrid Twp. by A. J. Wilson, J.P. on 5-25-1889

BOOK 2

Page 1

James Brooks of New Madrid Co. and Elizabeth C. Jones July 23, 1889 by T. J. O. Morrison, J.P.

Charles W. Davidson of New Madrid Co., Portage Twp. and Amanda Kelly of Portage Twp. on 7-26-1889 by John Young, J.P.

Page 2

James Strain of Como Twp. and Laura O'Neal of Como Twp. on May 23, 1889 by T.J.O. Morrison, J.P.

John McCannon of Marshall, New Madrid Co. and Medita Tempa of Marshall, New Madrid Co. on 5-29-1889 by Joel Cook, J.P.

Page 3

Thomas Mize of Big Prairie and Lizzie Brown of Big Prairie on 5-25-1889 by J.F. Bishop, M.G.

R.C. Boyes and Jenny Phesch of New Madrid Co. on 6-7-1889 by J.F. Bishop, M.G.

Page 4

James A. Jones and Margaret A. Ward of Ristine, New Madrid Co., consent for Margaret given by stepfather, John D. Holden, on 7-13-1889 by Joel Cook, J.P.

Dennis A. Carl and Zula A. Prudy of New Madrid town on 7-6-1889 by Joel Cook, J.P.

Page 5

Cyrus Porter of St. John Twp. and Nora Eiceman of St. John Twp. on 7-23-1889 by W. T. Peeler

Thomas Starr of New Madrid Twp. and Mrs. Parethena Noell of New Madrid Twp. on 7-22-1889 by T.J.O. Morrison, J.P.

Thomas Starr of New Madrid Twp. and Mrs. Parethena Noell (dup) of New Madrid Twp. on 7-22-1889 by T. J.O. Morrison, J.P.

Page 6

George Mims of Sugar Tree Ridge of Co. and Catharine Harris of same place on 6-5-1889 by G. W. Clark, J.P.

Benjamin F. Wilburn of East Twp. and Mamie L. M. J. Turner with consent of Louis Turner, father of Mamie, on 8-1-1889 by J. L. Shelby

Page 7

William Sheappard of Sugartree Ridge and Allie Blizzard of Sugartree, Sarah Green, mother of Allie consents, on 6-8-1889 by Geo. W. Clark, J.P.

George W. Porter of Ruddles point and Melinda Francis of Ruddles point on 6-11-1889 by W.G.Henson, M.G.

Page 8

George N. Brown of East Twp. and Catherine Smith of East Twp. on 6-15-1889 by J.L.Shelby

James Adcock of LeSieur Twp. and Bettie Blackwell of LeSieur Twp. William Adcock, father of James, consents, on 6-19-1889 by Jas. O'Bannon J.P.

Page 9

Louis Baher of New Madrid and Alice Ewing on 6-21-1889 by W.W.Ellis

Algeronon Donahue of New Madrid and Laura A. Moore of same place on 6-26-1889 by J.A.Curtis, M.G.

Page 10

John Gray of Paw Paw and Minnie Hendricks of New Madrid Twp. on 6-29-1889 by T. J.O.Morrison, J.P.

James A. Jones of LaForge and Margaret A. Ward of Ristine consent by stepfather (John D. Holden) 7-13-1889 (no return)

Page 11

Thomas Stan and Pauline Noell of New Madrid twp. on 7-22-1889 (no return)

George A. Hillsman of Mclean, Ky. and Ruth E. Powell of New Madrid on 7-23-1889 by J.F.Curtis, M.G.

Page 12

Gus W. Butt of Big Prairie and Annie Patterson of Big Prairie on 7-26-1889 (no return)

Ben Hart of New Madrid Twp. and Lucinda L. Waters of New Madrid consent of father, Wash Waters, on 7-26-1889 by W.T.Johnson, M.G.

Page 13

Charles W. Davidson of Portage Twp. and Almeda Kelly of Portage on 7-26-1889 (no return)

Page 13

James Henry of Brush Prairie and Sarah A. Cupp of Brush Prairie on 8-6-1889 by Conrad Seipler, J.P.

Page 14

John W. Hoguis of New Madrid Co. and Malinda Riggs of New Madrid Co., Carlin Riggs father consenting, on 8-13-1889 by Ira P. Eby, M.G.

Willie E. Jones of New Madrid and Laura McCreery of Portageville on 8-19-1889 by John Young, J.P.

Page 15

J. M. Cain of Obine Twp. Miss. Co. and Amanda C. Randolph of Miss. Co. on 8-19-1889

George Bradshaw of Portageville and Mary J. Crawshaw of Portageville on Aug. 19, 1889 by Tedford Hogan, M.G.

Page 16

Pleas Akers of Portage Twp. and Florence V. Arbuckle of Portage Twp. M. F. Akers, father of Pleas, consents and Florence's mother, Ann Augustine Vestal consents Aug. 22, 1889

Mr. John Vampeth of Scrub Ridge and Nancy Arbuckle of Scrub Ridge on 8-24-1889 by John Young, J.P.

Page 17

Raphel LeSieur of Portage Twp. and Lue Nicholus of Portage Twp. on 8-26-1889 by Joel Cook, J.P.

Charles R. McGee of LeSieur Twp and Bettie J. Knight of LeSieur, J.J.Knight, father of Bettie consents, on Aug. 27, 1889 by C. C. Hudspeth, J.P.

Page 18

John Coffee of New Madrid and Bell F. Marney of New Madrid on 8-27-1889 by Conrad Seissler, J.P.

Robert Frazer of Dunklin Co. to Eliza Paxton of Como on Aug. 31, 1889 by James Stewart, J.P.

Page 19

Tom Fox of New Madrid City to Sallie Hampton of New Madrid twp. on 8-31-1889 by Thos. Johnson, M.G.

Page 19

Isaac Bird of New Madrid Twp. and Maggie Henderson of New Madrid Twp., age of Maggie Henderson proved by Mrs. Sikes, Sep. 2, 1889 by James G. Biship, pastor

Page 20

William Parker of New Madrid and Amanda Jackson of New Madrid on 9-7-1889 by James Bishop, M.G.

Page 20

William Mainord of Brush Prairie and Mollie Magee with written consent of Ellen Bell, mother of Maggie, on Aug. 14, 1889 by James F. Bishop, M.G.

Page 21

Joseph Blizard of St. John Twp. and Mollie Wimp of St. John Twp on Oct 9, 1889 by W. T. Peeler, J.P.

Mr. John C. Pack of LaForge and Miss Emma Mitchell of New Madrid Twp. by J. F. Curtis on 9-11-1889

Page 22

Andrew Lawson of New Madrid and Matilda Patterson of New Madrid on 8-4-1889 by Henry Hunter, M.G.

William E. Johnson of East Twp. and Daisy Potts of East Twp., James H. Johnson, father of William consents, on Sept. 16, 1889 by J. M. Presson, M.G.

Page 23

Elias Lazell of New Madrid and Frankie Waters (Bettie Enlow, mother of Franklin consents, on 12-28-1889 by Henry Hunter, M.G.

Mr. James Alcott Shead of New Madrid and Miss Mary LaForge of New Madrid on 9-18-1889 by Phillip Brady, Catholic Priest of St. John Church, St. Louis

Page 24

John Ray of Tiptonville, Lake Co. Tenn. and Lizzie Burnum of same place on 9-20-1889 by T.J.O.Morrison, J.P.

Ben Millis of LeSieur Twp. and Lizzie Ross of LeSieur on 9-22-1889 by Jas. O'Bannon,J.P.

Page 25

J.J.Johnson of New Madrid and Julia Waters of New Madrid Emeline Thompkon, mother of Julia Waters consents, on 9-23-1889 by Henry Hunter, M.G.

Page 25

William B. Craig of Como and Eliza Guthrie of Como, J.L. Craig, father of William B., consents, on 9-24-1889 by James Stewart J.P.

Page 26

James Creason of Marshall Co. Ky and Mattie L. Mangum, J.I.Mangum, father of Mattie consents, on 9-25-1889 by T.J.O.Morrison,J.P.

Jessie L. Moore of New Madrid Twp. and Emma O. Ewing of New Madrid Twp. on 9-23-1889 by J. R. Morris

Page 27

George Brown of New Madrid City and Patsey Young on Oct. 5, 1889 by James W. Bishop, M.G.

Daniel Ogden of Big Prairie and Vina Woods of Big Prairie by R. F. Chine, M.G. on 10-6-1889

Page 28

James Upton of Barnes Ridge and Lucy Doss of Mississippi Co. on Oct 16, 1889 by W. T. Peeler, J.P.

Lidge A. Ash of LaForge and Mary Martin of LaForge with Matilda Martin, mother of Mary, consenting on 10-13-1889 by James F. Bishop. M.G.

Page 29

George V. Montague of New Madrid and Lilly A. Durocher of New Madrid by F. Brand, Minister of Catholic Church on 10-15-1889

Frank Worth of Scrub Ridge and Maggie A. Richardson of Scrub Ridge on 10-24-1889 by Jas. O'Bannon, J.P.

Page 30

David W. Jones of East Twp. and Ida M. Carter, Wm. S. Hollingsworth, stepfather of Ida consenting, on 11-6-1889 by J. W. Mitchell, J.P.

Wesley A. Willis of Donaldson Point and Susan Rogers of Donaldson Pt. on 11-3-1889 by T. J. O. Morrison

Page 31

Robert Dockery of LeSieur Twp. and Florence Rainwater with T. M. Rainwater, father of Florence, consenting on 11-6-1889 by Jas. D. Stine, J.P.

Page 31

William Whitehead of Nelson Co., Ky. and Ada Boyer of New Madrid on 11-7-1889 by W. W. Blalock, M.G.

Page 32

Frank LeSieur of New Madrid Twp. and Laura Williams on 11-10-1889 by James W. Bishop, M.G.

William Stockard of New Madrid and Mary E. Streets of New Madrid , age of Mary from testimony of Will LeSieur, her brother, on 9-28-1889 by Henry Hunter, M.G.

Page 33

Alfred F. McFadden of Brush Prairie and Minnie Bell Davis of New Madrid, Hardin Davis, father of Minnie Bell, consents, on Nov. 26, 1889 by Ira P. Eby, M.G.

James H. Butler of East Twp. and Matilda J. Holden of East Twp., Frances Holden, mother of Matilda, consenting, on Dec. 11, 1889 by J. W. Mitchell, J.P.

Page 34

Henry Willis of New Madrid Twp. and Bell Channy of New Madrid Twp. by T. J. O. Morrison J.P. on 12-15-1889

Ed Shanks of New Madrid Twp. and Bettie Henry of New Madrid Twp., Ed Shanks on oath says he is 23 and Bettie Henry is 20 years, on Dec. 15, 1889 by J.R. Morris, M.G.

Page 35

John Gamble of Como Twp. and Mary Bartlett of Como Twp. on Dec. 25, 1889 by James Stewart, J.P.

Willie Case of LeSieur Twp. and Annie Lewis of LeSieur Twp. on Dec. 26, 1889 by Charles Reed, M.G.

Page 36

Lucy Q. Nelson of East Twp. and Maggie Godwin of East Twp. J.M. and M.J. Godwin, father and mother of Maggie consent, on Dec. 22, 1889 by Louis W. Mott (deputy)(no other name)

George Fletcher of New Madrid and Ellen Scims of New Madrid on Dec. 25, 1889 of by James Wesley, M.G.

Page 37

Joseph Lindley of Barnes Ridge and Katie Upton of Barnes Ridge by W. T. Peeler J.P. on 12-29-1889

John Brown of New Madrid and Leoder Pikey of New Madrid Twp Augustus G. Pikey, father of Leoder consents, on Dec. 23, 1889 by T. J.O.Morrison, J.P.

Page 38

George W. Stull of Big Prairie Twp. and Sarah A. Patton of Big Prairie Twp, M.J.Stull, mother, consents for Sarah, on Dec. 25, 1889 by J.P. (no name)

John Williams of LeSieur Twp. and Laura Hampton of LeSieur Twp. by Henry Hunter, M.G. on Dec. 28, 1889

Page 39

Newton Smothers of Craighead Co., Ark. and Mary McCormick of Craighead Co., Ark. on Dec. 25, 1889 by Joel Cook, J.P.

James Martin of East Twp. and Ally Phillips of East Twp. on Dec. 29, 1889 by J.P. of Mississippi Co., Mo. at Pid Martins (no other name)

Page 40

William T. Umphries of East Prairie of Mississippi County and May Virginia Blankenship of East Prairie on Dec. 26, 1889 by Joel Cook, J.P.

William Mitchell of New Madrid and Ceola O'Bannon of New Madrid by James Furlong, Priest on Jan. 1, 1890

Page 41

Thomas B. Williams of Pt. Pleasant and Susie B. Lyons of LeSieur Twp. on 1-2-1890 by W. W. Blalock, M.G.

William Adkinson of New Madrid Twp. and Cassey Stoval of Portage Twp., John Adkinson, father of William, consents, on Jan. 1, 1890 by W. W. Blalock, M.G.

Page 42

Charles Hoglan of LeSieur Twp. and Mattie McKiney of LeSieur by W. W. Blalock, M.G. on 1-8-1890

Charles P. Toney of New Madrid Twp. and Clara Lamb of LeSieur Twp on 1-8-1890 by W.W.Blalock, Minister of Gospel of M.E.Church South at Bride's Mothers near Pt. Pleasant.

Page 43

John Pain of LeSieur Twp. and Matilda Young of LeSieur Twp. on 1-9-1890 by J.P. at his office (no name)

David L. Martin of New Madrid Co. and Lucy Neal of New Madrid Co. by Rev. James H. Bishop, M.G. on 1-11-1890

Page 44

Dick Fletcher of New Madrid Co. and Lucy Levy of New Madrid Co. by Minister of Gospel on 1-12-1890 (no name)

Joseph Davis of New Madrid Twp. and Hattie Fisher of New Madrid Twp. on 4-3-1890 by Rev. James F. Bishop

45

John P. Lee of Brush Prairie and Minnie Storey by A. J. Summers, J.P. on 1-15-1890

James C. Matheney of East Twp. and Margaret E. Buckman of East Twp., D. T. Buckman, father of Margaret Elizabeth consents, on Jan. 15, 1890 by Rev. John M. Prisson, M.G.

Page 46

James M. Thomas of LeSieur Twp. and Cene Craig of LeSieur on 1-18-1890 by Elder W. G. Henson, M.G.

Lewis Brown of Portageville and Ada Davis of Portageville on 1-22-1890 by R. L. LaFont, J.P.

Page 47

John W. Chaney of Scott Co. and Ella M. Moore on 1-31-1890 by F. Brand, Pastor

Mautthew J. Matsinger of Malden and Ella Dood of Rector(Ark) with E. J. Langdon, Guardian, consenting, on 1-27-1890 by W. H. Blalock, M.G.

Page 48

John Blocker of Como Twp. and Lucina Godard of Como Twp. on 1-30-1889 by David Walker, J.P.

J. H. Stout of Malden and Mary Stiles of Malden on 2-8-1890 by J. F. Curtis, M.G.

Page 49

Sam Allen of New Madrid Twp. and Tanner Willis of New Madrid Twp. on 2-9-1890 by James Wesley, M.G.

Perry J. Mays of New Madrid Co. and Louisa Early on 2-13-1890 by Conrad Leissler, J.P.

Page 50

Henry Conrad of Portage Twp. and Mary M. Baldwin of Portage Twp. on 4-23-1890 by Robert L. LaFont, J.P.

Edward Secoy of LeSieur Twp. and Mamie Willis of LeSieur Twp., S. T. Willis, mother of Mamie, consenting, on 2-18-1890 by T. J. O. Morrison, J.P.

Page 51

John Butler of New Madrid Twp. and Edward Jeffreys of New Madrid Twp. on Feb. 22, 1890 by Charles Reid, M.G.

Charlie Edwards of New Madrid Twp. and Fannie Simis of New Madrid Twp., Hanner Barber, mother of Charlie Edwards consents, and Henry Sims, father of Fannie, on Feb. 20, 1890 by James H. Bishop, M.G.

Page 52

James W. Merrill of New Madrid Twp. and Effa L. Samuels of New Madrid Twp. on 2-21-1890 by Rev. J. R. Morris.

Francis W. Hatten and Alicia Vetile of New Madrid Co. on 3-3-1890 by James Stewart, J.P.

Page 53

Herman Crisel of Hamilton, Ill. and Mary C. Trammell of Como, consent b y Jarsite Trammell, father of Mary C.

John T. Greer of Covington, Tipton, Tenn. and Laura Phelon of New Madrid by W. H. Blalock, M. G. on March 1, 1890

Page 54

L. P. Whitley of New Madrid Co. and Mrs. Nancy McClard on March 2, 1890 by Rev. IRVIN A. Ewing

King Williams of New Madrid and Laura Curr of New Madrid on March 10, 1890 by James H. Bishop, M.G.

Page 55

William A. Petty of Portage and Lasly Pope of Dunklin on Mar 12, 1890 by Joel Cook, J.P.

George McGarth of Big Prairie and Ida Jane Taylor of Big Prairie on Feb. 19, 1890

Page 56

James D. White of East? Memphis of Ark. and Ella McGeorge of Sciota Co. Ohio on 3-13-1890 by Joel Cook, J.P.

Thomas B. Porter of Lake Co., Tenn. and Rosalee B. Gaspeth of New Madrid on March 20, 1890 by T. J. O. Morrison, J.P.

Page 57

James Carroll of Big Prairie and Dora Walker of Big Prairie on Mar. 18, 1890 by E. P. McKinney, J.P.

Samuel Lindley of Barnes Ridge and Miss Jane Shultz of Barnes Ridge on Mar. 30, 1890 by W. T. Peeler, J.P.

Page 58

Rueben Trotter of Lewis Prairie and Anner Jones of Lewis Prairie, consent of Missoura Jones, on March 29, 1890 by (not given)

Monoroe Shanks of New Madrid Twp. and Alva Mippleton of New Madrid Twp. on 3-29-1890 by Joel Cook, J.P.

Page 59

Henry Rochell of New Madrid Twp. and Ella Toney of New Madrid Twp., W. H. Toney, father of Ella consents, on April 20, 1890 by Rev. Irvin A. Ewing

Edward J. Trammel of Como and Emma L. Shelfer of Como, T.E.Shelfer and M.E. Shelfer consent for Emma, on 4-3-1890 (no return)

Page 60

Matt King of Lewis Prairie and Lana Bell Dunn, John Dunn, father of Lana Bell consents, on 4-3-1889 by Henry Hunter

William F. Turner of Fulton Co., Ky. and Susie Smedley of Fulton Co., Ky, Wm. F. Turner consents, on 4-4-1890 by Irvin A. Ewing, M.G.

Page 61

William H. Hill of Portage Twp. and Sallie Keith of Portage on 4-5-1890 by Robt. L. Lafont, J.P.

Page 61

Samuel Walker of Sikeston, Scott Co. and Anna Carroll of Big Prairie, consent of mother, Mary Carroll, on 4-13-1890 by R. T. Hyde, J.P.

Page 62

Natt Thompkins of New Madrid Twp. and Laura Climmons of same place on 4-12-1890 by Henry Hunter

Charles Jones of New Madrid and Etta Ellis of New Madrid on April 14, 1890 by W. C. Blalock, M.G.

Page 63

Jessie Smith of LeSieur Twp. and Mary Cantral of New Madrid Twp. 4-17-1890 (Ret. May 4th, 1890 without certificate)

Jessie Smith of New Madrid and Annie Woods of New madrid on 4-6-1890 by James H. Bishop, M.G.

Page 64

James A. Baston and Celeste Moore of Webster Co., Ky. on 4-28-1890 by T. J. O. Morrison, J.P.

Andrew Banks of Big Prairie and Sarah Davis of Big Prairie on 4-30-1890 by A. J. Simmons, J.P.

Page 65

John J. Henson of LeSieur Twp. and Lucy A. Petty of LeSieur Twp. on 4-30-1890. (no return)

Clay W. Dawson of New Madrid and Bettie Ellis of New Madrid, John Ellis, father of Bettie, consents by James J. Furlong(Catholic Priest) on 4-30-1890

Page 66

William Farrie of New Madrid Twp. and Lou Waters on 5-1-1890 by Henry Hunter

Louis Prichett of New Madrid Co. and Mary L. Preston by J.M.Presson   May 12, 1890

Page 67

Ambrose Galloway of New Madrid Co. of Gray Ridge and Bell Day of LeSieur Twp. by John Young, J.P. on 5-12-1890

Tom Nickles of New Madrid Twp. and Jane Roberson of New Madrid Twp. by Elder Reed, M.G. on 7-23-1890

Page 68

Richard Bayne of New Madrid Twp. and Mamie F. Ransburgh on May 22, 1890 by W. W. Blalock, M.G.

Andrew Davis of New Madrid Twp. and Ellen Fletcher of New Madrid Twp. with consent of Susan Bird, mother of Ellen, by Elder Reed, M.G. on May 25, 1890

Page 69

Lawrence H. Bell of New Madrid and Ida Thompson on May 31, 1890 (no return)

James T. Ragsdale of LeSieur Twp. and Clara N. Blackwell of LeSieur, Thomas and Mary Blackwell consent for Clara, by Jas. O'Bannon on 6-19-1890

Page 70

Alfred W. Cravens of New Madrid and Cora Maulsby of New Madrid, John Maulsby, father of Cora, consents (no return) dated June 14, 1890

William Smith of New Madrid and Martha Beasley of New Madrid by Geo. W. Clark, June 19, 1890

Page 71

Silas Y. Barrett of Obion Co., Tenn. and Annie E. McGee of Como on 6-18-1890 by Joel Cook, j.P.

Dallas Stubbs and Alice Shelson with testimony of Dallas Stubbs that they are of age by T. J. O. Morrison on 6-26-1889

Page 72

Richard Carroll and Katie Helm of Big Prairie Twp. on Oct 9, 1890 by A. J. Simmons, J.P.

Wm. H. Murphy of New Madrid Twp. and Ida Bogard by Geo. W. Clark, J.P. on 6-27-1889

Page 73

James Hendricks of East Twp. and Elmer Wilbourn of East Twp. by J. L. Shelby, J.P. on 7-2-1890

Charles Tinnin of LeSieur and Nancy Jane Grant of LeSieur.Twp Martha Butler, mother of Charles Tinnin consents, on 7-10-1890 by T. J.O.Morrison, J.P.

Page 74

John T. Anderson of New Madrid Twp. and George A. Willis of New Madrid Twp. by T. J. O. Morrison, J.P. ON 7-21-1890

Page 74

James Reede of Sugar Tree Ridge and Nancy Medders of Sugar Tree by Geo. W. Clark, J.P. on 7-15-1890

Page 75

Edward Evans of St. Louis, Mo. and Louivisa Haislep of St. Louis by T. J. O. Morrison, J.P. on 7-17-1890

Joseph Morehead of Big Prairie and Fannie Overfield of Scott Co. by T. J. O. Morrison, J.P. on 7-20-1890

Page 76

Augustus Oiceman of Sugar Tree and Lena Lawfield of Sugar Tree by Geo. W. Clark, on July 27, 1890

Monroe Neely of Grays Ridge and James Kelley of Grays Ridge by J. D. Wren, J.P. on 8-3-1890

Page 77

Jerry Michell of New Madrid Twp. and Annie Randols of New Madrid by J. H. Bishop, M.G. on 8-20-1890

Ferman Williams of West Twp. and Mary A. Jones of same by J. L. Shelby J.P. on 8-10-1890

Page 78

David A. Patterson of East Twp. and Lotty Laster of East Twp. William Laster, guardian consents, on 8-5-1890 by J. H. MIchaels, J.P.

Daniel Waldrop of Morehouse and Miss Mary Shoat of Morehouse on 8-13-1890 by T. J. O. Morrison, J.P.

Page 79

George Matthews of New Madrid Twp. and Miss Ida Barnes of New Madrid Twp. on 8-16-1890 by E. P. McKinney, M.G.

John Ash of Laforge and Lizzie Marr, Mary E. Reis, mother of Lizzie Marr, consents, by A. J. Wilson, M.G. 8-17-1890

Page 80

Wallard Taylor of Big Prairie Twp. and Laura Peeples of Ogden, New Madrid Co. with consent of Benson W. Peeples (father) by A. J. Scimmones, J.P. on 8-17-1890

John Allison of East swamp of New Madrid and Rena Elldridge of East Swamp by J. H. Michael, J.P. on 8-24-1890

Page 81

Henry Dowdy of New Madrid Twp. and Jain Davis of New Madrid Twp. (Henry Dowdy says both are of age)by James Westley, M.G. on 8-28-1890

Ed Turner of Barnes Ridge and Susan Settles of Barnes Ridge Samuel Settles consenting to Susan's marriage, by W. T. Peeler, J.P. on 9-7-1891

Page 82

Louis Water (col) of New Madrid Twp. and Annie Bell of New Madrid by J.H.Bishop, M.G. on 9-6-1890

Andrew Carroll of Big Prairie and Mary Isabel Dewberry of Big Prairie on 9-8-1890 by Joel Cook, J.P.

Page 83

Robert Carson of Scrub Ridge of New Madrid Co. and Alberta Akers of Scrub Ridge on 9-8-1890 by John Young, J.P.

Columbus Shaver of Brush Prairie and Amanda Driver of Big Prairie by A. J. Simmons, J.P. on 9-13-1891

Page 84

John N. Chaney of Scott Co., Mo. and Ella M. Moore of Big Prairie Jan. 23, 1890 (no return)

Henderson Sturgeon of Como and Susan Ford of Como by Joel Cook J.P. on 9-15-1890

Page 85

David Ferrenberg of New Madrid Twp. and Mrs. Ida Newton of New Madrid by Ira P. Erby, M.G.

Ed Sims of James Bayou of Miss. Co., Mo. and Lela E. Doyle of same by Geo. W. Clark, J.P. on 9-17-1890

Page 86

James Underwood of Scrub Ridge and V. Admer by James O'Bannon J.P. 9-23-1890

Joseph Bartolomew and Mary E/ Detie of Portage Twp. on Oct 21, 1890 by Jas. O'Bannon.

Page 87

William M. Coleman and Anna K. Ransburgh of New Madrid Twp. by C. P. Mauchman, M.G. on 10-9-1890

Page 87

Sam Newberry of New Madrid Twp. and Ella Matthews of
Matthews by A. J, Scummons J.P. on 10-12-1890

Page 88

William Parrott of Lewis Prairie and Ada Young of New
Madrid by Stephen Lee on 10-12-1890

Daniel Matthews of Pt. Pleasant and Minnie Richardson
(consent of Amson Richardson, father of Minnie) by
James O'Bannon, J.P. on 10-19-1890

Page 89

Isie Manuel of New Madrid and Joe Gray of New Madrid
on Oct 21, 1890 by Joseph Peges, M.G.

Frank Wilson of New Madrid and Harriet Wilson of New
Madrid on Oct 21, 1890 by Joseph Pegges, M.G.

Page 90

Oseal Smith of New Madrid and Ada Low of New Madrid on
Oct 12, 1890 by Joseph Pegges, M.G.

Jacob Sutton of Big Prairie Twp. and Sallie Ann Dewitt
of Big Prairie on Oct 26, 1890 by J.M.Morgan, M.G.

Page 91

David Sims of New Madrid and Emma Johnson of New Madrid
on Oct 26, 1890 by Joseph Pegues, M.G.

John W. Brannum of New Madrid Twp. and Fathy E. Cunningham
of New Madrid Twp. Henry Cumingham consents, father of
Falhy, by Sa. Harburg M.G. at Farrenburg
Page 92
Henry M. Brown of Mamkah, county of Blue Earth, State of
Minn. and Louisa Newsum of New Madrid by Theo Hudson, M.G.
on 10-29-1890

John S. Martin of New Madrid County and Martha A. Stewart
of New Madrid Co. on 10-29-1890 by E. P. McKinney, M.G.

Page 93

Charles Nicholas of New Madrid and Mary Ida Phillips on
11-2-1890 by Henry Hunter, M.G.

William Manuel of New Madrid and Adale Smith of New
Madrid by Joseph Pegus, M.G. on 11-3-1890

Page 94

Arthur Dixon of New Madrid and CordeliaRichards of New Madrid with Rufus Richards, father of Cordia consenting on 11-3-1890 by C. P. Henchman, Methodist minister

Harrison Long of Brush Prairie and Delia Ann Brown of Brush Prairie with James Chapman, guardian consenting, on 11-5-1890 by A. J. Simmons, J.P.

Page 95

James F. Bishop of LaForge, Co. of N.M., and Sarah A. Alsup of LaForge, and Sarah A. Huffman, mother of Sarah Alsup, consenting, by J. F. Youem, M.G. on 11-9-1890

Emerson G. Blanch of LeSieur Twp. and Ida Damon of LeSieur Twp. , Angalow Damon consenting for Ida on 11-6-1890, by J. L. Knight, M.G.
Page 96
Benjamin F. Clayton of Big Prairie and Emma Thompson of Big Prairie on 11-8-1890 by A. J. Simmons J.P.

James A. McConnell of Big Prairie Twp. and Jessie Moss of Big Prairie by A. J. Simmons J.P. on 11-8-1890

Page 97

Benjamin F. Pikey of LeSieur Twp. and Lucy Henson of Pt. Pleasant by Rev. W. G. Henson, M.G. on 11-19-1890

James Tippet of New Madrid Co. and Elizabeth Perchy by J. A. Morris, M.G. on 11-19-1890

Page 98

Thead T. Key of Scrub Ridge and Tabitha Jane Chapman of Scrub Ridge by John Young, J.P. on 11-27-1890

Andrew Morra Of City of New Madrid and Lula Woods by Rev. Geo. G. Branon, M.G. on 11-20-1890

Page 99

James P. Ruddles of Pt. Pleasant and Mrs. Anny Miller by W. G. Henson, M.G. on 11-23-1890

Beuregard Simmons of Portage Twp. and Mary A. Crashard, Mary Bradshaw, mother of Mary Crashard consents, on 1123-1890 by John Young, J.P.

Page 100

William R. Wathen of New Madrid Twp and Nellie G. Mahar of same on Nov. 26 by Roman Catholic Priest James J. Furlong

Stephen W. St. Mary of New Madrid Twp. and Miss Nona Ewing of New Madrid Twp., Stephen St. Mary, father of Stephen W. consenting, on Nov. 26, 1890 by J. R. Morris, M.G

Page 101

Thos. W. Morgan, Lake Co. Tenn. and Annie Redin of Lake Co. Tenn., James Morgan, father of Thomas W. consents, by Joel Cook, J.P. on 11-29-1890

Hiram Morgan of Lake Co. Tenn and Anne Hogue of Lake Co. Tenn by Joel Cook, J.P. on 11-29-1890

Page 102

Robert McCormick of Big Prairie and Rachael Bolinger of Big Prairie by John N. Mills, J.P. on 12-7-1890

William Masterson of Big Prairie and Reanie Ford of Big Prairie by A. J. Simmons J.P. on 10-23-1890

Page 103

Daniel Bush of Ogden of New Madrid and Mollie Cantrell of Ogden by JohnN. Mills, J.P. 1890

Benjamin R. Strong of East Twp. and Ellen Robbins of East Twp. by J. M. Lee, Elder, M.G. on Dec. 8, 1890

Page 104

Romants S. Burgess of LaForge and Ida May Burgess of LaForge R.C.Burgess, father of Ida May consenting, by A.J. Wilson M.G. on 12-9-1890

Morgan Worth of LeSieur Twp. and Lizzie Adcock of LeSieur Twp. consent of J. F. Adcock, father of Lizzie, on 12-11-1890 by B. F. Boyce, Judge of Probate Court

Page 105

Willie N. Johnson, New Madrid Twp. and Miss Sarah J. Kenworthy by J. R. Morris, J.P. on 12-16-1890

John W. Randolph of LeSieur Twp. and Miss Addy Key of LeSieur by A. M. O'Quinn, M.G. on 12-17-1890

Page 106

Thomas Osby of Lewis Prairie and Nelly Parrott of Lewis Prairie with William Parrott, brother of Nellie giving testimony as to age of Nelly, by J. A. Wortham, M.G. on 12-21-1890

Page 106

James W. Maberry of West Twp. and Martha J. Ray of West Twp. by Ephraim Brown, J.P. on Dec. 25, 1890

Page 107

John Hall of new Madrid and Miss Kathy Raidt of New Madrid on Dec. 22, 1890 by J. R. Morris

Wm. Richard Gray of Lewis Prairie and Miss Lizzie Lemons of Lewis Prairie on Dec. 23, 1890 by J. R. Morris

Page 108 Mellici Ogdon of Big Prairie and Mary Pleas of Big Prairie by John N. Mills on Mar. 24, 1891

Robert F. Crevoisier of LeSieur Twp. and Miss Mary Smith of LeSieur Twp. on Dec. 24, 1890 by John Young, J.P.

Page 109

Adolph Crevoisier of LeSieur and Miss Adaline Meatt of Portage with consent of Luke Meatt , Guardian of Adaline by John Young, J.P. on Dec. 24, 1890

Andy Keys of New Madrid and Josey Jackson of Co. of New Madrid by W. T. Johnson, M.G. on Dec. 25, 1890
Page 110
Dan'l T. Richard of Ristine and Florence Brown of Ristine on Dec. 25, 1890 by James Wesley, M.G.

John Warren of New Madrid Co. and Martha Woods of New Madrid Co. on Dec. 24, 1890 by George Branan, M.G

Page 111

Stephen Burstett of New Madrid, and Amanda Hind of New Madrid by Joel Cook, J.P. on Dec. 25, 1890

William D. Trumper of Brush Prairie and Josay Sauls of Brush Prairie with consent of Abraham Sauls, father of J. Sauls by J. A. Workman, M.G. on Dec. 31, 1890

Page 112

Lee Hardin of New Madrid and Martha A. Forest with consent of father, S. M. Forest for Martha, on Jan. 1, 1891 by J. D. Stine, J.P.

Martin Pikey of Portage Twp. and Lizzie Sinks of Portage Twp. on Dec. 31, 1890 by John Young, J.P.

Page 113

John Cook of LaForge and Zelia Patterson of LaForge on 1-1-1891 by W. F. Johnson, M.G.

Page 113

Lilbourn JENKINS of New Madrid and Miss Maggie Dunn of Lewis Prairie on Jan. 1, 1891 by Henry Hunter, J.P.

Page 114

Jessie Jaynes of St. Johns Twp. and Miss Bettie J. Malone of St. Johns Township on Jan. 4, 1801 by W. T. Peeler, J.P.

George Morgan of Brush Prairie and Mediaa Banks of Brush Prairie on April 16, 1892 by W. T. Johnson, M.G.

Page 115

William H. Cook of Barnes Ridge and Ceinda Manion of Barnes Ridge by W. T. Peeler, J.P. on 1-11-1891

Page 115

John Adams of Portageville and Minnie Keith of Portage Twp. with Sallie Hill, mother of Minnie Keith, consenting, on Jan. 11, 1891 by John Young, J.P.

Page 116

Albert Cage of Louis Prairie and Clara Waters of Louis Prairie on Jan. 10, 1891 by Henry Hunter J.P.

Augustus J. Simms of LeSieur Twp. and Chinney Culat on Jan. 15, 1891 by John Young, J.P.

Page 117

John L. Penix of Pt. Pleasant and Mary Ray of Pt. Pleasant on Jan. 18, 1891 by J. J. Knight.

James Ward of East Twp. and Cyntha Ann Newman ofEast Twp. Joan Newman, mother of Cynthia Ann, consenting, by J. E. Shelby, on 1-19-1899

Page 118

William McGee of New Madrid Co. and Bettie Hunot of New Madrid Co. on 1-21-1891 by Joel Cook, J.P.

Page 118

Melvin F. Cackerham of Lotta and Rebecca Jane Orr with consent of Buford & Malisa Orr, parents of Rebecca Jane, on 1-25-1891 by James Stewart, J.P.

Page 119

Charles Cherry of New Madrid Twp. and Marih Green of New Madrid Twp. by W.T. Johnson, M.G. on 1-27-1891

Page 119

Jessie L. Smith of county of Fulton, Ky. and Ann Hunter of
LeSieur Twp., John Hunter, father of Ann, consents, on 1-26-1891
by J. J. Knight, M.G.

Page 120

Silas Wheeler of LeSieur Twp. and Fannie Blackwell of LeSieur
Twp. on 1-27-1891 by J.J.Knight, M.G.

John D. Dockery and Mary J. Anderson of LeSieur Twp. on 1-26-1891
by J. D. Stine, J.P.

Page 121

George E. Randolph of LeSieur Twp. and Miss Lou Key of
LeSieur Twp. on 1-28-1891 by J. D. Stine, J.P.

Thomas Gehan of LeSieur Twp. and Miss Linda Secoy of LeSieur
Twp. on 2-1-1891 by J. D. Stine, J.P.

Page 122

Charles W. England of New Madrid Co. and Miss Manah B. Simmons
on Feb. 1, 1891 by W. T. Peeler, J.P.

Charles Hall of West Twp. and Miss Mary Mays of West Twp.
on 1-30-1891 by Ephraim Brand J.P.

Page 123

Eugene Ray of James Bayou Twp. and Miss Rosa Dunn of James
Bayou Twp. on 1-29-1891 by Joel Cook, J.P.

Louis Moore of LeSieur Twp. and Sarah L. Knott of LeSieur Twp/
by Samuel Mecklem, M. G. on 2-5-1891

Page 124

William R. Myers of LeSieur Twp. and Miss Ella DeLisle of
Portageville on 2-5-1891 by James J. Furlong, Priest

W. E. Fields of LeSieur nwp. and Florence Proe, N. J. Fields,
father of W. E. Fields, consents and Sarah L. Knott, mother of
Florence Proe consents, on 2-5-1891 by Samuel Mecklem, M. G.

Page 125

William H. Counts of New Madrid and Cornelia Bellon of New Madrid
on Feb. 5, 1891 by Joel Cook, J.P.

Wm. D. Davis of Fulton, KY. and Martha J. Hinshaw of Fulton, Ky.
Thomas B. Hinshaw, father of Martha, consents, on Feb. 21, 1891
by Joel Cook, J.P.

Page 126

Henry R. Harris of Tiptonville, Lake Co., Tenn. and Mary J. Girvin of Portageville. John L. Girvin, father of Mary J., consents, on March 4, 1891, by D. A. Watkins, M.G.

Alexander Huntingdon of Riddles Pt. and Martha Brannack with Daniel Brannack, father of Martha consenting, on Feb. 29, 1891 by Henry Hunter, M. G.

Page 127

Samuel E. Thompson of Morehouse and Miss Josie Ryan of Morehouse with James Ryan, father of Josie consenting, on March 4, 1891 by J. W. Oliver, M. G. of Methodist Church

John Detie of New Madrid and Sallie Alexander of New Madrid with Eva Tegue, mother of Sallie, consenting, on March 2, 1891 by Joel Cook, J. P.

Page 128

Henry M. Lanin of Big Prairie and Katie Huston of Big Prairie on March 5, 1891 by J. T. Stepp, J. P.

Charles W. Cummingham of New Madrid Twp. and Miss May E. Burgess of New Madrid Twp. with W. L. Burgess, father of Mary Ellen, consenting, on Mar. 5, 1891 by Daniel Lerale, M. G.

Page 129

John Huffman of PawPaw and Miss Ida Phillips of PawPaw, Wm. B. Phillips, father of Ida consenting, by Joel Cook J.P. on 3-12-1891.

David Mann of New Madrid City and Lelia O'Bannon of New Madrid by James Furlong, Priest on March 17, 1891.

Page 130

Thomas Mitchell of East Twp and Srepty Ann Buckman with D. T. Buckman, father of Srepty Ann, consenting on 3-22-1891 by Elder J. L. Shirley.

Reuben Lewis of Morehouse and Eliza Davidson of same place on March 22, 1891 by John Goodman, M. G.

Page 131

Randolph Watson of New Madrid Twp. and Amanda Fox of New Madrid Twp by George Branan, M. G. on April 4, 1891

Louis Hufford of New Madrid Twp. and Elizabeth Weeks of New Madrid Twp. Thomas Weeks, father of Elizabeth consents, on April 5, 1891 by James Welsey, M. G.

Page 132

James Hunt of West Twp. and Ella Barrnett of West Twp.
Joseph Barnett, father of Ella consenting, by E. Browd, J.P.
on 4-9-1891

James Burns of East Twp. and Joann Newman of East Twp.
on April 12-, 1891 by J. L. Sheehy, M.G.

Page 133

Andrew J. Lane of Big Prairie and Mrs. Hattie Hix of Big
Prairie on 4-26-1891 by James F. Bishop, M.G.

Bob Fry of New Madrid and Maggie Davis with Gake Fry,
father of Bob and Minnie Green, mother of Maggie, consenting,
by Peter Hoehn J.P. on 4-26-1891

Page 134

Andrew I. McFaden of Big Prairie and Ida Byers of Big
Prairie, John T. Byers, father of Ida, consents, by John N.
Mills J.P. on 4-30-1891.

Shep Johnson of LeSieur Twp. and Candy Lewis of LeSieur Twp.
by A. Sniffer, M.G. on 5-30-1891

Page 135

Charles Greenwood of New Madrid Twp. and MRS. Maggie Martin
of New Madrid Twp. by Peter Hoehn J.P. on May 3, 1891

Ben F. C. Walker of Pt. Pleasant and Christine Jones of
New Madrid with consent of Josephine Jones, mother of
Christine, by Samuel Mecklem, J.P. on 5--5-1891.

Page 136

Franklin Cox of Lotta, Mo. and Sarah Simpson of Lotta, county
of New Madrid, by Joel Cook, J.P. on 5-6-1891

Charles Luke of James Bayou of New Madrid Co. and Elsie
Burton by George W. Clarke J.P. on May 10, 1891

Page137

Tonie Honard of New Madrid Twp. and Lizzie Jones of New Madrid
Twp on May 11, 1891 by Rev. James Wesley, M.G.

William Reeves of LeSieur Twp. and Mary Fry of LeSieur Twp.,
testimony of Robert Fry as to ages, on May 15, 1891 by Joel
Cook, M.G.

Page 138

Henry Hornburger of Big Prairie and Ida Dempsey of Big Prairie James Dempsey, father of Ida, consents, by John A. Mills, J.P. on May 17, 1891

John Sands of LeSieur Twp. and Alvey Cox by Rev. W. G. Hensley, M.G. on 5-17-1891

Page 139

A. J. Bacher of Big Prairie and Miss Janie Hopper of Big Prairie by E. Brown, J.P. on June 20, 1891

David C. Kinkade of Portageville and Mrs. Sarah Mc Githers b y W.W.Ellis, M.G. on 5-31-1891

Page 140

James Braglin of New Madrid and Amy Vaudrie of New Madrid Twp. by Chas. T. Voudin, father of Amy, on May 31, 1891 by Rev. Ervin A. Ewing, M.G.

James Ashford of LeSieur Twp. and Mary C. Alley of LeSieur Twp. on May 28, 1891 by L.F.LaFond, J.P.

Page 141

Mose Clark of New Madrid and Margaret Shay of New Madrid by George Brown, M.G. on 6-3-1891

Jackson Walker of St. John Twp. and Pearl Angelo of St. John Twp. by W.C.Peeler, J.P. on May 31, 1891

Page 142

Porter Byron of Big Prairie and Amanda Davis of Big Prairie on May 31, 1891 by Peter Hoehn, J.P.

James M. Hill of Brush Prairie and Hoda Mainord of Brush Prairie by John N. Mills, J.P. on 6-1-1891

Page 143

Willie Conner of LeSieur Twp. and Florence L. Burton of LeSieur Twp. on 6-3-1891 by L.O.C. LaFont, J.P.

William Van Felt of Scrub Ridge and Mary Ann Stokes of Scrub Ridge, John Benhan, guardian of Mary Ann consenting, by Rev. J.J.Knight, M.G. on 6-7-1891

Page 144

Jaspar Wilson of St. John Twp. and Mary Lynch of St. John Twp. on June 8, 1891 by Geo. W. Clark, J.P.

Henry Detie of Portageville and Clara Hanks of Portageville by L. F. LaFont J.P. on 6-7-1891

Page 145

John N. Hunter of New Madrid Twp. and Nancy Picket of New Madrid Twp. by Geo. W. Clark, J.P. on 6-22-1891

John Lang of New Madrid Twp. and Mollie Lucy of New Madrid Twp. on June 4, 1891 by John A. Mills, J.P.

Page 146

Stephen L. Colman of Big Prairie and Missouri M. Lumpkin of Big Prairie, Nancy Ann Lumpkin, mother of Missouri, consenting, by Jeff D. Stepp, J.P. on July 1, 1891

Franklin J. Key of Scrub Ridge and Annie Rhodes, Louisa Adkinson, mother of Annie, consenting, by Wm. King, A.L.M. on July 6, 1891

Page 147

Stephen Buckley of New Madrid and Rachael Waters of New Madrid by Henry M. Hunter, M.G. on 7-7-1891

Nute Peary of Big Prairie Twp. and Mary E. Fry with Emma Myers, mother of Mary, consenting, by E. P. McKinney, M. G. on July 15, 1891

Page 148

James Garner of Scrub Ridge and Beatrice Wiles, with Elizabeth Wiles, mother of Beatrice, consenting, by J. J. Knight, M. G. on 7-12-1891

Francis Sikes of New Madrid and Florence O'Bannon of New Madrid by Stephen Lee, M.G. on July 12, 1891

Page 149

Ed J. Williams of Ogden of New Madrid Co. and Ladusky Kilgon of same place by John L. Mills, on July 12, 1891

Joseph Masonville of LESieur Twp. and Elizabeth Barnes of LeSieur Twp. by L. F. LaFont, J.P. on 7-12-1891

Page 150

William F. Furgeson of Scrub Ridge and Mary Elizabeth Handy by L. F. LaFont, J.P. on July 14, 1891

Henry A. Maness of New Madrid Twp. and W.A.Conner of New Madrid Twp. on July 14, 1891 by J.P. (no name)

Page 151

William Tillman of Riddles Pt. and Alse Bucker of Riddle Pt. by Thomas Red, M. G. on July 21, 1891

John Arbuckell of LeSieur Twp. and Elizabeth Wiles of LeSieur Twp. by J. J. KNight, J.P. on July 23, 1891

Page 152

John Sims of Scrub Ridge and Annie Morrison of Scrub Ridge by R. L. Lafont J.P. on July 23, 1891

Manuel Little of James Bayou of New Madrid and Fannie Palmer of New Madrid by George W. Clark on July 24, 1891

Page 153

William Lemons of Scott Co. and Amanda Ogden of Big Prairie (no return)

Louy B. Ellis of Big Prairie and Miss Ida Carroll of Big Prairie by J. T. Snow on July 29, 1891

Page 154

Louis Hunot of Big Prairie Twp. and Sallie Brown of Big Prairie Twp. by J. D. Stepp, J.P. on 8-24-1891

Luther Gilbow of LeSieur twp. and Sallie Laws of LeSieur This was returned without certificate 9-15-1891 John Mott.

Page 155

Samuel Hufstetter of LeSieur Twp. and Ella Graham of LeSieur Twp. Julia Brookman, guardian of Samuel consenting, by L. F. Curtis M.G. 8-13-1891

Eli Samuel Willis of LeSieur Twp. and Arlie Mott of LeSieur Twp. Texanna Willis, mother of Samuel and Olive Mott, father of Arlie consenting, by Samuel Mecklem, J.P. on 8-11-1891

Page 156

Albert Wilson of Lotta, New Madrid Co., and Sarah Ann Miller of same, Mary Miller, mother of Sarah Ann, consenting, by James Stewart J.P. on 8-11-1891

Henry Vaiden of New Madrid Twp. and Mame Crawford of same by Stephen Lee, M.G. on 8- 1891

Page 157

John LaFont of Scrub Ridge of New Madrid County and Lucy Butts of same, Thomas M. Butts, father of Lucy consenting, by John Young, Judge of Co. Court on 8-20-1891

William R. Poe of LeSieur Twp. and Miss Laura LeSieur of same, James McCoy, guardian of Laura, consents, by Samuel Mecklem, J.P. on 7-30-1891

Page 158

Charles Hall of West Twp. and Miss Nancy Missouri of West Twp by Epraim Brown, J.P. on 1-31-1891

William Cagle of Big PRAIRIE and M. T. Ford of same by A. J. Simmons J.P. on May 16, 1890.

Page 159

Charles Marks of Big PRAIRIE and Miss Dora Colburn of same by John N. Mills, J.P. on 2-8-1891

John Robert Rose of New Madrid Twp. and Miss Josie Stuart of same by W.W.Ellis, M.G. on Oct. 15, 1890

Page 160

Owen Damon of LeSieur Twp. and Mattie Hunter of New Madrid Twp., Angeline Damon, mother of Owen consents, by J. J. Knight, M.G. on July 5, 1890

Ephraim Peace of Grap Ridge and Julia V. Evans of Grape Ridge by Joel Cook, J.P. on July 24, 1890

Page 161

Robert Lee Connell of New Madrid and Frances Ella King of New Madrid, Dinah Muke, mother of of Frances Ella consenting by Joel Cook, J.P. on 9-22-1890

Phillip Tinker of Lotta and Rose Pope (Marshall Co. of New Madrid) John Pope, father of Rosa consenting .

Page 162

William Jones of Ruddles Point and Ellen Rose of same by Samuel Mecklem J.P. 9-1-1891

Page 162

Allen Speller of Lotta and Lucinda Ford of Lotta by James Stewart J.P. on 9-19-1890

Page 163

Amos Brunson of Louis Prairie and Katy Richards of same (license issued 9-24-1891 - no return)

William Ferrell of New Madrid and Mary Bradshaw of same by Joel Cook, J.P. on Oct 12, 1890

Page 164

Benjamin M. Swank of Preis?? Landing in Scott Co. and Mahaley Masel of same by Joel Cook J.P. on 10-27-1890

Nacy F. Henson of Sikeston and Lelia Emory of Big Prairie by C. M. Ledbetter, M.G. of Methodist Church on 11-13-1891

Page 165

William Franklin Allen of East Twp. and Hannie McTouch of same on 9-2-1891 by James Winder

John Brown of Scott Co. and Agnes Holmes of Big Prairie. William Holmes consenting as father of Agnes, by E. Brown, J.P. 9-8-1891

Page 166

David Howard of West Twp. and Becky Cornwell of same by E. Brown J.P. on 8-23-1891

Samuel Green of New Madrid and Anna Wesley of same by Chas. Reed M.G. 9-6-1891

Page 167

Washington Ogden of New Madrid Twp. and Josephine Brooks of same by John N. Mills, J.P. on 9-22-1891

James Nunn of Brownville, county of Haywood and State of Tenn. and Fannie Settles of same by Joseph Peques, M.G. on 9-5-1891

Page 168

Geo. W. Baxter of Scrub Ridge and Pamela A. Beggs of Scrub Ridge by L. F. Lafond J.P. on 8-16-1891

Wm. T. Murphy of LeSieur Twp. and Miss Lucy A. Hardon of same Abraham Hardon consents, by Jas. D. Stone, J.P. 9-12-1891

Page 169

Robert Brunson of New Madrid Twp. and Harriet Hicks of same
Thomas Hicks, father of Harriet consenting, 9-13-1891 by
James Wesley, M. G.

John Dotson of Ristine and Annie Carroll of Ristine by
W. F. Johnson M. G. on 9-15-1891

Page 170

John Green and Alice Cornwell of New Madrid Twp. by W. R.
Howell, M. G. on 9-14-1891

William Moore of Ristine and Sallie Spencer by W. F. Johnson,
M. G. on 9-25-1891

Page 171

Milege F. Akins of LeSieur Twp. of New Madrid and Mary E.
Grubb of same by L. F. LaFond, J.P. on 12-27-1891

Samuel W. Sullivan of LESieur Twp. and Annie L. Adcock with
Wilburn Adcock, father of Annie consenting, on 10-22-1891
by J. J. Knight M. G.

Page 172

John Bougard of Big Prairie and Maggie Huggins of same by
John N. Mills, on Oct 4, 1891

William McClellande of Sandy Ridge and Rachel Akinson of same
by W. T. Peeler, J.P. on 10-11-1891

Page 173

William A. Wood of Elke Twp, StoddardCo. and Bettie Alsup of
New Madrid Twp. by Peter Hoehn J.P. on 10-11-1891

Edward L. Mirehand of Grandchain, Pulaski Co. Ill and Miss
Carrie Tony of New Madrid by L. T. Curtis, M. G. on 10-14-1891

Page 174

John Anderson of Lotta, New Madrid Co. and Jane Canny of same
James Stewart, J.P. on 10-25-1891

William Jones of Big Prairie and Dora Arkade of same by E.
Brown, J.P. on 11-1-1891

Page 175

William E. Jones of Marshall Co. Ky. and Rachael Nanney of New Madrid on testimony of James Nanny, brother of Rachael by John Young, Judge of Co. Court, 11-4-1891

Fred Phillips of LeSieur Twp. and Durutha Thompson of same by Stephen Lee, M.G. 10-29-1891

Page 176

Ross Tony of New Madrid Twp. and Mary Glass of same by Henry Hunter, J.P. on 11-14-1891

Joseph Presley of LeSieur Twp. and Etta Bratten of same by Samuel Mecklem J.P. on 11-12-1891

Page 177

Charles Matthews of New Madrid Twp. and Fanny Malone of Big Prairie by John M. Morgan, M.G. 9-27-1891

William M. Cook of Pemiscot Co., Mo. and Mrs. Ella Delashmuth of State of California by Joel Cook, J.P. on 11-14-1891

Page 178

William Thorn of Big Prairie and Nattie Young of same by John N. Mills on 11-23-1891

William McQuaque of Big Prairie and Frances Smruing?? of same by G. A. Shelby M.G. on 11-15-1891

Page 179

James W. Cronan of St. Louis and Ida Mary Young of Pt. Pleasant on 11-25-1891 by A. J. Curtis, M.G.

Joseph Ross of LeSieur Twp. and Emma V. Parker of same by A. B. Crumpler, M. G. on 11-25-1891

Page 180

Ephraim Atkinson of LeSieur and Columbia Ward of same by Samuel Mecklem J.P. on 12-3-1891

Jas. R. Gurley and Maggy Holmes of Big Prairie by E. Brower, J.P. on 12-8-1891

Page 181

Oliver Motte of LeSieur and Amanda Renion of same by James D. Stine J.P. on 12-11-1891

James F. Stubblefield of LeSieur and Clementine Rainwater of same with James Stubblefield father of James consenting, by L. F. LaFont J.P. on 12-13-1891

Page 182

Jas E. DeLisle of Portage and Francis LeSieur of Pt. Pleasant by Roman Catholic Clergyman, James J. Furlong, on 12-9-1891

Simon Golden of Lotta and Mary Judy of same by James Stewart, J.P. on 12-14-1891

Page 183

Joseph Tripp of Big Prairie and Nancy Parson of Sikeston, Scott Co. by John M. Crowe, M. G. on 1-17-1892

John Townson of St. John Twp. and Margaret Cavalenon of same on 12-13-1891 by W. T. Peeler J.P.

Page 184

John F. McKinney of Como and Elizabeth Trammell of same, Jewett Trammell, father of Elizabeth, consenting on Dec. 19 , 1891 by JamesStewart, J.P.

Page 185

Hosea Hornburger of Brush Prairie and Martha E. Shirkey of same by B. T. Boyce Judge of Probate on Dec. 21, 1891

J. C. Lester of Clay Co. Texas and Pauline Ross of Big Prairie by J. F. Bishop on Dec. 21, 1891

Page 186

Foster Clayton of LeSieur Twp. and Mary Shelby of same on Dec. 23, 1891 by Samuel Mecklem, J.P.

John Truman of Delanaw, Ind. and Josie Shirley of Pt. Pleasant by Allen McFarland, 'M. G. on Dec. 25, 1891

Page 187

John Jackson of Louis Prairie and Ida Jackson of same by Henry Hunter, M. G. on Dec. 24, 189<u>2</u> (probably 1891)

Edward Adcock of Portageville and Lilie Gibbs of same by John Young, J.P. on Dec. 24, 1891

Page 188

Jay McGlasslon of Como and Eliza Frazier of same by Peter Hoehn J.P. on Dec. 24, 1891

Frank Brown of James Bayou of Miss. Co. and Mrs. Dora Ayres of same by W. T. Peeler, J.P. on Dec. 24, 1891

Page 189

George Thompson of Dunklin Co. and Miss Flora Bell Kitchens by J. F. Curtis, M.G. on Dec. 28, 1891

Joseph O'Bannon Jr. of Scrubb Ridge and Nannie Brown with consent of Joseph O'Bannon, father of above Joseph, and S. L. Brown, father of Nannie (Spelled Brown, Bowin and Bower) by Allen Macfartan, M. G. on Dec. 30, 1891

Page 190

Henry T. Penrod of Portage and Jennie Knotgrass of same on Jan. 7, 1892 by L. F. LaFont, J.P.

Albert Shields and Annie M. Law of Pt. Pleasant by Allen Macfarlan, M. G. on 1-11-1892

Page 191

George W. Grubb of LeSieur Twp. and Miss Sallie J. McDonald by Joel Cook, J.P. on 1-16-1892

Davidson Brandon of New Madrid Twp. and Miss Margarit Nippen of Hubbard, Miss. Co. Mo. by Matthew Blasse, M. G. on 1-18-1892

Page 192

Asa V. Holmes of Big Prairie and Mrs. Visey Wells of Sikeston, Scott Co. by J. M. Morgan, M. G. on 1-29-1892

C. Q. Kelley of Rt. John and Mrs. Mary L. Williams of st. John by Geo. Clark, J.P. on 1-24-1892

Page 193

Charles H. Haynes of St. John Twp. and Lula Hardin of Union City, Obion Co., Tenn. by Geo. W. Clark, J.P. on 1-24-1892

John E. Atwell of Pt. Pleasant and Miss Viola Coats of LeSieur Twp. by Samuel Mecklem J.P. on 1-27-1892

Page 194

John Thompson of New Madrid and May A. Watson of New Madrid by Henry Hunter, M. G. on 1-30-1892

Robert W. McKinney of Portage Twp. and Alice M. Holland of same by Allen McFarland, M. G. 2-9-1892

Page 195

Olive Freeman of West Twp. and Margaret Terry of West Twp. by E. Bowen J.P. on Feb. 7, 1892

Daniel W. Poststen of Mississippi and Caroline H. Grun of Barnes Ridge on Feb. 11, 1892 by Geo. W. Clark, J.P.

Page 196

James E. Stepp of Big PRAirie and Grace Berryman of Irondale, Washington Co., Mo. Mrs. J. D. Stepp, father of said James E. consents, by G. W. Nollner, M. G. on 2-5-1892

David Wilkerson of New Madrid Twp. and Mary Brown of New Madrid Twp. on Feb. 16, 1892 by Peter Hoehn, J.P.

Page 197

Amos Paxton of Como and Ida Curford of Kennett, in Dunklin Co. by Joel Cook, J.P. on 2-18-1892

Wash Hunter of LaForge and Atline Jackson of LaForge, Neal Hunter, father of Wash and Clarrisa Hunter, Mollie and Charles Hopel, parents of Atline Jackson, consent on 2-17-1892

Page 198

Walter Higgerson of St. John Twp. and Mrs. Katie Shultz on 2-20-1892 by W. T. Peeler, J.P.

William H. Bell of Big Prairie Twp. and Cynthia A. Wheat of Big Prairie with Thanuse Wheat, father of Cynthia, consenting. On 2-23-1892 by James F. Bishop, M. G.

Page 199

James Minner of New Madrid and Mrs. Lenny R. Burgess of same R. C. Burgess, father of Lenny, consents, by J. G. Bishop, M.G. on March 2, 1892

Alphonse C. LaForge of New Madrid and Letitia A. Lewis of New Madrid on Mar. 1, 1892 by J. F. Curtis, M. G.

Page 200

Albert Shelby of LeSieur Twp. and Mollie Griffey of same on March 7, 1892 by Samuel Mecklem, J.P.

Robert LaFavens of New Madrid and Elmira Gaddis of same on March 10, 1892 by Joel Cook, J.P.

Page 201

William Fletcher of Pt. Pleasant and Neely Porter of same by Henry Hunter, M. G. on March 20, 1892

Willie E. Debre of New Madrid and Mary E. Kelly of same by Joel Cook J.P. on March 11, 1892

Page 202

Owen Damon of Portageville and Mary Adams of same by L.F. LaFont on March 10, 1892

Monroe Sands of LeSieur Twp. and Catherine Coats of same, John Coats, father of Catherine, consents, March 15, 1892 by Samuel Mecklem, J.P.

Page 203

William Anderson of New Madrid and Kitty Fry of same on March 17, 1892 by Joseph Pegus, M. G.

George Mason of New Madrid and Louise Bucker of same by Joseph Pegus, M. G. on March 19, 1892

Page 204

Jerry Logan of LaForge and Racheal Brown of New Madrid by W. J. Johnson, M. G. on March 20, 1892

Lonnie H. Bell of New Madrid and Ida Thompson of same by Joseph Pegus, M. G. on March 22, 1892

Page 205

Andrew Jackson of New Madrid Twp. and Ella Williams of same by Henry Hunter, M. G. on March 23, 1892

Robert Jenkins of New Madrid Twp. and Ella Williams of same on March 23, 1892 by Henry Hunter, M. G.

Page 206

Frank Parker of New Madrid Twp. and Sissie King of same on March 24, 1892 by Joseph Pegus, J.P.

Harrel C. Bird of St. John Twp. and Sarah A. Dunn of James Bayou of Miss. Co., Mo. on March 30, 1892 by W.T.Peeler, J.P.

Page 207

Max Hereitze of St. Louis, Mo. and Ada Slaughter of Dexter of Stoddard Co., Mo. by Joel Cook, J.P. on March 23, 1892

Page 207

Albert Hill of New Madrid Twp. and Katie Drake of same by
W. T. Johnson, M. G. on April 2, 1892

Page 208

Dennis Henry of New Madrid Twp. and Lizzie Ewing of same
on April 4, 1892 by A. B. Crumpler, M. G.

John A. Milhorn of Gayosa of Pemiscot Co. and Ellen Thorpe
of same on April 7, 1892

Page 209

William Norton of New Madrid Twp. and Mattie Hunter of same
by Joel Cook J.P. on April 7, 1892

Jeff Whitelow of New Madrid Twp. and Katie Augden on
April 16, 1892 by W. T. Jackson, M. G.

Page 210

Matt Hicks of New Madrid and Amelia Phelaber by W. R.
Nowell, M. G. pastor of C.M.E. Church

Tony Woods of New Madrid Twp. and Nettie Waide of same by
W.T.Johnson, M.G. on April 17, 1892

Page 211

David J. Thurston of New Madrid and Jennie Houben of same by
Joel Cook J.P. on 4-18-1892

Joseph P. Arnett and Jane Hayes of New Madrid Twp. on
4-18-1892 by Joel Cook J.P.

Page 212

Robert L. Lewis of New Madrid and Rosa McDonald of same, W.L.
Lewis and Malissa Lewis, parents of Robert consent, on
April 19, 1892 by Joel Cook, J.P.

Albert N. Whaley of Big Prairie and Janie Hudson of same on
April 20, 1892 by John N. Mills, J.P.

Page 213

Mitchell Ady and Mary A. Gunlis of New Madrid Twp. on
4-20-1892 by Robert R. Rudder, M. G., M. E. Church South

Harry B. Green of Cairo, Ill. and Marie W. LaForge of New
Madrid on April 27, 1892 by James Furlong, Catholic Prist

Page 214

Horrell C. Bird of St. John Twp. and Sarah A. Dunn of James Bayou, on March 26, 1892 (no return -see page 206)

James Bunson and Dorah Ann Beavers of Como Twp. by W. S. Farmer, M. G. on May 8, 1892

John W. M. Goth of Portageville and Lula Moore of same by L. F. LaFont J.P. on May 7, 1892

Fred Young of New Madrid and Clara Toney of same by Charles Reed, M. G. on May 7, 1892

Page 216

Allen McFarlan of New Madrid Co. and Miss Pattie Howard of Washington Co., Mo. on M-y 10, 1892 by A. B. Crumpler, M.G.

Edward T. Barrett of Como and Ida May Paxton of same, Thomas A. Paxton, father of Ida May, consents, on March 22, 1892 byCharles Massie, J.P. of Stoddard Co., Mo.

Page 217

Newton C. Laws of Scrub Ridge and Catherine Essary of same, Mary Maxwell, mother of Catherine consents, on May 15, 1892 by L. F. LaFont, J.P.

Perkins Basker of New Madrid and Mary Young of same by W. T. Johnson , M. G. on May 15, 1892

Page 218

Nathan Carter of Lotta, Mo. and Jewett Jackson of same on May 19, 1892 by James Stewart

George Wesley of New Madrid Twp. and Sallie Waters of same on May 29, 1892 by W. R. Nowell, M. G.

Page 219

William McGill of LeSieur Twp. and Sarah A. Bradley of same by James W. Sawyers, J.P. on June 21, 1892

William Weaks of Daonaldson Point of New Madrid and Betty Sudberry of Hickman Co., Ky. on June 16, 1892 by Joel Cook, J.P.

Page 220

Isaac Paxton of Como and Mary McCarmack by Charles Massie J.P. on June 24, 1892

Page 220

Balcet Waggoner of Como and Emma Sheefer of Como on
June 29, 1892 by A. J. Watson, M.G.

Page 221

Samuel F. Peeples of Lotta, New Madrid Co. and Mrs. Jane West
by A. J. Wilson, M. G. on July 6, 1892

Henry Rhodes of New Madrid Twp. and Ella Bishop of same by
Matthew M. Blalse, M. G. on 7-13-1892

Page 222

Louis Moore of Ruddles Point and Lucinda Rice of same on
July 25, 1892 by Samuel Mecklem, J.P.

David Walker of Lotta and Mary Stafford of same on Aug. 7,
1892 by Minister of Gospel (no name given)

Page 223

Sam Brandon of LeSieur and Clumbia Marion of New Madrid Twp.
by Joel Cook J.P. on Aug. 15, 1892

Paul H. Phillips of New Madrid and Miss Lula W. Powell of
New Madrid, Albert B. Hunter, guardian of Paul Phillips,
consents, on Aug. 10, 1892 by A. B. Crumpler, M. G.

Page 224

Joseph Jones of West Twp. and Alice Monaham of same on
Aug. 13, 1892 by J. W. Oliver, M. G. of ME South

William Day of New Madrid and Minnie Parker of same on
August 14, 1892 by Joel Cook, J.P.

Page 225

Willis Elmer Allen of Big Prairie Twp. and Nancy Elizabeth
Sisco, Daniel B. and Julia Sisco, mother and father of Nancy,
consent, Eliza J. Allen and David T. Allen, father and mother
of Willie, consent, by J. M. Morgan, M.G. on 8-14-1892

James McLemore of Scrub Ridge and Emma Welshans of New
Madrid Twp. by Allen MacFarlan on 8-18-1892

Page 226

Robert Adams of Portageville and Martha Roberts of same by
John Young, Judge, on 8-21-1892

Page 226

James C. Price of Portage Twp. and Mary Davis of same by
Peter Hoehn, J.P. on 8-25-1892

Page 227

Benjamin Neal of East Twp. and Martha Adams of same, M. J.
Adams, mother of Martha, consents, by F. M. Holden M.G.
on 8-28-1892

William Weeks of New Madrid Twp. Manerary Carlisle of same
by W. T. Peeler, J.P. on 8-28-1892

Page 228

Daniel Dell of New Madrid Co. and Della Gibbs of same, Margaret
Elizabeth Dell, mother, consents, on 9-3-1892 by A.J.Wilson,M.G.

Mathame Wheat of Brush Prairie and Sarah Mershall of same by
James Stepp, J.P. on 9-11-1892

Page 229

Robert W. Van Amburgh of New Madrid and Miss Mattie Lee of
same by Rev. A. B. Crumpler on 9-14-1892

Thomas S. Cline of Morehouse and Addy Murphy of West Twp.
on Oct 9, 1892 by W. L. Loudermuch, M.G.

Page 230

John W. Gillian of Portage Twp. and Tilda Gills of same by W. G.
Henson, M.G. on 9-28-1892

William Jackson of Pt. Pleasant and Anna Lewis of same on
Sept. 25, 1892 by Henry Hunter, M. G.

Page 231

Benjamin W. Peeples of Big Prairie and Emma H. Patten of same
by J. N. Mills, J.P. on 9-29-1892

Tom Johnson of East Twp. and Caroline Moore of same on Oct 6,
1892 by James Winders, J.P.

Page 232

Owens Hawthorn of New Madrid Twp. and Martha Lay by Rev.
James Wesley on 9-29-1892

Page 232

Albert A. Jones of Hickman Co., Fulton, Ky. and Beula A. Cole of Hayward, Pemiscot County, Mo. G. S. Jones, father of Albert and F. A. Cole, father and M. E. Cole, mother of Beula, consent. Married on Oct. 1, 1892 by E. L. D. C. Downing, M.G.

Page 233

John M. Rodgers of New Madrid City and Martha Hale of same City, John Hale, father of Martha, consents. Married on Oct 3, 1892 by Irwin A. Ewing, M. G.

William Case of Pt. Pleasant and Margaret Hampton of same by Samuel Mecklem J.P. on Oct. 4, 1892

Page 234

Lafayette Wiseman of New Madrid Twp. and Susie Steward of same by J. J. Knight, M.G. on Oct. 5, 1892

William Wood of East Twp. and Ida M. Whitson of same on Aug. 28 by J. L. Shelby M. G.

Page 235

Horan Stack of Lotta and Miss Annie Farmer of New Madrid Co. by A. J. Wilson, M. G. on Oct 16, 1892

Sid Curdy of New Madrid Co. and Sarah Butler of same, W. C. Butler, father of Sara consents, by James D. Stine, J.P. on Oct. 12, 1892

Page 236

Mike Abbott of New Madrid Twp. and Annie Likins of same by George Clark, J.P. on Oct. 15, 1892

William H. Sneab of Como and Miss Allie Miller of same on Oct. 14, 1892 by A. J. Wilson, M.G.

Page 237

Nathan Young of New Madrid Twp. and Lula Brown of same by W. W. Johnson M.G. on Oct. 15, 1892

James Rounds of New Madrid and Nellie Frost of Paw Paw with William Counts, guardian of Nellie Frost consenting, on Oct. 20, 1892 by Robert D. Kennedy, M.G. Methodist South

Page 238

Luke Montgomery of New Madrid Twp. and Mary E. Davis of same Jasper Montgomery, father of Luke and Mavis Davis, father of Mary E. Davis consenting, on Oct. 23, 1892 by John A.M.W.W. Johnson, M.G.

Page 238

Patrick H. Aldridge of LeSieur Twp. and Mattie E. Schink of St. John Twp. by J. L. Atwood, M.G. on Oct 12, 1892

Page 239

Marqus S. Whitley and Lucinda B. Godair of New Madrid Twp. on Oct. 25, 1892 by A. J. Wilson

William Shelton of Ogden of New Madrid and Miss Betty Childers of Ogden on Oct 29, 1892 by J. N. Mills, J.P.

Page 240

Ralph Floro of Portage Twp. and L. Angeline Manus with G. T. Maness, father of Angeline consenting, on Oct. 27, 1892 by L. F. LaFont, J.P.

Joseph L. Allison of LeSieur Twp. and Rosa L. Stine of same with Joseph D. Stine, father of Rosa consenting, by L. G. LaFont J.P. on Nov. 6, 1892

Page 241

Walter L. Boyce of New Madrid and Lotta E. Shidler of same Mary Jasper, mother of Walter Boyce consenting, by James J. Furlong, Priest on Nov. 8, 1892

Samuel Carr of Big Prairie Twp. and Elizabeth Ray of same by J.N.Mills J.P. on Nov. 6, 1892

Page 242

Thomas H. Beymer and Miss Maggie Lewis of New Madrid, Mrs. C. A. Sparks, Mother of Maggie, consents on Nov. 7, 1892 by Robert D. Kennedy, M. E. Church South

Rivers D. Owens of LeSieur Twp. and Nanie Davis of same by J. J. Knight M.G. on Nov. 8, 1892

Page 243

George F. Dean of Big Prairie and Amanda Barnhart of same Sarah A. Dean, Mother of George and James Rodgers, guardian of said Amanda consents, by J. N. Mills, on Oct 20, 1892

Adam L. LeSieur of LeSieur Twp. and Ella Kimes of same by W. T. Talley, M. G. on Nov. 9, 1892

Page 244

William Markahm of West Twp. and Sarah Cammel of same by E. Brower J.P. on Nov 5, 1892

Page 244

Charles Dockery of LeSieur and Mary Robbins of same J. M. Dockery, father of Charles consents, on Oct 9, 1892 by L.F.LaFont, J.P.

Page 245

George Roseberry of Big Prairie and Mattie E. Lumsdem, Green Lumsden, father of Mattie consents, by John N. Mills, J.P. on Nov. 13, 1892

Henry T. Green of Grape Ridge and Laura J. Johnson of Fulton, Ky. on Nov. 15, 1892 by Joel Cook, J.P.

Page 246

Henry Alexander of New Madrid and Alice Johnson of same on Nov. 24, 1892 by Joseph Peggus, M.G.

William Lee of New Madrid Twp. and Ella Dawson of same by W. T. Johnson, M.G. on Nov. 27, 1892

Page 247

Pompy Till of New Madrid and Dixey Willoughby.

Clarence Waters of New Madrid and Pearl Thompkins, Betsy Thompkins, mother of Pearl consents, on Dec. 1, 1892 by H. W. Owesley.

Page 248

Thomas B. Allen of Madison Co., Mo. and Emma G. Hunter of New Madrid on Nov. 10, 1892 by Wisel Beal, M. G. of Jackson, Mo. Prebyterian Minister

James Forks and Emelia Beavers of New Madrid Twp. on Dec. 7, 1892 by Jno. D. Doherty, M. E. Church South

Page 249

Richard Hayes of Sugar Tree Ridge and Barbara Soloman of same on Sept. 23, 1892 b y Geo. W. Clark, M.G.

William Hawkins of New Madrid Twp. and Jennie Hanner of same on Dec. 11, 1892 by W. T. Johnson, M.G.

Page 250

James M. Waltrip of Dunklin Co., Mo. and Mrs. Amelia Whitson of Portageville, Mo. on Dec. 11, 1892 by M/V.Baird, M.G.

Page 250

James W. Ferguson of Lake Co. Tenn and Bell McAdoo of same by Joel Cook, J.P. on Dec. 19, 1892

Page 251

Alex Griffen of Pt. Pleasant and Eliza Walker of same by Albert Treadwell, M.G. on 11-27-1892

Washington Tony of New Madrid and May Young of same on testimony of Fred Young, brother of said May, on Dec. 23, 1892 by John Paris, M. G.

Page 252

Albert Davis of New Madrid and Molly Brown by J. W. Ousley, M.G. on Dec. 24, 1892

Fred E. Gross and Peal Edna Shideter of New Madrid on Dec. 21, 1892 by J. P. White, M.G.

Page 253

Thomas Woods of New Madrid and Melissa Smith of same on Dec. 27, 1892 by J. W. Ousley, M.G.

Amos J. Thomas of East Twp. and Sarah M. Gillbrith of same M. E. Buckman, mother of Sarah consenting by R. G. Pearsonan, M.G. on Jan. 3, 1893.

Page 254

Burris D. Doss of Mississippi Co., Mo. and Matty Kelly of same on Jan. 3, 1893 by J.P.

Wm. J. Smith of New Madrid and Mary Seaton of Pemiscot Co., Mo. on Jan. 5, 1893 by L. F. LaFont, J.P.

Page 255

Seth Priutt of Portage Twp. and Mrs. Anna Speakman of same on Jan. 13, 1893 by A. M. O'Quinn, M.G.

James L. Badlwin of New Madrid and Louisa May Baker of same by John D. Doherty, M. G. M.E.South on Dec. 6, 1892.

Page 256

Thomas Loomis of St. John Twp. and Susie Birdwell of same on Jan. 15, 1893 by W. T. Peeler, J.P.

Richard Hicks of Lotta and Anna Sisk of same by A. J. Wilson, M.G. on Jan. 24, 1893

Page 257

George Dickson of Lotta Miss Katy Corbin of Lotta by
A. J. Wilson, M. G. on Jan. 24, 1893.

Bradford Hogan of Portageville and MRS. Lotta Rittenhouse of
Portage Twp. on Jan. 29, 1893 by W. W. Ellis, M.G.

Page 258

Edward Dunn of New Madrid Twp. and Nannie Wesley of same
by Henry Hunter, M. G. on Jan. 21, 1893

Calvin Farmer of St. John Twp. and May Wimp of same by
W.T.Peeler, J.P. on Jan. 24, 1893

Page 259

John F. Rainwater of Big Prairie and Miss Ida Long of same
by J. N. Mills, J.P. on Jan. 24, 1893.

Thomas Van Bibber or Big Prairie and Miss Mary Lumsden
of same, Green Lumsden, father of Mary, consents, on
Jan. 24, 1893 by J. N. Mills, J.P.

Page 260

Otis Shaver of Big Prairie and Maggie Acord of same, Marty
Johnson, Mother of Otis Shaver, consents, Hamilton Acord,
guardian consents by J. N. Mills, J.P. on 1-26-1893

John N. Sands of New Madrid Co. and Miss Bell McLemore of
Scrub Ridge, Mrs. A. J. McLemon, Mother of Bell consents,
by James D. Stine, J.P. of LeSieur Twp. on 1-29-1893

Page 261

Charles C. Ferrenberg of New Madrid Twp. and Minnie B.
Lynch of same by Ira P. Eby, M. G. on 10-23-1893.

George Loving of Madrid Bend, Ky. county of Fulton and May
Duke of same by Joel Cook, J.P. on Feb. 14, 1893

Page 262

James M. Hill of New Madrid Twp. and Ida Henry of same
by Joel Cook J.P. on 2-7-1893

James Midget of New Madrid Twp. and Cora Swan of Big
PRAirie, Angeline Panell, mother of Cora consents, by
J.N. Melts, J.P. on Feb. 14, 1893.

Page 263

James A. Gassett of West Twp. and Miss Mary Waddell of East by E. Barnes on Feb. 19, 1893

George F. Bowlin of Morehouse and Malinda Bullinger of Morehouse on Feb. 20, 1893 by J. M. Morgan, M.G.

Page 264

Robert C. Sanders of LeSieur and Miss Mary M. Till of same William Till, father of Mary, consents, on Feb. 23, 1893 by J. A. Workman, M.G.

John Harrell of New Madrid Twp. and Lissie Knight of same Annie Nolan, mother of Lissie, consents on Feb. 29, 1893 by Joseph Peggus, M. G.

Page 265

James Cammack of Madrid Bend, Fulton Co., Ky. and Miss Minnie Tharp of same by Joel Cook, J.P. on 3-21-1893

John Meatt of Portage and Velma Godard of Pemiscot Co., Mo. by E.L.D. Downing, M.G. on March 12, 1893

Page 266

Louis Johnson of New Madrid Twp. and Sarah Farmer of same by D. C. Phillips, J.P. on March 13, 1893

George W. Demint of Big Prairie and Mattie Adkerson of same by Justice of County Court on March 14, 1893

Page 267

Christopher B. Mooring of Barnes Ridge and Miss Mary LaPlant of same by W. T. Peeler, J.P. on March 22, 1893

Reeder Gray of LeSieur Twp. and Miss Jinny Gray of New Madrid Twp. by Charles Reede M.G. on March 19, 1893

Page 268

Robert Tucker of Ruddles Point and Mrs. Dora Barnes of same by W. C. Henson, M. G. on March 18, 1893

John Bozarke of Riddles Pt. and Mrs. Rosa Tucker of same by W. G. Henson, M. G. on March 19, 1893

Page 269

Toliver Hardy of Lotta and Sussana Whitehead of same by A. G. Wilson M.G. on March 21, 1893

Page 269

Thomas Franklin of New Madrid and Mariah Lay of same by Joel Cook J.P. on 3-27-1893

Page 270

John Watson of Lake Co. Tenn and Manda Roper of same by Robert D. Kennedy M.G. on 2-6-1893

James Holt of Como and Martha E. Thompson of same by J. J. Knight J.P. on 4-25-1893

Page 271

John H. Coats of LeSieur and Cela Macke of same by J. J. Knight M.G. on 4-2-1893

Edgar Davis of Portage Twp. and Mrs. Mary Dunn of same by J.C. Huffman J.P. on 4-6-1893

Page 272

John Ross of New Madrid Twp. and Jane Witherspoon of same by James Wesley, M.G. April 10, 1893

Cyrus Porter of St. John Twp. and Minnie Paterson in Fulton Ky. by W. T. Peeler, J.P. on 5-7-1893

Page 273

Robert Hogan of Portageville and Lida Nicholas of same by G. S. Jones, M.G. on 4-16-1893

James A. Westman of West Twp. and Mary A. Cagle, John Cagle, father of Mary, consents on April 19, 1893 by E. Brand, J.P.

Page 274

John Ash of Brush Prairie and Miss Daisey L. Lee of same, O.A. Patterson, Mother of Daisy consents, by John N. Miller J.P. on April 23, 1893

Frederick T. Piggot of Pt Pleasant and Annie T. Watson of New Madrid Twp. by James J. Furlong, Roman Catholic priest, on April 26, 1893

Page 275

William Bredenstined of New Madrid and Miss Thersia Gleuck of same, Christopher Gleuck, father of Theresia consents, by James J. Furlong, Roman Catholic priest, on May 2, 1893.

Page 276

George Trammell of Como and Laura B. Crisel of same by A.J.Wilson, M.G. on May 3, 1893

Isaac Caldwell of Big Prairie Twp. and Anna Taylor of same by John N. Mills, J.P. on May 9, 1893

Page 277

Cullen Barnes of Brush Prairie and Mary Jones of same by John M. Crow, Methodist minister on May 18, 1893

Robert McGrow of New Madrid Twp. and Lizzie Brown of LaForge by Joel Cook, J.P. on May 21, 1893

Page 278

Charles Moore of Big Prairie and Lizzie Brown of same by J.N. Mills J.P. on May 28, 1893

Allen Sweat of Como Twp. and Cordelia Cox of same, William Webb guardian of Allen Sweat consents, by W. S. Tanner, M.G.. on May 29, 1893

Page 279

Horton Byers of Big Prairie and Amanda J. Phillips of same by A. A. Harrison, J.P. on June 3, 1893

David J. F. Gower of East Twp. and Martha E. Jones of same by Joel Cook, J.P. on June 3, 1893

Page 280

William Carrol of Big Prairie and Miss Nancy Malone of same J.H.Malone, father of Nancy, consents, by O.J.Scimmones,J.P. on June 8, 1893

Robert W. Welles of East Twp. and Miss Tabitha C. Presson Henry T. Presson, father of Tabitha, consents, by J. M. Presson, J.P. on June 18, 1893

Page 281

Benjamin O'Bryan of Big Prairie Twp. and Teda Sullivan of same by D. C. Phillips, J.P. on June 25, 1893

Andrew Pankey of New Madrid Twp. and Maggie Mann of same, May Rose, Mother of Maggie, consents, by D. C. Phillips,J.P. on June 25, 1893

Page 282

Daniel Presson of East Twp. and Mary E. Maynar of same by Joel Cook, J.P. on 7-2-1893

Robert Morris of Big Prairie Twp. and Alley Williams of same by J. N. Mills J.P. on 7-16-1893

Page 283

Julius Hall of Big Prairie and Miss Mattie Willis of same by A. J. Scimmons J.P. on 7-4-1893

John Wesley of New Madrid Twp. and Dixie Davis of same on 7-8-1893

Page 284

R. M. McKinney of New Madrid Twp. and Ella Jacobs of same by Joel Cook J.P. on 7-15-1893

Grant Neil of Sikeston, Scott Co. and Steller Pierce of East Twp. with William Peirce, father of Stella, consenting on July 23, 1893 by S. P. Carlisle, M.G.

Page 285

Geary W. Coon of Whiting, Mississippi County, and Mrs. Georgia Richardson, County of Ohio, Ky. b y Joel Cook, J.P. on 7-20-1893

Saml Bell of Brush Prairie and Lucy Ann Wheat of same, Mott Wheat, father of Lucy consents, by John N. Mills, J.P. on July 30, 1893

Page 286

John Trogden of Como Twp. and Alice M. Brevard of Como, Joseph Brevard, father of Alice, consents. by A. J. Wilson,M.G on Aug. 5, 1893

Luther Gilbow of LeSieur Twp. and Jennie Penrod of LeSieur Twp. by L. F. LaFont J.P. on May 31, 1893

Page 287

Hamp Carroll of New Madrid and Mariah Ross of same by W.T.Johnson M.G. on 8-13-1893

William Walls of New Madrid and Ada Philibow(returned Sept. 6, 1893 John Mott Recorder

Page 288

Wm. F. Kimes of Portage Twp. and Luella Mukum of same, Frank D. Kimes, father of W. F. and Sarah F. Adcock, mother of Luella, consent on August 24, 1893 by J.D.Stein, J.P.

Albert Lee Carter of New Madrid Co. and Mollie Massey, James Massey, father of Mollie, consents, by Ira P. Eby, M. G. on Aug. 27, 1893

Page 289

Matthew Brooks of Big Prairie and Ada A. Mainord of same, W.W.Mainord, father of Ada, consents on 8-27-1893 by J.J.Presson, M.G.

Jacob Ward of Big Prairie and Maudy Moore of same, J.H.Ward, Mother of Jacob, consents. W.H.Marre, father of Maudy consents, by R.P. Peurman, M.G. on 8-31-1893

Page 290

Henry C. Ford of Como Twp. and Mrs. Anes Inman of same by W.S.Farmer, M.G. on 8-21-1893

William C. Bell of West twp. and Mrs. Lyia Terry of West Twp. on 8-21-1893 by Joel Cook J.P.

Page 291

Robert Drake of Fulton Co., Ky. and Mrs. Cora Hampton of same J.W.Ellington, guardian of Robert, consents, by Robert D. Kennedy, Deacon of M.E.Church S. on 9-6-1893

Charles Samuel Harrison of James Bayou, Miss. Co. Mo. and Helen Branham with George W. Harrison, father of Charles Samuel and Herum Brannum, father of Helen, consenting by Geor. W. Clark J.P. on 9-3-1893

Page 292

James T. Stewart of New Madrid Twp. and Mrs. Louisa Hutchins of same by A.M.O'Quin on 9-20-1893

Samuel Waters of New Madrid Twp. and Mattie Jackson of New Madrid City by P.P.Payton, M. G. on 9-13-1893

Page 293

Charley Ridley of LaForge and Margaret Robinson of same by P.P.Payton M.G. on 9-21-1893

John Hawley of Morehouse and Mollie Malone of same on 9-20-1893 by E. Brow J.P. of West Twp.

Page 294

Albert Winchester of East Twp. and Cordelia Constant of same
Mrs. Sallie Davis, mother of Cordelia, consents by E. Brow, J.P.
on Oct 1, 1893

Page 295

John M. Stewart of Portage Twp. and Miss Bell Hess of same
Lerrsa Riddle, Mother of Bell Hess, consents by E. J. T. Hart,
Elder on Oct 8, 1893

James D. Webb of Como Twp. and Miss Emily McWilliams of same
George W. McWilliams, father of Emily, consents by James
Stewart, J.P. on Oct 11, 1893

Page 296

Edward Bartholamy of LeSieur Twp. and Laura Detie of same,
Andrew Detie, guardian of Laura consents, by J.J.Knight, M.G.
on Nov. 4, 1893

George Martin of New Madrid Twp. and Hester Greer of same
by J. W. Owsby, M.G. on Oct 15, 1893

Page 297

Elder Burkett of New Madrid Twp. and Miss Sallie Willis of same
by Joel Cook, J.P. on Oct 16, 1893

Mr. Morton Nicholson of New Madrid Co. and Eura Holcomb of same
by W. C. Edwards, M.G. on Oct 19, 1893

Page 298

Henry Dallas of LaForge and Mrs. Kitty Hampton of same on
Oct. 22, 1893 by W. T. Johnson, M.G.

Charles F. Herring of Malden, Dunklin Co., and Mrs. Nanny A.
Lazell of Riddles Pt. by C. S. Mills (M.E.C.S.) on Oct 25, 1893

Page 299

Joseph Dark of Grape Ridge and Miss Fanny Adams of same, Mrs.
Sophia Dark, mother of Joseph consents, by J.J.Knight, M.G.
on Nov. 4, 1893

Page 300

James Martin of New Madrid Twp. and Amanda Jane Stewart of
same, Sarah Riggs, mother of ? consents, by Joel Cook, J.P.
on Nov. 10, 1893

Warwell C. Girvin of Riddles Pt. and Miss Carey M. Wiley of
same by W. H. Batton, M.G. on Nov. 22, 1893

Page 301

James A. Jones of Portage Twp. and Miss Hester Tesoy (could be Troy) of Portage(Mainy Tesoy, mother of Hester, consents, (no return)

W.T.Parker of Montgomery, Texas and Miss Florence Smith of Dolph, Texas by W. C. Enochs, M.G. on 11-19-1893

Page 302

Eugene Smith of Portage Twp. and Molly Harris of same, J.W.Moore, guardian of Molly consents, on 11-21-1893 by L.F.LaFont, J.P.

George Henderson of New Madrid Twp. and Carrie Palmer of same by Henry Hunter, M.G. on 11-25-1893

Page 303

Richard Morgan of New Madrid Co. and Fanny Blackman of same by Chas. Reid, M.G. on 12-6-1893

James A. Smith of New Madrid Co. and Sarah H. Stewart of same on 12-5-1893 by Joel Cook, J.P.

Page 304

Roger D. Waring of Paw Paw and Tishy Eulett of New Madrid Co. by Joel Cook, J.P. on 12-11-1893

William Coats of New Madrid Twp. and Caroline Wayde of same Louis Wayde, father of Caroline consents, by W. T. Johnson, M.G. on 12-25-1893

Page 305

Charles A. Johnson of LeSieur Twp. and Mary M. Webster of same by W. H. Batten, M. G. on 12-25-1893

Elam Henderson of New Madrid Twp. and Franky Wiley of same by Lewis Samuel Hill, M.G. on 12-21-1893

Page 306

Thomas Rhoads of Pt. Pleasant and Ellen Williams of same by Henry Hunter M.G on 12-25-1893

John Williams of New Madrid Twp. and Elizabeth Raglon of same John Raglon, father of Elizabeth consents, by W. T. Johnson,M.G. on Dec. 25, 1893

Page 307

George W. Malone of Pt. Pleasant and Drury Williams of same by Samuel Mecklem, J.P. on 12-25-1893

Henderson Fish of New Madrid Twp. and Rilla Watson of same by J. V. Ousley, M.G. on 12-24-1893

Page 308

Lymus Porter of LeSieur Twp. and Rena LaFont of same by
Albert Treadwell at Pt. Pleasant on 12-31-1893

William Waters (col) of New Madrid Twp. and Fannie
Phillips by J. W. Ousley, M.G. on 12-31-1893

Page 309

William S. Hufstudler of LeSieur Twp. and Miss Linda Lamb
of Portage by W. H. Batten, M.G. on 1-3-1894

John E. Clarke of LeSieur Twp. and Miss Ella O'Bannon of
same by W. H. Batten, M.G. on 1-31-1894

Page 310

John W. Haggens of New Madrid Twp. and Margaret Massey of
same by Ira P. Eby, M.G. on 1-7-1894

John W. Johnson of Riddle Pt. and Maggie Norton of same
by Samuel Mecklem J.P. on 1-14-1894

Page 311

Carrol D. Furgeson of Memphis, Shelby Co. Tenn., and Lula N.
Neel of New Madrid by W. S. Enochs, M.G. on 1-17-1894

James R. Alexander of New Madrid Twp. and Nannie Parker
of Point Pleasant by W. C. Enochs M.G. on 1-21-1894

Page 312

Clarence S. DeFields of Miss. Co. and Annie L. Webb of Como
Twp. David DeFields, father of Clarence S. consents, by
W.S.Farmer M.G. on 1-25-1894

Joseph Everett of Fulton Co., Ky. and Ada Sexton of Lake
County, Tenn. by Joel Cook, J.P. on 1-24-1894

Page 313

John H.Gilbert of Paw Paw of New Madrid Co. and Mary Fields
of Paw Paw by Joel Cook, J.P. on Jan. 25, 1894

Frank Henry of New Madrid Twp. and Miss Mary Jonte of same
by C. H. Riley, J.P. on 1-28-1894

Page 314

Albert W. LaFont of Lewis Twp. and Masitite LeSieur of Portage by L.F.LaFont, J.P. on 1-31-1894

Summers Toney of New Madrid Twp. and Miss Emery Klein of same by W. C. Enochs, M. G. on 1-39-1894

Page 315

Peter Ruble of New Madrid Co. and Miss Cora Majors, Sara Roland, mother of Cora consents, by W. C. Enochs, M.G. on 2-2-1894

Joseph Ruck Edmondson of Big Prairie and Miss Tinie Disminey of same by William Carlisle, Feb. 11, 1894

Page 316

Bius Richards of New Madrid Twp. and Netty Morgan of same (no return)

John C. Conrade of Pt. Pleasant and Miss Hattie Watson of same by C. H. Riley, J.P. on 2-11-1894

Page 317

Walter M. Hubbard of Clarkton, Dunklin Co. and Mrs. Maggie Young of Portage by M. V. Baird, M G on 2-14-1894

John M. Thom of Donaldson Pt. and Miss Agness E. Carlisle of same by W. T. Peeler, J.P. on 3-4-1894

Page 318

Robert Lee Gray of New Madrid Twp. and Luncinda Nicholas of same Mar. 3, 1894 (no return)

Page 319

Lee R. Bayliss of Sikeston, Scott Co., and Amanda Ogden of same by John N. Mills, J.P. on 3-18-1894

George H. Bartlett of Como Twp. and Rosa Franklin of same. James F. Jewell, guardian of Rosa consents, by W. S. Farmer, M.G. on 3-18-1894

Page 320

Armstrong Waters of Ruddles Pt. and Henryetta Vinson of same. Errion and Bell Vinson, father and mother of Henryetta consent, by W. G. Henson, M. G. on 4-1-1894

Page 321

William H. McCormick of LeSieur Twp. and Nora Elizabeth Bowen of same on March 21, 1894 by Joel Cook, J.P.

Samuel R. Shy of New Madrid and Miss Laura L. Wathen by James J. Furlong, Roman Catholic Priest, on 4-4-1894

Page 322

Chas. C. Hutton of Lotta of New Madrid and Mary Jane Jones of New Madrid by Joel Cook, J.P. on 5-12-1894

Thomas Lewis of New Madrid Twp. and Miss Mary Hunt of New Madrid by Charles Reed on 4-11-1894

Page 323

Samuel Oliver of East Twp. and Jenette Morris of same Robert M. Morris, father of Jenette consents, on 4-19-1894 by J. E. Shelby, J.P.

Wm. W. Laws of Pt. Pleasant and Miss Elza Davis of same by John D. Fleming M. G. on 4-29-1894

Page 324

Parker Cherry of LaForge and Hattie Richardson of New Madrid by E. A. McKenny, M. G. on 5-2-1894

Henry Cavender of Pemiscot County and Gerty Cavender of Pemiscot County by R. M. Morgan M.G. on May 11, 1894

Page 325

William Brunson of New Madrid Twp. and Maggie Dorsey of same, Gem Brunson, father of William consents, and Emeline Young, Mother of Maggie consents, by Chas. Reed, M. G. on 5-20-1894

Henry Loomis of New Madrid Twp. and Adaline Dees of same by J. H. Howard, J.P. on 5-18-1894

Page 326

John Huntington of Lotta and Mandy Harris of same by A. J. Wilson M.G. on 4-25-1894

Joseph E. Terry of West Twp. and Mary Alice Brower of same, Ephraim Brower, father of Mary Alice consents, by J. N. Mills, J.P. on 5-24-1894

Page 327

William Henry Seward of New Madrid and Rosa Bell Gassett
of New Madrid Co. by Joel Cook J.P. on 5-24-1894

Pope Stowe of Madrid Bend, Fulton Co. Ky., and Miss Francis
Watson of same on 5-29-1894 by W. C. Edwards M.G.

Page 328

Robert D. Harris of New Madrid Co. and Miss Adelia A.
Brannum of same by Matthew A. Moore, M. G. on 5-30-1894
at Big Prairie Church

Joseph Bradshaw of New Madrid and Lillie Ball with
William Farrell, guardian of Lillie Ball, by Joel Cook, J.P.
on 5-26-1894

Page 329

Henry Roland, New Madrid Co. and Miss Amanda Whitt of
Lewis Prairie by Henry Hunter, M. G. on 5-27-1894

Daniel Pebyhouse of St. John Twp. and Miss Elby Jones of
same by W. T. Peele J.P. on 6-17-1894

Page 330

Robert Shultz of St. John Twp. and Miss Tompy Ailes of
same by Joel Cook, J.P. on 6-7-1894

Albert Lee Burns of New Madrid Twp. and Miss Katie Carter
William; Graham guardian of Katie consents, by Joel Cook, J.P.
on June 16, 1894

Page 331

Henry Tilbert of West Twp. and Rosa Revelle of same by
E. Brower, J. P. on 6-18-1894

Edward Snider of New Madrid Twp. and Kathie Higgerson of
same by Joel Cook, J.P. on 6-21-1894

Page 332

Julius Logan of Donaldson Pt. and Amanda Horner of same on
June 23, 1894 by W. C. Enoch, M. G.

William D. Schultz, Pemiscot Co., Mo. and Miss Nelly Reno of
New Madrid on 6-28-1894 by James J. Furlong, Roman Catholic Priest

Page 333

Frances M. Allen of Scrub Ridge, New Madrid Co. and Tabitha J.
Chatman of same by W. C. Enochs, M. G. on 6-27-1894

James A. Dodson of Barnes Ridge and Bethe Clark of St. Johns
Twp. on 6-30-1894 by W. T. Peeler, J.P. of St. Johns Twp.

Page 334

Robert F. Gilmore of Grape Ridge and Fidelia Holdneary of same on July 3, 1894 by J. J. Knight, M.G.

James F. Gray of Paw Paw and Miss Rosa Banks of same by Joel Cook, J.P. on July 5, 1894

Page 335

Dailey O. Prisson of East Twp. and Miss Mary L. Wells, Z. T. Wells, father of Mary L. Wells consents, on July 10, 1894 by J. M. Presson, M. G.

Base Hudspeth of Calavry, Ky. and Ida Thompson of New Madrid by Ira P. Irby M. G. on 7-14-1894

Page 336

John D. Parker of New Madrid and Sarah Rolan of same by W. C. Enochs, M. G. on 7-14-1894

Eugene P. Thomas of Morehouse and Miss Jennie L. Hoehn of New Madrid by W. C. Enochs, M. G. on 7-16-1894

Page 337

Albert Wilson of Lotta and Miss Matty Kenworthy of LaForge on 7-17-1894 by John A. Wilson, M. G.

Thodius Williams of Paragould, Ark. and Lena Jones of New Madrid by W. C. Enochs, M.G. on 7-16-1894

Page 338

Monroe Milikin of Lotta of New Madrid Co. and Miss Ella Simon of Lotta on July 20, 1894 by James Stewart, J.P.

Page 339

David V. Rackley of Miss. Co., Ark. and Catherine Isbell of Miss. Co., Ark. by Joel Cook J.P. on 8-1-1894

John Digman of New Madrid and Miss Anna Ratcliff by Rev. J. A. Bell M.G. on 8-6-1894

Page 340

Henry Johnson of New Madrid Co. and Holly Ross of same by T. L. Mulligan on 8-12-1894

James R. Cullion of Barnes Ridge and Miss Lucinda England of same consent of Joseph D. England, father of Lucinda, b y W. T. Peele, J.P. on 8-8-1894

Page 341

Reubon Trotter of New Madrid and Sallie Nicholas of same consented to by David Nicholas, father of Sallie, by James Wesley, M. G. on 8-8-1894

Roy Hurle of LeSieur Twp. and Amanda Pippen of same on 8-10-1894 by W. H. Patton, M. G.

Page 342

James M. Williams of New Madrid and Fannie Jackson of same on 8-11-1894 by P. P. Payton, M. G.

Henry J. Baker of New Madrid Co. and Mary Summers of same consent of James Summers, father of Mary, on 8-11-1894

Page 343 Louis Renfro of LeSieur Twp. and Amandy Wright of same on 8-13-1894 by Jos. D. Stine, J.P.

Robert Clayton of Avonie Landing, Pemiscot Co. and Susie Riley of same on 8-15-1894 by Joel Cook, J.P.

Page 344

Sidney Ruggles of Paw Paw and Katy Frenso of same by Joel Cook, J.P. on 8-14-1894

J. A. P. Willett of New Madrid and Miss Eddie Neal of same by W. C. Encohs M. G. on 8-29-1894

Page 345

Lee Constant of New Madrid Co. and Miss Katy Graham of same by W. C. Enochs M. G. on 9-3-1894

Mr. William Dobbins of Scrub Ridge and Miss Fanny Hole of same by L. F. LaFont, County Judge of 2nd District on 9-4-1894

Page 346

George Bailey of Fulton, Ky. and Miss Cora Parker of New Madrid, consent of P. C. Parker, Mother of Cora, by W. C. Enochs M. G. on 9-4-1894

James E. Henry of Louis Prairie and Miss Laura E. Lee of New Madrid on 9-5-1894 b y W. C. Enochs, M. G.

Page 347

Thomas D. Spencer of New Madrid Twp. and Minnie Rushing of same on 9-8-1894 by Joel Cook, J.P.

Page 347

Thomas Davis of New Madrid Twp. and Ada Philabar of same by W. T. Johnson J.P. on 9-9-1894

Page 348

George Hampton of Pt. Pleasant and Mittie Guinn of same by Samuel Mecklem J.P. on 9-16-1894

Noland Johnson of Pt. Pleasant and Maggie Morrow of same on 9-19-1894 b y L. F. LaFont county Judge of 2nd District

Page 349

John Kirby of Portageville and Adaline Morrell of same Mary Rice, mother of Adaline consents, by L. F. LaFont on 9-20-1894

Benjamin O. Kitterman of Como Twp. and Sarah Drivall of same by A. J. Wilson M. G.

Page 350

Jessie L. Ham of Portage Twp. and Miss Viola L. Estes of same with consent of Wm. Estes, father of Viola, by John Young, J.P. on 9-30-1894

Miles Moore of Pemiscot Co., Mo. and Emma Channey of same with consent of Betsy Chaney, Mother of Emma, by A. F. Parker, J.P. on 10-7-1894

Page 351

Samuel A. Crabtree of Portage Twp. and Miss Mollie Meatte of same, Samuel Crabtree, father of Samuel A. consents by John Young, J.P. on 10-1-1894

George Johnson of St. John Twp. and Mrs. Lula Moore of New Madrid on Oct 8, 1894 by Joel Cook, J.P.

Page 352

Frank Evans of LeSieur Twp. and Miss Bertha Adcock of same Wilburn Adcock, father of Bertha consents, on Nov. 1, 1894 by J. J. Knight, M.G.

J. F. Poe of Lotta and Mattie J. Sutherland of same on 10-19-1894 by James Stewart, J.P.

Page 353

William Graham of New Madrid Co. and Susan Davis of same
on Oct. 21, 1894 by E. A. McKinney, M.G.

Joseph A. Hanes of Como Twp. and Lizzie A. Taylor of same
on Oct 23, 1894 by W. S. Farmer, M. G.

Page 354

William Henry Murphy of New Madrid Twp. and Minnie A. Burnes
of same, J. G. Hawkins, guardian of Minnie consents,
on Oct 25, 1894 by Joel Cook, J.P.

Jonot DeLisle of Portageville and Katie Bloomfield of NEW
Madrid on Oct 25, 1894 by James J. Furlong, Roman Cath. Priest

Page 355

William H. Presson of East Twp. and Minnie B. Watson of same
by James Winders J.P. on 10-19-1894

John Ash of New Madrid Twp. and Lizzie Marr of same by
L. F. LaFont, County Justice 2nd Dist on Oct 30, 1894

Page 356

J. S. Linsey, Marshall Co., Ky. and Nola V. Marning of same
on Nov. 5, 1894 by Joel Cook, J.P.

Henry Hampton of Pt. Pleasant and Laura Walker of same on
Nov. 10, 1894 by J. S. Law, J.P.

Page 357

Martin Alexander of LeSieur Twp. and Emma Jackson of same
bought Nov. 12, 1894 (no return)

Charles P. Phillips of St. Louis Co. and Corda M. Gant of
same on Nov. 24, 1894 by J. H. Ewing, M.G

Page 358

Charles Conley and Eliza Logan of New Madrid Twp. on Nov. 12,
1894 by W. T. Johnson, M. G.

Edward Rodes of LeSieur Twp. and Matilda LaFont of same on
Nov. 18, 1894 by Henry Hunter, M. G.

Page 359

William Gregory of New Madrid and Lizzie Hampton of same,
Sallie Fox, mother of Lizzie consents by Thomas Mulligan, M.G.
on Nov. 14, 1894

Page 359

Mack Abar (Ab ad) of LeSieur Twp. and Maggie Roots of same by Joseph D. Stine J.P. on 11-15-1894

Page 360

Miles A. Butler of LeSieur Twp. and Miss Rosie E. Butler of same, William C. Butler, father of said Rosie consents by J.J.Knight, M. G. on Nov. 18, 1894

Martin Alexander of LeSieur Twp. and Emma Osburn of same on Nov. 20, 1894 by John Paine, M.G.

Page 361

James Winders Jr. of East Twp. and Francis Fox of same by James Winders, J.P. on Nov. 6, 1894

Albert A. Stepp of New Madrid Co. and Miss Ida C. Hart of same by P. H. Roberts, M.G.

Page 362

Walter Dodson of St. John Twp. and Bulah Hyles of same by W. T. Peeler J.P. on Nov. 28, 1894

George Lawfield of Barnes Ridge and June Hyles of same by Joel Cook, J.P. on Dec. 5, 1894

Page 363

Thomas Legate of LeSieur Twp. and Miss Ida Johnson of Lewis Twp. by J. J. Knight, M.G. on Dec. 9, 1894

John T. B ooker of Como and Mattie Colule of same b y James Stewart J.P. on Dec. 6, 1894

Page 364

James Davis of New Madrid Twp. and Miss Sarah E. Jont of same on Dec. 12, 1894

G. A. Draffin of Portage and Bette Allin of same on Dec. 17, 1894 by G. S. Jones, M.G.

Page 365

James A. Higgerson of West Twp. and Mary Hector of same by Jno. D. Satterwhite, M. G. of C. P.Church on 12-23-1894

John Williams of Memphis, Shelby Co., Tenn. and Lula Johnson of New Madrid by Joel Cook, J.P. on 12-24-1894

Page 366

Edward Gray of Pt. Pleasant and Mary Howard of same on Dec. 24, 1894 by Henry Hunter M.G.

Samuel Dean of Barnes Ridge and Miss Dora Peeler of same by C. Q. Kelley J.P. on Dec. 24, 1894

Page 367

Thomas L. Jackson of New Madrid and Laura A. Castleberry of same on Dec. 29, 1894 by W. C. Enochs, M.G.

W. H. McCormick of LeSieur Twp. and R. V. Branham on 12-24-1894 by Joel Cook, J.P.

Page 368

William M. Vedetae of Como Twp. and Ada Bell E. Balder of same, Alexander Bolder, father of Ada Bell consents by James Stewart, J.P. on 1-5-1895

E. H. Brew (Brue) (Brewer) of Grape Ridge and Mary E. Wheeler of same on 1-7-1895 by A. M. O'Quinn, M.G.

Page 369

Edward Case of Scrub Ridge and Allie Brown of same by Albert Treadwell on 1-7-1895

Major Green of New Madrid Twp. and Laura Mitchell of same on 1-7-1894 by W. T. Johnson, M.G.

Page 370

J.W.Morris of Grape Ridge and Ruth B. West of Como Twp. W.H.Morris, father of J.W.C. Morris consents, M J. Ruples, only living parent of Ruth consents, by W. S. Farmer, M.G. on 1-7-1895

J. Lee Hampton of Ruddles Point and Miss Hatty E. Aldridge of same, P. H. Aldridge, father of Hattie, consents, by Samuel Mecklem, J.P. on 1-9-1895

Page 371

Ham Echord of Big Prairie and Miss Ellen Brent of same by J. N. Mills J.P. on 1-9-1895

Moses R. DeWitt of East Twp. and Lillie M. Siggers of same John W. Siggers, father of Lilly consents, on 1-12-1895 by R. P. Pearman, M.G.

Page 372

James C. Inman of Lotta and Katie McColum of same, Anise Forde, mother of James consents by James Stewart J.P. on 1-15-1895

J. A. Beck of Lotta and Buthly Stanley of same by James Stewart, J.P. on 1-15-1895

Page 373

William Sweat of Como Twp. and Cordelia Banham of same Enoch Banham, father of Cordelia consents, Jan 12, 1895 by James Stewart, J.P.

Page 373

William M. Brown of New Madrid Twp. and Altha Parrot of same by P. P. Patton, M. G. on 1-19-1895

INDEX
(New Madrid, Co., MO. Marriages Vol #2)

ABAR,MACK	152	. J.F.	111	ALDREDGE,ANNIE	82
MAGGIE ROOTS	152	. JAMES	96	P.H.	82
ABBOTT,ANNIE LIKINS	132	. LILIE GIBBS	124	ALDRIDGE,HATTY	153
. ELIJAH	32	. LIZZIE	111	. MATTIE SCHINK	133
. MARY E. STALLINGS	32	. WILBURN	150	. P.H.	153
. MIKE	132	. WILLIAM	96,122	. PATRICK H.	133
. NANCY	73	ADDA,CORA DAVIS	48	ALEXANDER,	
ACORD,HAMILTON	136	JOSEPH	48	. ALICE JOHNSON	134
MAGGIE	136	ADKERSON,MATTIE	137	. ELIZABETH	7
ADAMS,A.M. INMAN	67	ADKINS,BENJAMIN C.	2	. EMMA JACKSON	151
. ABRAHAM B.	43	. MELISSA	61	. EMMA OSBURN	152
. ALBERT	68	. SALLIE ANN HOWE	2	. EVA	73
. ALEMEN CONRAD	68	ADKINSON,		. GEORGE	43
. ALSA R.	67	. CASSEY STOVAL	101	. HENRY	134
. BELL WHITE	52	. JOHN	101	. IDA LATHAM	87
. EMMA	15	. WILLIAM	101	. INA B. REED	16
. FANNY	142	ADMER,V.	108	. JAMES R.	144
. JAMES	20	ADY,MARY A. GUNLIS	128	. JEFFERSON M.	20
. JEFF D.	19	MITCHELL	128	. JENNY	59
. JOHN	113	AESTERMAN,JAMES	33	. JOHN	43
. JOSEPHINE RIDDLE	40	MARTHA CANCELL	33	. JOHN ALFRED	16
, M.J.	131	AILES,TOMPY	147	. JUDY WARD	43
. MARTHA .	131	AKERS,ALBERTA	108	. JULY ANN WATSON	43
. MARTHA ROBERTS	130	. BETTY BAKER	62	. LULA McFARLAND	43
. MARY	127	. FLORENCE ARBUCKLE	97	. MARTIN	151-152
. MARY ANN STAUBIN	20	. JOHN	92	. MARY STRINGFIELD	25
. MARY ARBUCKLE	19	. LOU HERRING	92	. MOLLIE THOMAS	20
. MINNIE KEITH	113	. M.F.	97	. NANNIE PARKER	144
. MOLLIE HAYES	43	. PLEAS	97	. ROBERT	25,59
. MOLLIE McELHANY	37	. WILLIAM	62	. SALLIE	115
. NANNY	51	AKIN,BENTON	16-17,19-20	. SCOTT	43,56
. ROBERT	37,52,130	.	22,28,36	. WILLIAM W.	87
. TEARCE	48	. OLA R.	94	ALFORD,NANCY A.	8
. WILLIAM	40	AKINS,B.	25	ALISON,MARG.	3
ADCOCK,ANNIE	122	. BENTON	26-27,35	ALLEN,ANN	12
. BERTHA	150	. MARY GRUBB	122	. ANNIE CALDWELL	8
. BETTIE BLACKWELL	96	. MILEGE F.	122	. AZALEE	67
. EDWARD	124	AKINSON,RACHEL	122	. BENJAMIN F.	11

INDEX
(New Madrid, Co., MO. Marriages Vol #2)

. CHARLES	10	. JAMES W.	3	ARKADE, DORA	122		
. DAVID T.	130	. JOHN	107	ARNETT, JANE HAYES	128		
. DELLA LOU	23	. JOSAPHINE	22	JOSEPH P.	128		
. ELIZA J.	130	. JOSEPH L.	133	ASH, DAISEY L. LEE	138		
. ELIZABETH STALLCUP	1	. RENA ELLDRIDGE	107	. JOHN	107,138,151		
. EMMA HUNTER	134	. ROENA SMULLINS	3	. LIDGE A.	99		
. FLONNA	28	. ROSA STINE	133	. LIZZIE MARR	107,151		
. FRANCES J. WATERS	48	ALLSUP, BETTY	39	. MARY	12		
. FRANCES M.	147	ALSUP, ANNIE HOEFMAN	88	. MARY MARTIN	99		
. HANNAH BRATTON	27	. BETTIE	122	ASHBY, DEEK	69		
. HANNER	93	. SARAH	110	. DUB	69		
. HANNIE McTOUCH	121	. THOMAS	88	. FANNY	69		
. JAMES	69	ANDERSON,		. MARY	59		
. JAMES C.	8	. GEORGE WILLIS	106	ASHFORD, JAMES	117		
. JENNY HOGAN	62	. JANE CANNY	122	MARY C. ALLEY	117		
. JOSEPH L.	62	. JOHN	122	ASPLEY, L.F.	5		
. JULIA CANTRELL	10	. JOHN T.	106	ATCHESON, GEROGE	55		
. LORENA	35	. JOHN W.	3	LUCY HENSON	55		
. MARY BAKER	69	. KITTY FRY	127	ATE, JOSEPHINE HAMPTON	57		
. NANCY E. SISCO	130	. MARY	114	SAMUEL	57		
. RICHARD	27	. MARY LEFERNEY	3	ATES,			
. ROBERT HATCHER	48	. WILLIAM	127	. CATHARINE BABTEST	85		
. SAM	103	ANDREWS, EMMA INGRAM	34	. CHARLES	37,85		
. SAMUEL	1	WILLIAM H.	34	. JOSEPHINE BRANSON	56		
. SUSAN J. WILLET	11	ANGEL, SALLIE WATSON	91	. JOSEPHINE BUNSON	56		
. TABITHA J. CHATMAN	147	WILLIAM	91	. LOUISE BRUNNER	56		
. TANNER WILLIS	103	ANGELO, PEARL	117	. LUCINDA DIRSEY	37		
. THOMAS B.	134	ANTHONY, W.A.	3	. SAMUEL	56		
. W.B.	48	APPLEGATE, R.G.	14	ATKINSON,			
. WILLIAM FRANKLIN	121	ARBUCKELL,		. COLUMBIA WARD	123		
. WILLIS ELMER	130	. ELIZABETH WILES	119	. EPHRAIM	123		
ALLEY, IDA DEAS	86	. JOHN	119	. JAMES	3		
. JAMES M.	35	ARBUCKLE, FLORENCE	97	ATTERBERRY, SUSAN BLUE	29		
. JANE BLACK	35	. J.W.	19,21	WILLIAM	29		
. M.N.	86	. LUCY	19	ATTERBURY, ELIZABETH	8		
. MARY C.	117	. MARY	19	. JOSEPH N.	23		
ALLIN, BETTE	152	. NANCY	97	. MARTHA DARNALL	23		
ALLISON, ELIZABETH	47	. VICTORIA	21	. THOMAS	8		

INDEX
(New Madrid, Co., MO. Marriages Vol #2)

Name	Page	Name	Page	Name	Page
ATWELL, JOHN	22	. FRANCIS O.	28	BARNES, ADA F.	35
. JOHN E.	125	. HENRY J.	149	. ALEXANDER L.	73
. VIOLA COATS	125	. LOUISA	135	. AMOS	44
ATWOOD, J.L.	133	. MARY	69	. CULLEN	139
AUBIN, POLINA SAINT	16	. MARY SUMMERS	149	. DIXIE POWELL	63
AUCTINE, C.J.	82	. PETER	28	. DORA	137
AUGDEN, KATIE	128	. SARAH	11	. E.	137
AULDRICH, EMMA GIRVIN	90	. SUSAN	64	. ELISHA	2
SAM	90	BALDER, ADA BELL	153	. ELIZABETH	118
AUSTIN, PAULINA	19	BALDWIN, GEORGE	8	. IDA	107
AUSTINE, C.J.	82	. JAMES L.	135	. JOSEPH	2
AUTRY, JAMES	66	. LOUISA BAKER	135	. LINDA FRISKE	73
. MARGARET CAMPBELL	66	. MARY M.	103	. MARTHA ROBERTSON	2
. MARTHA EVANS	27	. MARY PATRICK	8	. MARY	90
. OUBJBET	27	. METILDA	70	. MARY ANN HARDEN	44
AVERY, CHARLES	4	BALL, LILLIE	147	. MARY JONES	139
DALSEY LOUIS	4	BANDY, ELLEN	9	. MATTIE LAFONT	41
AYRES, DORA	125	BANHAM, CORDELIA	154	. MELISSA J.	4
BABB, ANDREW W.	61	ENOCH	154	. RANK	41
. ETTA	36	BANKS, ANDREW	105	. RANKIN	63
. HENRIETTA NELSON	8	. ELLEN McCARRIE	86	. SARAH E. JONES	2
. MARY ETTA CRAVENS	61	. GEORGE	19	BARNETT, E.A.	67
. THOMAS	8	. GEORGE W.	19	. JOSAPHINE	15
BABTEST, CATHARINE	85	. LANCY TAYLOR	94	. ROSA MITCHELL	67
BABTESTE, CATHARINE	28	. MACK	86	BARNHART, AMANDA	133
BACHER, A.J.	117	. MARY	38	SARAH	9
JANIE HOPPER	117	. MARY J. MARSH	19	BARNHILL, BENJAMIN F.	20
BAEHR, JACOB	88	. MEDIA	113	THEODOCIN PARKER	20
. LEE W.	81	. RICHARD M.	94	BARNS, SARAH C.	12
. RENY MAXEY	88	. ROSA	148	BARR, FRANCIS GRAHAM	67
BAHER, ALICE EWING	96	. SARAH DAVIS	105	THOMAS	67
LOUIS	96	BARBER, HANNER	103	BARRET, T.C.	9
BAILEY, CORA PARKER	149	BARBOUR, HANNAH MOTT	66	BARRETT,	
. GEORGE	149	RICHARD	66	. ANNIE E. McGEE	106
. JOSEPHINE	33	BARKER, LACKEY J.	19	. EDWARD T.	129
BAINES, JERRY	38	BARKLEY, HENRY	66	. IDA M. PAXTON	129
BAIRD, M.V.	134, 145	BARLEY, ANNIE E. HEDGE	54	. SILAS Y.	106
BAKER, BETTY	62	C.A.	54	BARRNETT, ELLA	116

INDEX
(New Madrid, Co., MO. Marriages Vol #2)

Name	Page	Name	Page	Name	Page
BARRON, FANNIE	46	PAMELA BEGGS	121	. ELLEN	98
W.J.	46	BAYLISS, AMANDA OGDEN	145	. IDA THOMPSON	106,127
BARRY, EBLEN	86	LEE R.	145	. J.A.	148
. LAURA M. HENSON	9	BAYNE,		. JAMES R.	12
. NANNIE WATHEN	86	. MAMIE RANSBURGH	106	. KATY M.	27
. THOMAS J.	9	. NORA	88	. LAWRENCE H.	106
BARTHOLAMY, EDWARD	142	. RICHARD	106	. LONNIE H.	127
LAURA DETIE	142	BAYNES, LAVENIA	9	. LUCY ANN WHEAT	140
BARTHOLEMY,		BAYOU, JAMES	50,127	. LUELLA	19
NAPOLEON B.	21	BEACLLES, KATIE	83	. LYIA TERRY	141
BARTLETT, DORA WILSON	31	BEAL, WISEL	134	. SAMUEL	27,140
. GEORGE H.	145	BEALE, WEISEL	69	. SARAH J. BROWN	12
. HENRY S.	31	BEALL, WASEL	66	. WILLIAM C.	141
. MARY	100	WESEL	55	. WILLIAM H.	126
. ROSA FRANKLIN	145	BEARD, CHARLES H.	73	BELLANT, DAVID	83
BARTOLOMEW, JOSEPH	108	. JOSEPHINE McELAVY	73	. KATIE FRANSO	83
MARY E. DETIE	108	. NANCY E.	9	. MOLLIE	83
BARTON, ANIE GAMBLE	86	BEARDE,		BELLON, AMELIA TONEY	85
JOHN	86	. AMANDA HUTCHENS	65	. BOURBON	36
BASCOMB, NANCY A.	3	. JAMES B.	65	. CORNELIA	114
BASHAM, COLUMBUS	20	. PAUSHY	47	. RUTH McGARIN	36
. HARDAN	25	BEASLEY, MARTHA	106	. TALBOT E.	85
. HENRIETTA CARILTON	20	BEASY, MARY	40	BELSON,	
. LETHA NELSON	25	BEAVERS, AMANDA U.	12	. MATTY A. BETTIS	63
BASKEN, LIZZIE MERLEN	31	. BETTY	51	. ROBERT	63
RICHARD	31	. CATHERINE	57	BENEDICT, ALICE SANDS	22
BASKER, MARY YOUNG	129	. DORAH ANN	129	CHARLES W.	22
PERKINS	129	. EMELIA	134	BENHAN, JOHN	117
BASS, M.	55	. JOHN	61	BENNET, MARY CHISM	18
BASSET, ROSA	76	. MARTHA DILLARD	61	WILSON	18
BASTON, CELESTE MOORE	105	BEAVORS, CHARLES	27	BENNETT, AMANDA	43
JAMES A.	105	KATY M. BELL	27	. BARNEY	92
BATES,		BECK, J.A.	154	. MARTHA	55
. MINERVA J. SPARKS	7	RUTHLY STANLEY	154	. MELINDA HARDIN	92
. SAMUEL D.	7	BEGGS, PAMELA	121	BENTON, CLEIN J.	61
BATTEN, W.H.	143-144	BELCHER, MARY J.	8	ELLEN MURPHY	61
BATTON, W.H.	142	BELL, ANNIE	108	BERRYMAN, GRACE	126
BAXTER, GEORGE W.	121	. CYNTHIA WHEAT	126	BERTHOLINN, N.B.	67

INDEX
(New Madrid, Co., MO. Marriages Vol #2)

BERTHOLISON, AMELIA	67	. J.G.	126	. FANNY	143		
BERTHOTOMY,		. J.H.	74,107-108	. MARY GUITON	72		
. JENNY LAFONT	69	. J.P.	91	BLACKWELL, BETTIE	96		
. N.B.	69	. JAMES	61,65,77,89,98	. CLARA	106		
. THOMAS N.	69	. JAMES A.	57	. FANNIE	114		
BESHEARS,		. JAMES F.	54,56,58-63	. MARY	106		
. MAGGIE WALLACE	92	. 66,69,78,94,98-99,110		. THOMAS	106		
. ROBERT A.	92	.	116,126	BLAIR, SARAH	54		
BETTIS, MATTY A.	63	. JAMES G.	98	BLALOCK, W.C.	105		
BEVINS, BETTIE	5	. JAMES H.	89-90,92	. W.H.	102-103		
BEYMER, MAGGIE LEWIS	133	.	102-103,105	. W.W.	100-101,106		
THOMAS H.	133	. JAMES L.	80	BLALSE, MATTHEW M.	130		
BIAS, MARY CUNNINGHAM	9	. JAMES W.	99-100	BLANCH, EMERSON G.	110		
THOMAS A.	9	. JOHN A.	61	IDA DAMON	110		
BINKLEY, F.M.	13	. JONES	78	BLANKENSHIP, MAY	101		
. JOHN H.	41	. L.F.	55	BLASSE, MATTHEW	125		
. MARY J. GIBBIN	13	. MARY	63,87	BLEDSOE, EMILY TOWNSEND	4		
. NANNIE JACKSON	41	. MILES L.	67	. EMMER	90		
BIRD, A. RUDDLE	9	. NARCISSUS GRAW	69	. JANE DANIELS	11		
. ANNA	42	. NELLIE HALL	67	. VIRGINIA BOLTON	19		
. ELIJAH	68	. RENE JONES	81	. W.	91		
. HARREL C.	127	. SARAH ALSUP	110	. WALKER	11		
. HORRELL C.	129	. THOMAS F.	66	. WALKER A.	19		
. ISAAC	98	BLACK,		. WARREN	4		
. MAGGIE HENDERSON	98	. AMANDA E. KUNCKELS	23	BLESSING, CHARLES	20		
. PATSY CHERRY	68	. AMANDA KNUCKLES	22	LEVINA HAYES	20		
. SALLIE M. HUNTER	9	. EMMA PARKERSON	56	BLIZARD, JOSEPH	98		
. SARAH A. DUNN	127,129	. H.C.	18	MOLLIE WIMP	98		
. SUSAN	106	. JANE	35	BLIZZARD, ALLIE	96		
BIRDWELL, SUSIE	135	. MARY E. FORD	18	. MARY E. SHELTON	12		
BISHIP, JAMES G.	98	. ROBERT M.	56	. RANCILY	12		
. MILES L.	67	. WILLIAM F.	22	. SARAH	50		
. NELLIE HALL	67	. WILLIAM T.	23	BLOCKER, JOHN	102		
BISHOP, ELLA	130	BLACKBURN, S.F.	33	LUCINA GODARD	102		
. EMMA	4	BLACKEN, JERE	22	BLOOMFIELD, JAMES	28,34		
. HARRIET	78	MARTHA	22	KATIE	151		
. J.F.	71,79,82,93,95	BLACKMAN, CRISTINE	18	BLOT, EXER	82		
.	124	. ED A.	72	BLUE, SUSAN	29		

INDEX
(New Madrid, Co., MO. Marriages Vol #2)

BOGARD, IDA	106	. B.J.	82	. DAVIDSON	125
BOGGAN, G.P.	54	. B.T.	124	. MARGARIT NIPPEN	125
BOGGS, ALICE	78	. LOTTA SHIDLER	133	. SAM	130
BOHANNON, A.J.	23	. MARY H.	87	BRANHAM,	
JENNY	23	. WALTER L.	133	. CLARRISSA WILLIAMS	28
BOLIN,		BOYD, W.S.	57	. HELEN	141
. BARBARY BRODHACKER	65	BOYER, ADA	100	. HESTER	53
. JAMES E.	65	BOYES, JENNY PHESCH	95	. LAURA	77
BOLINGER, RACHEL	111	R.C.	95	. R.V.	153
BOLTON, VIRGINIA	19	BOZARK, NELLIE	93	. THOMAS ALEXANDER	28
BOOKER, DINAH	35	BOZARKE, JOHN	137	BRANNACK, DANIEL	115
. JOHN T.	152	ROSA TUCKER	137	MARTHA	115
. MATTIE COLULE	152	BRACY, MARY	40	BRANNUM, ADELIA	147
. MAUDE	63	BRADEN, POLLY A.C.	23	. ADOLPHUS M.	16
BOON, ADELE	58	BRADLEY, SARAH	129	. EMMA MORLAND	16
. G.W.	55	BRADSHAW, ADALE	17	. FATHY CUNNINGHAM	109
. MARY	58	. ALICE	22	. HERUM	141
BOOTON, JERUSHA RANKIN	26	. EMILY	44-45	. JOHN W.	109
JOHN A.	26	. GEORGE	97	. NOAH	77
BOROUGH, J.W. ROSE	32	. JOSEPH	147	BRANON, GEORGE C.	110
BOTTON, MINTY	91	. LILLIE BALL	147	BRANSCOM, ELIZABETH	7
BOUGARD, JOHN	122	. MARY	110,121	BRANSFORD, E.K.	20
MAGGIE HUGGINS	122	. MARY CRAWSHAW	97	BRANSON, JOSEPHINE	56
BOUNDS, SARAH HENDRICKS	7	BRADY, KATIE F.	44	BRANSSUCES, ROBERT	50
WILLIAM B.	7	. P.P.	1,6	BRATTEN, ETTA	123
BOWEN, E.	126	. PHILIP	82	BRATTON, HANNAH	27
NORA E.	146	. PHILLIP	98	LINDA	93
BOWENS, LULA	45	BRAGLIN, AMY VAUDRIE	117	BRAVOIS, MARTHA	13
BOWER, NANNIE	125	JAMES	117	BRAY,	
BOWERS, FRANCIS	73	BRANAN, GEORGE	112,115	. ANN DELIA PHILLIPS	6
BOWIN, NANNIE	125	BRANCH, JOHN S.	87	. P.A.	6
BOWLIN, GEORGE F.	137	NANCY NICHOLAS	87	BREDENSTINED,	
. JOHN	88	BRANCI, FRANCES	87	. THERSIA GLEUCK	138
. MALINDA BULLINGER	137	BRAND, E.	138	. WILLIAM	138
. ROSALEE McDANIEL	88	. EPHRAIM	114	BRENT, ELLEN	153
BOWMAN, T.A.	34	. F.	87,91,99,102	BREVARD, ALICE	140
BOYCE, B.F.	37,45,67-68	BRANDON,	78	JOSEPH	140
.	84,87,92-93,111	. CLUMBIA MARION	130	BREW, E.H.	153

INDEX
(New Madrid, Co., MO. Marriages Vol #2)

MARY E. WHEELER	153	. LIBBIE	15	. JOSEPH L.	29
BREWER, E.H.	153	. NANNIE HUNTER	14	. JOSEPH S.	25
BRIDGEMAN,		. SALLIE	15	. JOSEPHINE	40
. AMELIA WINCHESTER	74	. SALLIE STEWART	68	. KATE	14
. JOHN	74	BROW, E.	141-142	. LEODER PIKEY	101
BRINE, DELLA O.	49	BROWD, E.	116	. LEWIS	102
BRINKLEY, JAMES D.	43	BROWER, E.	123,133,147	. LIZZIE	95,139
MARY E. HAY	43	. EPHRAIM	146	. LOUISA NEWSUM	109
BRISTOL, HATTY	80	. MARY A.	146	. LUCY	85-86
BRODHACKER, BARBARY	65	BROWN, ADA DAVIS	102	. LULA	132
BRODHAEKER,		. ADELL	58	. MAGGIE WITTER	69
. ADELE LASSLER	64	. AGNES HOLMES	121	. MANDY	50
. WILLIAM M.	64	. ALLIE	153	. MARGARET RATLIFF	91
BROODSHACKER,		. ALTHA PARROT	154	. MARY	13,58,126
. BARBARA ROBBINS	28	. ANNETTA COTTON	15	. MARY BARNES	90
. CHARLES	28	. ANNIE TUCKER	84	. MARY STOLDER	54
BROOKMAN, JULIA	119	. CATHERINE SMITH	96	. MATTIE	52
BROOKS,		. DELIA	110	. MELISSA	21
. ADA A. MAINORD	141	. DOLPH	94	. MOLLY	135
. ELIZA ANN	50	. DORA AYRES	125	. NANCY A. PAXTON	4
. ELIZABETH C. JONES	95	. E.	117,121-122	. NANCY E.	79
. GEORGE W.	25	. ELIZA	55	. NANNIE	125
. JAMES	95	. EPHRAIM	112	. PATSEY YOUNG	99
. JOSEPHINE	121	. EPRAIM	120	. POLLY MORGAN	94
. LIZZIE	82	. FLORENCE	112	. PRESS	51
. MARTHA E. DUNN	25	. FRANCIS	15	. RACHEAL	127
. MATTHEW	141	. FRANK	125	. ROSA LEE ENGLE	73
. REBECCA	23	. GEORGE	99,117	. S.L.	125
. W.M.	41	. GEORGE N.	96	. SALLIE	119
BROUGHTON, ARTHUR	14	. HENRY M.	109	. SARAH A.A. GROVIS	25
. CHARLES	15	. HESTER	53	. SARAH J.	12
. CHARLES H.	68	. J.A.	73,90	. SYLVANNIS	84
. CLARA MOTT	57	. J.F.	23	. WILLIAM	15,91
. HENRY E.	57	. J.L.	22,32	. WILLIAM M.	154
. J.M.	15	. JAMES	84	. WILLIAM THOMAS	4
. JAMES EDWARD	43	. JAMES R.	25	BROWNELL,	44
. JESSIE DORCH	43	. JOHN	54,101,121	. CORRIE	76
. JESSIE TONEY	43	. JOHN T.	69	. JOHN WILL	10

INDEX
(New Madrid, Co., MO. Marriages Vol #2)

. NANNIE BUFORD	10	BULLOCK, ELLEN	56	. NANCY HENRY	11		
BRUCKMAN, DAVID F.	51	BUNCH, AMANDA	10	. THOMAS J.	2		
MARTHA GILBERT	51	BUNSON,		BURNUM, LIZZIE	98		
BRUE, E.H.	153	. DORAH ANN BEAVERS	129	BURNY, MAGGIE	53		
BRUH, LAURA YOUNG	91	. JAMES	129	BURRUS, J.A.	73		
WILLIAM T.	91	. JOSEPHINE	56	BURSTETT, AMANDA HIND	112		
BRUNNER, LOUISE	56	BUNTING,		STEPHEN	112		
BRUNSON, AMOS	121	. ELIZABETH MANUEL	36	BURTON, ELSIE	116		
. ANNY GRAHAM	23	. WEBSTER	36	FLORENCE	117		
. EVA DAVIS	45	BURCHELL, ELIZA	19	BUSBY, ERIVN	43		
. GEM	146	BURGESS, HENRY	79	. NANCY M.	16		
. HARRIET HICKS	122	. IDA M.	111	. VIOLA G.	15		
. KATY RICHARDS	121	. IDA M. BURGESS	111	BUSH, ARCHILAND	58		
. MAGGIE DORSEY	146	. LENNY	126	. DANIEL	111		
. MARY	28	. MARTHA	79	. ELISA	52		
. ROBERT	122	. MARY	115	. ELIZABETH FORD	11		
. WILLIAM	23,45,146	. MAY	115	. GEORGE P.	11		
BRUNSTON,		. R.C.	111,126	. MARY McWILLIAMS	58		
. ADALE BRADSHAW	17	. ROMANTS S.	111	. MOLLIE CANTRELL	111		
. JAMES	17	. W.L.	115	BUSHY, ERION	48		
BRYANT, JANE	25	BURKETT, ELDER	142	BUTLER, DORA	62		
MAGGIE	15	SALLIE WILLIS	142	. EDWARD JEFFREYS	103		
BRYCE, B.F.	77	BURKHART, NANCY C.	44	. JAMES H.	100		
BUCHANAN, BETTY	48	BURKINSON, SAUNDRA	28	. JANE ROBINSON	87		
JOHN	42	BURKS, DICEY	5	. JOHN	103		
BUCKER, ALSE	119	BURNES, MINNIE	151	. JOHN A.	87		
LOUISE	127	BURNETT, AMOS	27	. LENA WATERS	63		
BUCKLEY,		. JEFFERSON	24	. MARTHA	106		
. RACHEL WATERS	118	. LUCY CUNINGHAM	27	. MARY MINNEWEATHER	69		
. STEPHEN	118	. MARY SANVILLE	24	. MATILDA HOLDEN	100		
BUCKMAN, D.T.	102,115	BURNEY, M.C.	53	. MILES A.	152		
. M.E.	135	BURNS, ALBERT LEE	147	. PRUDE	2		
. MARGARET	102	. ELISHA	11	. ROSIE E.	152		
. SREPTY	115	. ELIZABETH C. KEW	2	. ROSIE E. BUTLER	152		
BUCKNER, LEALA FOX	63	. JAMES	116	. SARAH	132		
LEROY R.	63	. JOANN NEWMAN	116	. W.C.	132		
BUFORD, NANNIE	10	. KATIE CARTER	147	. WILLIAM	63		
BULLINGER, MALINDA	137	. MARY E.	60	. WILLIAM C.	152		

INDEX
(New Madrid, Co., MO. Marriages Vol #2)

. WOODSON	69	. ISAAC	139	. S.P.	140
BUTT, ANNIE PATTERSON	96	. ISAAC FRANKLIN	52	. WILLIAM	26,145
GUS W.	96	. LARKIN	31	CARNEY, MARY	2
BUTTS, LUCY	120	. MARGARET FLANNERY	52	CARPENTER, ANNA	62
THOMAS M.	120	. MARGARET PRESLEY	45	. MARMGARET	5
BYERS,		. MARGRETT	87	. T.W.	13
. AMANDA J. PHILLIPS	139	. SALLIE	44	CARR, AMANDA	42
. HORTON	139	. WILLIAM	14	. ELIZABETH RAY	133
. IDA	116	. WILLIAM J.	45	. JAMES	81
. JOHN R.	116	CALL, ANCIE D.	33	. JOSEPH J.	25
BYMUNE,	32	CAMACK, JAMES	137	. MADARY WILLIS	81
BYOWS, MISSOURI DOWDY	84	MINNIE THARP	137	. SAMUEL	133
WILLIAM	84	CAMMEL, SARAH	133	. SUSIE L. PHILLIPS	25
BYRON, AMANDA DAVIS	117	CAMPBELL, ALICE	25	CARROL, ANDREW	34
PORTER	117	. C.J.	36	. MAGGIE J.	34
CABLES, SALLIE	14	. ELIZA FORDE	52	. NANCY MALONE	139
CACKERHAM, MELVIN F.	113	. JAMES N.	52	. WILLIAM	139
REBECCA ORR	113	. MARGARET	66	CARROLL, ANDREW	35,51,108
CADE, ELIZABETH MADRAY	14	. MARY	62	. ANNA	105
. JACOB	39	. MARY JANE RIACH	36	. ANNIE	122
. JACOB S.	14	CANCELL, MARTHA	33	. CAROLINE SHELBY	58
. S.A.L.	39	CANDER, C.C.	41	. DORA WALKER	104
CADSON, ANCIE D. HALL	33	CANNY, JANE	122	. HAMP	140
E.J.	33	CANOY, MARGARET	21	. IDA	119
CAGE, ALBERT	113	CANTRAL, MARY	105	. JAMES	104
CLARA WATERS	113	CANTRELL, JULIA	10	. JEFF D.	58
CAGLE, JOHN	138	MOLLIE	111	. KATIE HELM	106
. M.T. FORD	120	CARAL, MARY	44	. M.I. HELM	51
. MARY A.	138	CAREY, JOHN	10	. MAGGIE J.	35
. WILLIAM	120	NANCY DEITMORE	10	. MARIAH ROSS	140
CAIN, AMANDA RANDOLPH	97	CARILTON, HENRIETTA	20	. MARY	105
J.M.	97	CARL, DENNIS A.	95	. MARY DEWBERRY	108
CALDWELL, ALICE	30	ZULA A. PRUDY	95	. MOLLIE	44
. AMANDA E. MOORE	31	CARLISLE, ADA E. DEWEN	3	. P.J.	63,68,70
. AMY	87	. AGNESS	145	. R.J.	63
. ANNA TAYLOR	139	. BETTY UNDERWOOD	26	. RICHARD	106
. ANNIE	8	. CHARLES	3	CARRS, SUSAN	94
. HARRIETE SUMNER	14	. MANERARY	131	CARSON, ALBERTA AKERS	108

INDEX
(New Madrid, Co., MO. Marriages Vol #2)

Name	Page	Name	Page	Name	Page
. EMMA WORKMAN	88	CATT, MARY RUCKETTS	81	CHATMAN, J.	79
. MARY	60	SIMON F.	81	. LUCY SULLIVAN	79
. MARY C.	4	CAUSLY, REBECCA A.	10	. MARY E.	7
. ROBERT	88,108	CAVELENON, MARGARET	124	. TABITHA J.	147
. SARAH	46	CAVENDER, GERTY	146	. THOMAS D.	79
. TABITHE J.	10	. GERTY CAVENDER	146	CHERRY; CARELINE ROSS	89
. WILLIAM R.	4	. HENRY	146	. CHARLES	113
CARTEE, NELLY ANN	23	CERNE, SARAH	46	. HATTIE RICHARDSON	146
CARTER, ALBERT LEE	141	CHAMBERLAIN, THERESA	16	. MARIA GREEN	113
. ALTHIA JACKSON	84	. WILLIAM J.	90	. PARKER	146
. AMANDA ROSS	45	. WILLIE WILBURN	90	. PATSY	68
. C.F.	84	CHAMBERLIN,		. RICHARD	89
. ELIZABETH	43	. ALLEY JACOBS	72	. TISHY	46
. ESTHER WOODS	25	. WILLIAM E.	72	CHILDERS, BETTY	133
. IDA M.	99	CHAMPION, BELL PARKER	53	. GEORGE E.	83
. JANE	43	JAMES	53	. MARY MAINORD	83
. JEWETT JACKSON	129	CHANDLER, MARY	15	CHINE, R.F.	99
. KATIE	147	CHANEY, BELL	84	CHISM, MARY	18
. LUVENE SIMPSON	93	. BENJAMIN F.	14	CHOAT, SARAH E.	47
. MOLLIE MASSEY	141	. ELLA M. MOORE	102,108	CHRISTESTEN, JOSEPH	3
. NATHAN	45,69,89,129	. JOHN N.	108	MARG. ALISON	3
. SARAH NORMAN	86	. JOHN W.	102	CHROU, LUCINDA T.	40
. WILLIAM C.	25	. KATE BROWN	14	CLACK, MARY JANE	72
. WILLIAM DUDLEY	86	. ROSA	150	CLARK, BETHE	147
. WILLIAM H.	93	CHANNEY, EMMA	150	. FLORENCE OSBURN	70
CASE, ALLIE BROWN	153	CHANNY, BELL	100	. G.W.	53,77,95
. ANNIE LEWIS	100	CHAPMAN, BERDIN	72	. GEORGE	33,81,132
. EDWARD	153	. BERDINE	74	. GEORGE W.	7,9,12,41,47
. ELLEN	37	. H.	83	.	56-57,67-68,79-80,88
. MARGARET HAMPTON	132	. JAMES	57,110	.	92,96,106-108,118-119
. WILLIAM	132	. MARY A. HUNOTT	74	.	125-126,134,141
. WILLIE	100	. NANNEY R. ELLIS	57	. MARGARET SHAY	117
CASTLEBERRY, JANE	42	. TABITHA	110	. MARY	59
. LAURA	153	CHAPPEL, A.W.	77	. MOSE	117
. LAURA JONES	77	NOAH BRANNUM	77	. NANNIE	42
. THOMAS	77	CHARTER,		. NATT	70
CATHERAN, AMANDA	2	. ELIZA BURCHELL	19	. NETTIE	52
CATHRELL, MELVINA	11	. GEORGE W.	19	. SARAH S. PARKER	57

INDEX
(New Madrid, Co., MO. Marriages Vol #2)

CLARKE, ELLA OBANNON	144	. WILLIAM	143	COMPTON, GEORGE	24
. GEORGE W.	116	COBB, ELIZA O.	26	JULIA McGOWAN	24
. JOHN E.	144	COCHRAN, DANIA	30	CONLEY, CHARLES	151
CLARKSON, ALFORD	11	. MARY E. ORR	75	. ELIZA LOGAN	151
PHEBE OGDEN	11	. W.E.	75	. ELLA	55
CLAY, HENRY	93	COE, HURELEUS	28	CONNELL, FRANCES KING	120
MATTIE GRIMES	93	MINNIE CUNNINGHAM	28	ROBERT LEE	120
CLAYTON, BENJAMIN F.	110	COFFEE, BELL F. MARNEY	97	CONNELLY, J.A.	14
. EMMA THOMPSON	110	JOHN	97	. LOO	12
. FOSTER	124	COKER, IRENE C.	1	. MARY McDONOUGH	11
. HANNAH	15	COLBURN, DORA	120	. RICHARD	11
. JAMES B.	51	COLE, BEULA A.	132	CONNER,	
. JAMES M.	37	. F.A.	132	. FLORENCE BURTON	117
. JENNY LIGON	51	. M.E.	132	. W.A.	119
. KATY MINNER	37	COLEMAN, ANGELINE	62	. WILLIE	117
. MARY SHELBY	124	. ANGELINE MIDGETT	8	CONNOLLY, J.A.	10,13,16
. ROBERT	149	. ANNA RANSBURGH	108	CONNOR, BELL	60
. SUSIE RILEY	149	. GEORGE W.	68	. JOHN L.	53
CLEMENS, MATTY	65	. HARVEY	90	. MINERVA SLOAS	53
CLEMENT, JOHN W.	86	. J.J.	8	. SALLY	47
NANCY McCORMIC	86	. LOUISA MITCHELL	90	. SELENA B. DARNELL	9
CLEMENTS, T.W.	62	. MORLEY	8	. THOMAS M.	9
CLEMON, T.W.	38	. TENNESSEE MAXEY	68	CONRAD, ALEMEN	68
CLEMONS, MOLLIE	32	. WILLIAM M.	108	. GEORGE W.	58
. T.M.	43	COLMAN,		. HENRY	103
. T.W.	44	. MISSOURI LUMPKIN	118	. IDA	62
CLIMMONS, LAURA	105	. STEPHEN L.	118	. JEFFERSON	68
CLINE, ADDY MURPHY	131	COLSON,		. MARY M. BALDWIN	103
. HENRY	79	. CAROLINE JOHNSON	80	. MATT J.A.	89
. LENA KLEIN	79	. JOHN W.	7,24,80	. TEARESA HOWARD	58
. THOMAS S.	131	. MARY FARMER	24	CONRADE,	
COATS, CAROLINE WAYDE	143	. NANCY E. BEARD	9	. HATTIE WATSON	145
. CATHERINE	127	. ROBERT F.	9	. JOHN C.	145
. CELA MACKE	138	. SAMANTHA ROBERSON	7	CONRAN, MATT J.A.	88,91
. JOHN	127	COLULE, MATTIE	152	. MATT J.C.	86
. JOHN H.	138	COMBS, MARY S.Q.	2	. SALLIE	6
. SARAH	4	COMER, BARBERRY FULLER	85	CONSTANT, CORDELIA	142
. VIOLA	125	JOHN	85	. KATY GRAHAM	149

INDEX
(New Madrid, Co., MO. Marriages Vol #2)

. LEE	149	. MINERVA MOODY	12	MARY STRATTON	61
COOK, ABEL D.	1	. VIRGINIA HANCOCK	62	CRAIG, CENE	102
. ADENE E.	82	COPELAND, MARGRETT	87	. ELIZA GUTHRIE	99
. CEINDA MANION	113	COPS, MARTIN	14	. J.L.	99
. ELIZABETH	70	CORBETT, GEORGE	3	. SUSAN	93
. ELLA DELASHMUTH	123	SARAH SHULTZ	3	. WILLIAM B.	99
. HARRIET	66	CORBIN, KATY	136	CRAMON, ARSULA	94
. JO	10	CORNALL, J.A.	32	CRASHARD, MARY	110
. JOE	34,37	LUCY RILEY	32	CRATER, LUCINDA DAVIS	18
. JOEL	2,4,6-8,10,14	CORNWELL, ALICE	122	WILLIAM	18
.	17-20,23-24-25,27,30	BECKY	121	CRAVENS, ALFRED W.	106
.	32,37,39-40,42,44-45	CORSKY, F.C.	83	. CORA MAULSBY	106
.	47,50,57,59,63-64,92	COSBY, JOSEPHINE	75	. LETITIA	66
.	93,95,97,101,104,106	COTTON, ANNETTA	15	. MARY ETTA	61
.	108,111-116,120-121	COUNTS,		CRAWFORD,	
.	123,125-130,134-135	. CORNELIA BELLON	114	. ELIZABETH JONES	4
.	136-144,146-149,151	. WILLIAM	132	. JAMES	4
.	152-153	. WILLIAM H.	114	. LELIA P.	24
. JOHN	112	COURTNEY,		. MAME	119
. MOEL	26	. ELIZA WALDROP	83	CRAWSHAW, MARY	97
. SARAH UNDERWOOD	10	. FRANKLIN P.	83	CREASON, JAMES	99
. WILLIAM H.	113	COUSINS,		MATTIE L. MANGUM	99
. WILLIAM M.	123	. FLORENCE GEORGE	85	CRESAP, BELL NEWTON	48
. ZELIA PATTERSON	112	. KEULLEN	85	JOSEPH A.	48
COOKE, JOEL	51,54	COX, ALVEY	117	CREVISIEUR, EDWARD	5
JOHN	26	. CORDELIA	139	REBECCA DOCKERY	5
COOKSY, T.C.	85,88	. FRANKLIN	116	CREVOISIER,	
COOLEY, MATTIE	31	. M.C.	22,27,32,36,46-47	. ADALINE MEATT	112
COON, GEARY W.	140	. MARTIN	40	. ADOLPH	112
GEORGIA RICHARDSON	140	. SARAH SIMPSON	116	. ELLEN	89
COOPER, BERL	65	. W.C.	65	. MARY SMITH	112
. DANIEL S.	47	CRABTREE, CLARA	18	. ROBERT F.	112
. ELIZABETH SHUMAKER	47	. MARY	18,82	CREVOISIEUR, AUGUSTUS	3
. ISA	86	. MOLLIE MEATTE	150	CRISEL, HERMAN	103
. ISAAC C.	62	. S.S.	82	. LAURA	139
. JOHN	12	. SAMUEL	18,82,150	. MARY TRAMMELL	103
. MARY E. SETTLE	65	. SAMUEL A.	150	CROCKETT, ELIZABETH	39
. MINERVA	64	CRAFTON, GEORGE W.	61	. JOHN	67

INDEX
(New Madrid, Co., MO. Marriages Vol #2)

. MOLLIE WALKER	67	CUNNINGHAM, FATHY	109	DAMON, ANGALOW	110
CRONAN,		. JAMES H.	3	. ANGELINE	84,120
. IDA MARY YOUNG	123	. JOSEPH	3	. CLEMENTINE RAMATTER	84
. JAMES W.	123	. JOSEPH J.	23	. IDA	110
CROW, A.B.	71	. JOSEPHINE	81	. MARY ADAMS	127
. B.B.	56	. MALESSA	81	. MATTIE HUNTER	120
. BASIL B.	71	. MARY	9	. OWEN	84,120,127
. ELIZABETH CROCKETT	39	. MINNIE	28	DANIELS, JAMES P.	4
. JOHN M.	139	. MOLLIE	91	. JANE	11
. LUCINDA T.	40	. NELLY ANN CARTEE	23	. MARY E. DAVIS	4
. PERMINCE J. SIMMONS	71	. REBECCA	9	. S.A.L. CADE	39
. SARAH J. MARTIN	56	. REBECCA HOUSELE	3	. WILLIAM	39
. THOMAS B.	56	CUPP, ANDREW J.	93	DAPRON,	
. WILLIAM H.	39	. ELLEN HELMS	93	. JOSAPHINE EWING	22
CROWDER, ALSY JOHNSON	41	. LEUMEL	38	. OSCAR	22
. C.C.	35	. MARY ORRALL	38	DARK, FANNY ADAMS	142
. KANE	41	. RUFES	87	. JOSEPH	142
. SUSIE	92	. SARAH A.	97	. LOUIS	3
CROWE, JOHN M.	124	. SARAH HOLLOWAY	87	. SOPHIA	142
CROWNSHAW, EASTER	86	CURDY, SARAH BUTLER	132	DARNALL, MARTHA	23
CROWSHAW, MARY J.	86	SID	132	DARNELL, GAYLE L.	47
CRUCHON, DAVID J.	89	CURFORD, IDA	126	. SALLY CONNOR	47
LIZZIE HENZE	89	CURLEY, CAROLINE	29	. SELENA B.	9
CRUMP, BENITA DOWNING	64	. ELIZABETH THOMPSON	32	DASSETT, ELIZABETH	62
. GIRUMB	64	. F.H.	32	DATIEE,	
. JENNIE	64	CURR, LAURA	103	. MARY MASONVILLE	13
CRUMPLER, A.B.	123	CURRY, GLEEN	22	. PETER	13
	128-131	CURTIS, A.J.	123	DAUGHERTY, DABNEYM.	34
CULAT, CHINNEY	113	. J.A.	94,96	. JOSEPH	39
CULBERTSON, ELMINA	22	. J.F. 80,83-84,90,96,98		. SAMANTHA GRAY	34
CULLION, JAMES R.	148	.	102,125-126	. SARAH FLETCHER	39
LUCINDA ENGLAND	148	. L.F.	119	DAUGHTERY, SYLVIA	50
CUMINGHAM, HENRY	109	. L.T.	122	DAVIDSON, ALMEDA KELLY	96
CUMMINGHAM,		CUTLER,		. AMANDA KELLY	95
. CHARLES W.	115	. FLORINDA PASQUIN	3	. CHARLES W.	95-96
. MARY BURGESS	115	. MANUEL	3	. ELIZA	115
. MAY BURGESS	115	DALLAS, HENRY	142	DAVIS, ADA	102
CUNINGHAM, LUCY	27	KITTY HAMPTON	142	. ADA PHILABAR	150

INDEX
(New Madrid, Co., MO. Marriages Vol #2)

Name	Page	Name	Page	Name	Page
. ALBERT	135	. MAGGIE	116	. JULIA	7
. ALBERT S.	49	. MARIAH	63	. LENA	1
. AMANDA	46,117	. MARTHA ENLOW	67	. MARIAH HOWARD	32
. AMERICA STEIMAN	2	. MARTHA HINSHAW	114	. MARY L.	10
. ANDREW	106	. MARY	131-132	. NANCY	85
. B.F.	67	. MARY ANN WATERS	47	. NANCY MIZELL	85
. CARRIE DAWSON	49	. MARY DUNN	138	. WASH	85
. COLA	78	. MARY E.	4	. WILLIAM	1
. CORA	48	. MAVIS	132	DAY,BELL	105
. DIXIE	140	. MINNIE	100	. HATTIE	76
. E.T.	13	. MOLLY BROWN	135	. MINNIE PARKER	130
. EDGAR	138	. MORRIS	45	. WILLIAM	130
. ELIZA	34	. NANIE	133	DAZAN,HARRIET L.	30
. ELIZA DAVIS	34	. NELSON	1	DEAN,AMANDA BARNHART	133
. ELIZABETH	10,50	. NEWTON	24	. DORA PEELER	153
. ELLA	46	. PEGGY	25,92	. GEORGE F.	133
. ELLEN FLETCHER	106	. ROBERT	34	. JIMMY	74
. ELZA	146	. SALLIE	142	. MARY C.	87
. EMMALINE	84	. SARAH	105	. SALLY	58
. EVA	45	. SARAH E. JONT	152	. SAMUEL	153
. FRANK	57	. STEPHEN A.	47	. SARAH A.	133
. G.W.	20	. SUSAN	151	DEAS,IDA	86
. GEORGE	5	. SUSAN A. MORRIS	1	DEBOE,W.J.	33
. H.	18	. SUSY	24	DEBRE,MARY E. KELLY	127
. HARDIN	100	. THOMAS	150	WILLIE E.	127
. HARRIET MUDD	24	. VINA A.	7	DEES,ADA	75
. HETTIE FISHER	102	. WILLIAM D.	114	. ADALINE	146
. JAIN	108	DAWSON,BETTIE ELLIS	105	. ADRIAN	73
. JAMES	152	. CARRIE	49	. IDA	76
. JOHN	2	. CHARLES E.	85	DEFIELDS,	
. JOHN A.	46	. CLAY W.	105	. ANNIE L. WEBB	144
. JOSEPH	102	. ELIZA	14,31	. CLARENCE S.	144
. LAURA K.	35	. ELLA	134	. DAVID	144
. LIZZIE	43	. ELLA H. HUNTER	1	DEITMORE,NANCY	10
. LOTTIE	83	. FRANCES	85	DELASHMUTH,ELLA	123
. LOU	81	. G.W.	6	DELISLE,ALFRED	64
. LUCINDA	18	. GEORGE W.	32	. ALPHONSE	15
. LUCY	29	. JENNIE	6	. AMELIA	10

INDEX
(New Madrid, Co., MO. Marriages Vol #2)

. ANDREW	49	DENBOW, E.J.	89	DICKERSON,	
. ANNA TOMISOON	60	. J.W.	89	. PAMELA WILLIS	53
. COLUMBUS	7	. W.J.	28	. SAMUEL	53
. COLUMBUS B.	60	DENHART,	27	DICKSON, GEORGE	136
. ELLA	114	. SARAH W.	20	KATY CORBIN	136
. EMMA LESIEUR	70	. WILLIAM J.	1-5,10-12	DIGGES, THOMAS HENRY	6
. FRANCIS LESIEUR	124	. 18-19,21-23,26,28,34		DIGMAN, ANNA RATCLIFF	148
. IDA WOOD	16	DENNIS, BETTY BUCHANAN	48	JOHN	148
. JAMES E.	124	HESEKIAH	48	DILLARD, AMANDA HOGAN	41
. JESSE	70	DENSORY, JULIA	73	. JAMES	20,61
. JONOT	151	DENTON, WILLIAM J.	2	. MALBERRY	20
. KATIE BLOOMFIELD	151	DEPRO, LEONA	15	. MARTHA	61
. LAVALLE	60	DEPROW, JOSEPH	64	. NAOMIA	52
. LIZZIE STONE	64	. LAURA	9	. WILLIAM H.	41
. MARY	49	. MARY STURGEON	64	DIRSEY, LUCINDA	37
. MARY CARSON	60	DEROCHER, LENA	6	DISMINEY, TINIE	145
. MARY DELISLE	49	DETIE, ANDREW	142	DIVINNY,	
. MODEST MEATTE	15	. CLARA HANKS	118	. ELIZA STONEBRAKER	61
. OLIVE	16	. HENRY	118	. JAMES R.	61
. PARALEE	16	. JOHN	115	DIXON, ARTHUR	110
. SARAH MITCHEL	7	. LAURA	142	. CORDELIA RICHARDS	110
DELL, DANIEL	131	. MARY E.	108	. GREER	26
. DELLA GIBBS	131	. SALLIE ALEXANDER	115	. MARTHA TRIGNED	26
. MARGARET ELIZABETH	131	DEVERS, JAMES	39	DOBBINS, FANNY HOLE	149
DELMAN, LUTHER B.	4	REBECCA HARNEY	39	WILLIAM	149
MARY L. HATCHER	4	DEVINNEY, C.C.	17	DOCKERY, BEN	92
DELURY, ANN ALLEN	12	C.E.	10,15-16	. CHARLES	134
THOMAS	12	DEWBERRY, MARY	108	. FLORENCE RAINWATER	99
DEMENT, A.J.	36	DEWEN, ADA E.	3	. J.B.	3
ANNA J. HILL	36	DEWITT, H.Y.	89	. J.M.	71,73,76,84,89
DEMINT, GEORGE W.	137	. JERRY L.	21	.	134
. MARTHA J.	11	. KATIE SHELBY	21	. J.W.M.	10
. MATTIE ADKERSON	137	. LILLIE SIGGERS	153	. JAMES M.	3-5,7,13-14
. SARAH	8	. M.L. McDOWELL	89	.	16-18,20-21
DEMPSEY, IDA	117	. MOSES R.	153	. JOHN D.	114
JAMES	117	. SALLIE	109	. MARY ANDERSON	114
DENAZIER, JHN B.	12	DIBBREL, GEORGE	43	. MARY ROBBINS	134
MARY ASH	12	JANE CARTER	43	. REBECCA	5

INDEX
(New Madrid, Co., MO. Marriages Vol #2)

Name	Page	Name	Page	Name	Page
. ROBERT	99	PRESS BROWN	51	DUKE,EMMA JOHNSON	71
. ROSA LEGRAND	92	DOW,ANNIE	94	. H.H.	71
DOCKING,JAMES M.	26	. CARRY	50	. MAY	136
DODD,JAMES H.	91	. JENNIE WILSON	81	DUNHAM,DELELAH WATSON	89
MARY McCONNELL	91	. MARTIN	81	LEVI	89
DODSON,BETHE CLARK	147	DOWDY,CROCKET	7	DUNKLIN,ADALE	60
. BULAH HYLES	152	. HENRY	108	. AMANDA	49
. ELIZABETH HART	48	. IDA PETTIE	74	. ANNA KEELER	36
. JAMES A.	147	. JAIN DAVIS	108	. ARCHY	38
. MARY F. POE	67	. JAMES H.	74	. AUBY	37
. W.J.	48	. MARY A. JULIEN	7	. BETTIE	6
. WALTER	152	. MISSOURI	84	. BIAS	33,36
. WILLIAM J.	67	. NANCY E.	49	. DANIEL	49,73
DOHERTY,JOHN D.	134-135	DOWNING,BENITA	64	. FRANCIS BOWERS	73
DONAHUE,ALGERONON	96	. CULLEN	37-38,55,68	. GEORGE W.	6
LAURA MOORE	96	. CULLIN	5,33	. JOHN	40
DONAVAN,MARY	2	. E.L.D.	137	. MARTHA WOODS	40
DOOD,ELLA	102	. E.L.D.C.	132	. MARTIN T.	36
DOODS,J.H.	81	DOWNS,DAVID	7	. MARY LATIMORE	6
MARGAT RATLIFF	81	JULIA DAWSON	7	. MATTIE WILLIAMS	33,36
DORCH,JESSIE	43	DOYLE,GEORGE M.	29	. PATSEY HARRIS	37
DORSEY,ALFORD	52	. KATY E. MAULSBY	29	DUNLOP,ANNA LEE	40
. JACK	17	. LELA E.	108	GEORGE	40
. MAGGIE	146	DRAFFIN,BETTE ALLIN	152	DUNN,EDWARD	136
. NETTIE CLARK	52	G.A.	152	. JOHN	104
DORSON,NANCY ANN	21	DRAKE,CORA HAMPTON	141	. LANA BELL	104
DOSS,BURRIS D.	135	. KATIE	128	. MAGGIE	113
. LUCY	99	. KATY LOGAN	68	. MARTHA E.	25
. MARY	90	. ROBERT	141	. MARY	138
. MATTY KELLY	135	. SIDNEY	68	. MARY WESLEY	57
DOTIE,GEORGIA MUNSON	84	DREW,JOHN R.	2	. NANNIE WESLEY	136
JOHN	84	DRIVALL,SARAH	150	. ROSA	114
DOTSON,ANNIE CARROLL	122	DRIVER,AMANDA	108	. SARAH A.	127,129
JOHN	122	DUCKETT,ELIZA	75	. WILLIAM	57
DOUGLAS,JOHN T.	66	MARY LINSON	75	DUROCHER,LILLY	99
. LOUIS	62	DUDLEY,FRANK	12	DUW,MAGGIE	92
. MARY ANN WEAVER	66	VINA HORTON	12	DUYSON,FRITCHES	30
DOUGLASS,LUKE	51	DUFFY,SARAH JANE	63	EACKUS,	

INDEX
(New Madrid, Co., MO. Marriages Vol #2)

Name	Page	Name	Page	Name	Page
. ELIZABETH ALLISON	47	EICEMAN, NORA	95	. MANAH SIMMONS	114
. JAMES	47	ELLDRIDGE, RENA	107	. NANNIE CLARK	42
EAKIN,	43	ELLINGTON, J.W.	141	ENGLE, ROSA LEE	73
EARINGTON, ELIZABETH	52	. MARTHA McMILLAN	45	ENGLISH, MARY	35
EARLE, JULIA KEASTER	12	. WINSTON P.	45	ENLOW, MARTHA	67
SAMUEL J.	12	ELLIOTT, ALONZO	4	ENOCH, W.C.	147
EARLES, JULIA H.	48	ELLIS,	16	ENOCHS, W.C.	143,145
MARIE E.	8	. BETTIE	105	.	147-149,153
EARLEY, MARY M.	75	. ELIZABETH BRANSCOM	7	. W.S.	144
EARLY, CHARLES	78	. ETTA	105	ENSLOW, HELENA McMANN	88
. FRANCIS	59	. FRANCIS K.	40	JOHN W.W.	88
. HARRIET BISHOP	78	. GEORGE	29	ERBY, IRA P.	108
. LOUISA	103	. IDA CARROLL	119	ERVILL, HENRY W.	77
EASLE, ALICE BRADSHAW	22	. JOHN	72,105	LOUISA J. GARRETT	77
AUGUSTUS	22	. KATE	94	ESSARY, CATHERINE	129
EASTWOOD, ARTHUR F.	1	. LIZZIE	46	ESTES, VIOLA	150
MARY H. WATERS	1	. LOUY B.	119	WILLIAM	150
EBY, IRA P.	97,100,136	. MARTHA	29	EUGRAM, ELIZA	21
	141,144	. MARTHA ELLIS	29	EULETT, TISHY	143
ECHORD, ELLEN BRENT	153	. MARY	39	EVANS, ALFORD	7
HAM.	153	. MARY NEWBAUER	72	. ANNA	32,36
EDMONDSON, ANNA HENSON	59	. NANCY A. BASCOMB	3	. BERTHA ADCOCK	150
. ELIZABETH	6	. NANNEY R.	57	. CATHERINE	78
. ELLEN POTTER	76	. W.W.	45,77,94,96,117	. DUKE	30
. JAMES	76	.	120,136	. EDWARD	107
. JOSEPH RUCK	145	. WILLIAM J.	3,7	. FRANK	150
. TINIE DISMINEY	145	EMLOW, BETTIE	98	. HARRIETT	55
. WILLIAM J.	59	EMORY, JAMES S.	8	. JULIA	120
EDMONSTON, JOHN	59	. KATIE	16	. LOUIVISA HAISLEP	107
EDWARDS, CHARLIE	103	. LELIA	121	. MARTHA	27
. FANNIE SIMIS	103	. MARY FLETCHER	8	. MARTHA TREADWELL	30
. JOSEPH	75	ENGLAND, AMANDA	68	. MARY E. CHATMAN	7
. LENA PALMER	75	. CHARLES W.	114	. MATTIE E. WATSON	63
. MARY E.	69	. CORRINEY MORRIS	94	. WILLIAM E.	63
. MARY E. JONES	21	. GID THOMAS	94	EVANSURLIE, W.	36
. MISSOURI	85	. ISAAC P.	42	EVERETT, ADA SEXTON	144
. W.C.	142,147	. JOSEPH D.	148	. JOSEPH	144
. WILLIAM H.	21	. LUCINDA	148	. LAVENIA BAYNES	9

INDEX
(New Madrid, Co., MO. Marriages Vol #2)

Name	Page	Name	Page	Name	Page
. LAWRENCE	9	. WILLIAM W.	15	. HETTIE	102
EVERHART, LEVI J.	28	FARRELL, MARY CLARK	59	. JENNIE DAWSON	6
. MARY E. HORN	28	. WILLIAM	147	. JOHN J.	31
. SUSAN	43	. WILLIAM J.	59	. MAGGIE ROAN	91
EVINS,		FARRENBURG, ALICE	34	. ROBERT A.	38
. CALONY F. HORNES	83	FARRIE, LOU WATERS	105	. SIDNEY FRAZER	38
. WILLIAM	83	WILLIAM	105	. WILLIAM	64
EWING, A.	40	FAULESS, JAMES R.	72	FISKE, JAMES	56
. ALICE	96	SARAH HODGE	72	LUCY E.	56
. ALICE M.	71	FELPS, JOSEPHINE	57	FITZPATRICK, FANNIE	74
. ANNA B. SHIELDS	54	FERGUSON, BELL McADOO	135	MAURIE	74
. EMELINE	22	JAMES W.	135	FLANNERY, MARGARET	52
. EMMA O.	99	FERREL, MATTY	76	FLARE, MARK	35
. ERVIN A.	6,117	FERRELL,		SARAH L.	35
. IRVIN A.	9,15,19-20,50	. MARY BRADSHAW	121	FLEMING, DANIEL	2
	54,59,61,69,71-72,80	. WILLIAM	121	. JOHN D.	146
	85,103-104	FERRENBERG,		. MARY DONAVAN	2
. IRVIN H.	57	. CHARLES C.	136	FLETCHER, DICK	102
. IRWIN	26,41	. DAVID	108	. ELLEN	106
. IRWIN A.	132	. IDA NEWTON	108	. ELLEN SCIMS	100
. J.A.	50	. MINNIE LYNCH	136	. GEORGE	100
. J.H.	151	FERRENBURG, ALEX	18	. JAMES H.	8
. JOSAPHINE	22	. SARAH BAKER	11	. LUCY LEVY	102
. LIZZIE	128	. WILLIAM A.	11	. MARY	8
. MARY J.	8	FIELDS, FLORENCE PROE	114	. NEELY PORTER	127
. NONA	111	. MARY	144	. SARAH	39
FAILL, W.	21	. N.J.	114	. SUSAN	54
FARMER, A.J.	70	. W.E.	114	. WILLIAM	127
. ALICE NEAL	40	FIGUE, EVA ALEXANDER	73	FLORE, SARAH LIE	35
. ANNIE	132	WILLIAM	73	FLORO, FRANCES	49
. CALVIN	136	FINN, ELIZA ANN	50	. L. ANGELINE MANUS	133
. MARY	24	. ELIZA ANN FINN	50	. MARCUS	10
. MAY WIMP	136	. JAMES E.	50	. RALPH	133
. MINNIE	73	FISH, HENDERSON	143	. TABITHE J. CARSON	10
. SARAH	137	RILLA WATSON	143	FOLEY, HATTIE	76
. W.S.	129,141,144-145	FISHER, CHARLES W.	91	FOLKS, SUSAN BAKER	64
	151,153	. FANY LEWIS	31	WILLIAM	64
. WILLIAM H.	40	. GEORGE W.	6	FONTAINE,	

INDEX
(New Madrid, Co., MO. Marriages Vol #2)

Name	Page	Name	Page	Name	Page
. MATTY E. HALL	36	. LEALA	63	. KITTY	127
. THOMAS J.	36	. LENA SHELTON	33	. LOUISA E.	70
FORD, ANES INMAN	141	. SALLIE	151	. MAGGIE DAVIS	116
. ELIZABETH	11	. SALLIE HAMPTON	97	. MARY	116
. HENRY C.	141	. THOMAS	91	. MARY E.	118
. HENRY H.	93	. TOM	97	. ROBERT	116
. LEWANDA MOOREHEAD	93	FOXE, NELLY SMITH	49	FUGATE, CARRIE GIBSON	88
. LUCINDA	120	UPTON B.	49	JOHN	88
. M.T.	120	FOY, JAMES M.	11	FULL, W.	27
. MAGGIE A.	64	MARTHA J. DEMINT	11	WEBSTER	22-23,33,61,63
. MARY E.	12,18	FRANCIS, MELINDA	96	FULLER, BARBERRY	85
. POWELL	26	FRANKLIN, HENRY	76	THERESA	47
. REANIE	111	. MARIAH LAY	138	FURGESON, CARROL D.	144
. SUSAN	108	. MISSOURI SCOTT	76	. LULA NEEL	144
FORDE, ANISE	154	. ROSA	145	. MARY HANDY	119
ELIZA	52	. THOMAS	138	. WILLIAM F.	119
FORE, LENA V.	57	FRANSO, KATIE	83	FURLONG, JAMES	101,115
FOREST,		FRAZER, ELIZA PAXTON	97	.	128
. CATHARINE MITCHELL	5	. ROBERT	38,97	. JAMES J.	105,111,114
. CHARLES	5	. SIDNEY	38	.	124,133,138,146-147
. MARTHA	112	FRAZIER,		.	151
. S.M.	112	. CARRIE STEWART	86	. LEVENA	29
FORKS, EMELIA BEAVERS	134	. ELIZA	125	. NANCY	57
JAMES	134	. JAMES A.	86	GADDIE, ELMIRE	126
FORSYTHE, AMELIA	91	. R.B.	38	GAINGNE, PLASELDIN	8
FORTEST, ALBERT D.	46	. ROBERT	29	GALLAGHER, JAMES	9
SARAH A. MOTE	46	FREEMAN, HARRIET MUDD	54	MARGARET PAXTON	9
FOSTER, ALICE	11	. JAMES	54	GALLANT, MINNIE FARMER	73
ELIZA B.	54	. MARGARET TERRY	126	W.M.	73
FOUNTAIN, STELLA	19	. OLIVE	126	GALLOWAY, AMBROSE	105
FOUST, EMMA	26	FRENSO, KATY	149	BELL DAY	105
FOWLER, MATTIE	88	FREY, NAPOLEON	2	GAMBLE, ALFRED	89
FOWNS, ASALEE MORRIS	58	FRISKE, LINDA	73	. ANIE	86
BERRY	58	FROST, NELLIE	132	. JOHN	100
FOX, AMANDA	115	FROWHALK, JOHN S.	85	. MARY BARTLETT	100
. AMANDA JACKSON	91	MISSOURI EDWARDS	85	. MARY J. GRIFFY	89
. FRANCIS	152	FRY, BOB	116	GANT, CORDA M.	151
. JEFF	33	. GAKE	116	GARDEN, S.C. HOGWOOD	32

INDEX
(New Madrid, Co., MO. Marriages Vol #2)

Z.T.	32	. MOLLIE	35	GITTON,MARGARET		42
GARNED,L.J.	28	. NANCY	45	GLASS,MARY		123
GARNER,		. SARAH O. WYATT	55	GLEUCK,CHRISOPHER		138
. BEATRICE WILES	118	GIDEON,D.W.	66	THERSIA		138
. JAMES	118	GILBERT,HENRIETTA	59	GLISSON,MELA McLENNON		71
GARRETT,LOUISA J.	77	. JENNIE RALSTON	24	ROBERT		71
GARRISON,		. JOHN H.	144	GLOVER,		9
. CHINCY HARRISON	87	. LIZZIE PREWITT	72	NANCY		9
. ISACK	87	. MARTHA	51	GLUECK,CHRIS		75
GARTNEY,ED	34	. MARY FIELDS	144	MARY M. EARLEY		75
EM. C. MOORE	34	. WILLIAM	24	GODAIR,ADOLPHUS		9
GARTON,JOHN	18	. WILLIAM H.	72	. ALFRED		76
GASPETH,ROSALEE	104	GILBOW,ALFRED	71	. ANDREW		3,18,89
GASSET,JOHN	82	. JENNIE PENROD	140	. AUGUSTUS		5
GASSETT,JAMES A.	137	. LUTHER	66,119,140	. CHRISTINE LESSIEUR		5
. MARY WADDELL	137	. SALLIE LAWS	119	. JANIEVE		18
. ROSA BELL	147	. VICTORIA ARBUCKLE	21	. LAURA DEPROW		9
GAY,SILVIA	7	. WILLIAM	21	. LUCINDA		133
GEEHAM,JOSEPH	12	GILLBRITH,SARAH	135	. LUCY		36
LOO CONNELLY	12	GILLIAN,JOHN W.	131	. LUCY GODAIR		36
GEHEN,LINDA SECOY	114	TILDA GILLS	131	. MARY		18
THOMAS	114	GILLMAN,W.D.	70	. MARY E. NICHOLAS		3
GENRTY,JAMES	63	GILLS,HENRY	92	. ROBERT		36
RILLIE PEARIE	63	. PEGGY DAVIS	92	. ROSETTA McWILLIAMS		76
GENTRY,AMY CALDWELL	87	. TILDA	131	. SIDNEY		21
. JAMES L.	15,87	GILMORE,BETTIE	27	. TEREASY		13
. VIOLA G. BUSBY	15	. BETTY	34	GODAIRD,ELIZAH		60
GEORGE,FLORENCE	85	. FIDELLA HOLDNEARY	148	GODARD,EMMA WARD		60
GIBBIN,MARY J.	13	. ROBERT F.	148	. LUCINA		102
GIBBS,DELLA	131	GINY,HATTIE	41	. ROBERT L.		60
LILIE	124	GIRVIN,		. VELMA		137
GIBONY,LILLY	66	. CAREY M. WILEY	142	GODIAR,MAGGIE BURNY		53
GIBSON,CARRIE	88	. EMMA	90	VALLEE		53
. FRANK	33	. FLORENCE MORRISON	82	GODWIN,M.J.		100
. JAMES	33	. J.G.	82	MAGGIE		100
. LAFAYETTE	55	. JOHN L.	115	GOINS,HESTER		53
. MARY I. LANDERS	33	. MARY J.	115	GOLD,DRUZILA WARD		44
. MARY M. PETTY	33	. WARWELL C.	142	JAMES A.		44

INDEX
(New Madrid, Co., MO. Marriages Vol #2)

Name	Page	Name	Page	Name	Page
GOLDEN, MARY JUDY	124	. NANCY J.	106	. W.J.	43
. SIMEON	44	. SARAH SNIDER	45	. WILLIAM ALEXANDER	54
. SIMON	124	GRAVES, DORA	39	. WILLIAM RICHARD	112
. SUSAN EVERHART	43	. ISAAC	38	GREEN, ALICE CORNWELL	122
. WILLIAM H.	43	. LEVERNA PORTER	38	. ANNA WESLEY	121
GOLDON, SIMEON	45	GRAVIS, JOSEPH A.	25	. CHARLES	50,70
GOODIN, ALVIN	14	GRAW, C.J.	69	. CORNELIA KELLY	59
. JENNIE HEMPSTEAD	14	NARCISSUS	69	. EVERLINER WATERS	80
. MAUDE	15	GRAY, ANTONETTE	11	. GENNIS	86
GOODLIN, JACOB	84	. EDWARD	153	. HARRY B.	128
GOODMAN, JOHN	115	. ELIZA B. FOSTER	54	. HENRY T.	134
ROSA	83	. ELLA	63	. JOHN	122
GORDON, JOHN H.	22	. FLORENCE	36	. JORDAN	11
VICK WATERS	22	. GEORGE W.	56	. KITTEY WHITE	11
GORTON, JOHN	20	. JAMES	67	. LAURA JOHNSON	134
GOSSETT, ALICE	19	. JAMES F.	148	. LAURA MITCHELL	153
. ELLEN	21	. JINNY	137	. MAJOR	80,153
. MARTHA E. MOODY	21	. JINNY GRAY	137	. MARIA	113
. WILLIAM A.	21	. JOE	109	. MARIE LAFORGE	128
GOTH, JOHN W.M.	129	. JOHN	96	. MINNIE	116
LULA MOORE	129	. JOHN R.	9	. MISSIE RENFOE	86
GOWER, DAVID J.F.	139	. JOHN W.	43	. PETTIE SNOW	70
MARTHA E. JONES	139	. LIZZIE DAVIS	43	. SAMUEL	121
GRAHAM, AMELIA WALLS	13	. LIZZIE LEMONS	112	. SARAH	96
. ANNA	1	. LOTTY PORTER	67	. SARAH BLIZZARD	50
. ANNY	23	. LUCINDA NICHOLAS	145	. WILLIAM A.	59
. EDWARD	89	. LUCY E. FISKE	56	GREENWOOD, CHARLES	116
. ELLA	119	. MARY F.	1	MAGGIE MARTIN	116
. FRANCIS	67	. MARY HOWARD	153	GREER, HESTER	142
. JAMES	92	. MELINDA	25	. JOHN T.	103
. JENNY JORDIN	89	. MINNIE HENDRICKS	96	. LAURA PHELON	103
. KATY	149	. REEDER	137	GREGORY,	
. ROBERT	13	. ROBERT LEE	145	. LIZZIE HAMPTON	151
. SUSAN DAVIS	151	. ROSA BANKS	148	. MOLLIE REED	20
. SUSIE CROWDER	92	. SAMANTHA	34	. REBECCA	20
. WILLIAM	38,68,78,147	. SAMANTHA SUTTON	9	. REBECCA GREGORY	20
	151	. SETH W.	25	. SUSAN	5
GRANT, CHARLES	45	. VINA	4	. WESLEY	20

175

INDEX
(New Madrid, Co., MO. Marriages Vol #2)

Name	Page	Name	Page	Name	Page
. WILLIAM	20,151	GUTDRIDGE, JULIA	55	. MOLLIE CARROLL	44
GRIFFEN, ALEX	135	GUTHRIDGE, JULIA M.	55	. NANCY MISSOURI	120
. ELIZA WALKER	135	GUTHRIE, ELIZA	99	. NELLIE	67
. NEWTON	86	GUY, SYLVA	56	. SARAH	44
GRIFFEY, MOLLIE	126	HAAS, A.	34	. WILLIAM	44
GRIFFITH, NEWTON	3	ELLA SLAYTON	34	HALLIBURTON,	
GRIFFY, MARY J.	89	HACKNEY, BART	47	. LECRETIA KEITH	75
GRIMES, ALFRED GILBOW	71	CORNELIA WILSON	47	. M.J.	75
. HENRY	71	HADEN, PERNELIA J.	11	HAM, JESSIE L.	150
. MATTIE	30,93	HADSON, ANCIE D. HALL	33	VIOLA ESTES	150
GRIMUS, SHIRIRK	18	E.J.	33	HAMBURGER, HOSIA	63
GROSS, CAROLINE	4	HAGGENS, JOHN W.	144	. MATTIE HOLMES	63
. FRED E.	135	MARGARET MASSEY	144	. ROBERT	63
. PEAL E. SHIDETER	135	HAISLEP, LOUIVISA	107	HAMILTON, ALEX	24
GROVER, JOHN	10	HALE, EMMER BLEDSOE	90	MATTIE	22,24
REBECCA A. CAUSLY	10	. JOHN	132	HAMPTON, AMANDA	3
GROVES, CORA	46	. MADISON	57	. CORA	141
GROVIS, SARAH A.A.	25	. MARTHA	132	. ELLA	67
GRUBB, GEORGE W.	125	. ROBERT	90	. EMMA	89
. MARY	122	HALERY, JOE M.	40	. GEORGE	150
. SALLIE McDONALD	125	. LUCINDA T. CHROU	40	. HARRIETT	7
GRUBS, MARY E.	82	. LUCINDA T. CROW	40	. HATTY ALDRIDGE	153
GRUN, CAROLINE	126	HALL, ALBERT	128	. HENRY	151
GUINN, MITTIE	150	. ALICE	41	. IKE	79
GUITON, MARY	72	. ANCIE D.	33	. ISAAC	77,89
GULION, AMANDA J. NEILL	7	. ATLAS	11	. J. LEE	153
. JEREMIAH	7	. BETTIE TONEY	11	. JOSEPHINE	57
. SUSAN F.	9	. BETTY BEAVERS	51	. KITTY	79,142
GUNLIS, MARY A.	128	. CHARLES	114,120	. LAURA	101
GUNN, IDA	93	. HENRY	51	. LAURA WALKER	151
WILLIAM J.	93	. JENNIE	14	. LIZZIE	151
GURLEY, JAMES R.	123	. JOHN	112	. LORENA ALLEN	35
MAGGY HOLMES	123	. JULIUS	140	. LOUISE	57
GURR, JENNIE	19	. KATHY RAIDT	112	. MARGARET	132
JOHN	19	. KATIE DRAKE	128	. MARY	77
GURTEY,		. MARY MAYS	114	. MITTIE GUINN	150
. ISABEL ROBBERTS	66	. MATTIE WILLIS	140	. NANCY	29
. JOHN H.	66	. MATTY E.	36	. SALLIE	97

INDEX
(New Madrid, Co., MO. Marriages Vol #2)

Name	Page	Name	Page	Name	Page
. SALLY	13	. SUSSANA WHITEHEAD	137	. MINTY BOTTON	91
. SAM	13	. TOLIVER	137	. MOLLY	143
. WADE	35	HARLAN, C.C.	44	. NANCY M. BUSBY	16
HANCOCK, A.E.	16	HARLAND, NEHEMEAH	23	. PATSEY	37
. LOUISE	62	REBECCA BROOKS	23	. PATSY	93
. VIRGINIA	62	HARNER, NANCY	39	. ROBERT	91
HANDY,	5	HARNEY, REBECCA	39	. ROBERT D.	147
. MARY	119	HARNISCH, F.A.	8	. THOMS	43
. NOAH	14	MOLLIE MURPHY	8	. WILLIAM	37
HANES, JOSEPH A.	151	HARNS, FRANK	88	HARRISON, A.A.	139
LIZZIE A. TAYLOR	151	MELIE JONES	88	. CARRY	46
HANESWORTH, HENRY	4	HARPER, MALINDA J. REED	1	. CHARLES SAMUEL	141
HANEY, HENRY C.	66	WILLIAM Y.	1	. CHINCY	87
MODEST MASONVILLE	66	HARRELL, JOHN	137	. GEORGE W.	141
HANIPHAN, ARLEE WILLIS	37	. LISSIE KNIGHT	137	. HELEN BRANHAM	141
JOHN	37	. MARY	29	. JUNIOR SCOTT	44
HANKS, CLARA	118	HARRIS, ADA DEES	75	. KATIE F. BRADY	44
HANNER, JENNIE	134	. ADELIA BRANNUM	147	. SQUIRE	46
HANY, FANNY	34	. ALEX	66	HART, BEN	96
HAPPY, MARY L.	94	. AMELSON	93	. E.J.T.	142
HARBOLD, FRANK	55	. C.H.	7-8,15-16,18-19	. ELIZABETH	48
LELIA REEDER	55	. C.M.	16	. IDA C.	152
HARBURG, S.	109	. CATHARINE	95	. JOHN	42
HARDEN, JOHN	72	. CHRISTOPHER M.	59	. LUCINDA WATERS	96
. MARY ANN	44	. ELIZA	62	. M.	66,74,76,78-79,85
. MARY JANE CLACK	72	. ELIZA MERRETT	41	. MARTIN	68
. MELINDA LAY	13	. ELLEN CASE	37	HARVER,	12
. WALTER	13	. FRANCIS EARLY	59	HARVEY, LOUIS F.	23
HARDIN, EMMALINE DAVIS	84	. HARRIET COOK	66	ROSANA RILEFORD	23
. LEE	112	. HENRY	41	HAST, M.	72
. LULA	125	. HENRY R.	115	HATCHEL, MARGIE	34
. MARTHA FOREST	112	. HITA	16	HATCHER, MARY L.	4
. MARY	53	. JOHN R.	75	HATCHLEY, JAMES	7
. MELINDA	92	. LINDA BRATTON	93	MARY E. THURMON	7
. WALTER	84	. MANDY	146	HATHWICK, C.B.	79
HARDON, ABRAHAM	121	. MARY E.	68	MARTHA BURGESS	79
LUCY	121	. MARY J. GIRVIN	115	HATTEN, ALICIA VETILE	103
HARDY,		. MATTIE HENDERSON	43	FRANCIS W.	103

INDEX
(New Madrid, Co., MO. Marriages Vol #2)

HAWKINS, J.G.	151	H.E. JOHNSON	64	THOMAS J.	66
. J.N.	9-10	HELM, KATIE	106	HENRY, ALICE M. EWING	71
. JENNIE HANNER	134	M.I.	51	. BETTIE	100
. MAGGIE J. HAY	33	HELMS,	23	. DENNIS	128
. WILLIAM	33,134	ELLEN	93	. DENNIS C.	71
HAWLEY, JOHN	141	HEMPSTEAD, JENNIE	14	. FRANK	144
MOLLIE MALONE	141	HENCHMAN, C.P.	110	. JAMES	71,97
HAWTHORN, MARTHA LAY	131	HENDERSON,		. JAMES E.	149
OWENS	131	. AMANDA BENNETT	43	. LAURA E. LEE	149
HAY, MAGGIE J.	33	. CARRIE PALMER	143	. LIZZIE EWING	128
MARY E.	43	. CARRIE RANDOLPH	90	. MARY JONTE	144
HAYES, ALICE BOGGS	78	. ELAM	143	. NANCY	11
. BARBARA SOLOMAN	134	. FRANKY WILEY	143	. SARAH A. CUPP	97
. CATHERINE JOHNSON	33	. GEORGE	90,143	. W.W.	73
. CHARLES H.	125	. HARRISON	80	HENSLEY, W.G.	117
. JAMES	78	. IDA NEILL	37	HENSON, ANNA	59
. JANE	128	. J.	80	. G.W.	55
. JOHN	33	. JULIA	29	. HATTIE GINY	41
. LEVINA	20	. MAGGIE	98	. HATTIE TONEY	39
. LULA HARDIN	125	. MARY BROWN	13	. HENRY F.	39,41
. MOLLIE	43	. MATTIE	43	. JOHN J.	105
. PENESE MAYES	54	. PUD	13	. LAURA M.	9
. RALEIGH	6	. SALLY	72	. LELIA EMORY	121
. RICHARD	134	. SAMUEL	43	. LUCY	55,110
. WILLIAM	54	. SHADRACK	37	. LUCY A. PETTY	105
HAYNEY, CHARLES W.	94	. SMITH	14	. NACY F.	121
MARY L. HAPPY	94	. SYLVIA WATSON	75	. W.	82
HEAD, GEORGE W.	3	. WILLIAM	75	. W.C.	137
MARY LAWRENCE	3	HENDRICKS,		. W.G.	23,32,37,49,53,56
HEATH, CHARLES W.	46	. ELMER WILBOURN	106	.	59,63-64,83,87,90,93
ELIZA SETTLES	46	. JAMES	25,106	.	96,102,110,131,137
HEATON, HENRY	10	. MELENY ROBBINS	25	.	145
TILLIE POE	10	. MINNIE	96	HENZE, LIZZIE	89
HECKLE, HENRY	80	. SARAH	7	HERBERT, MAMIE READE	54
J. HENDERSON	80	HENDRIX, CAROLINE	5	WILLIE H.	54
HECTOR, MARY	152	. NANCY J. MEADORS	45	HEREFORD, LENA OAITAIN	61
HEDGE, ANNIE E.	54	. WILLIAM C.	45	WILLIAM	61
HEDGES, GREENUP J.	64	HENLON, ELIZA LAURY	66	HEREITZE,	

INDEX
(New Madrid, Co., MO. Marriages Vol #2)

Name	Page	Name	Page	Name	Page
. ADA SLAUGHTER	127	. KATIE SHULTZ	126	HINSHAW, MARTHA	114
. MAX	127	. MARY HECTOR	152	THOMAS B.	114
HERNDON, BEATRICE	90	. MOLLIE PICKETT	50	HIX, HATTIE	116
ROXANA	90	. PARIELEE JONES	67	. JOHN	52
HEROLDE, ISABEL	24	. WALTER	126	. MARY MOODY	52
HERON, ALICE FOSTER	11	. WALTER B.	67	HOARD, BETTIE DUNKLIN	6
. BENJAMIN	49	. WILLIAM	50	. JOE	85
. JOHN	11	HIGGIN, J.M.	64	. LENA LAFOE	85
. LUE PARKER	49	MARY JANE WOOD	64	. LEWIS	6
HERRING, CHARLES F.	142	HIGGS, JAMES P.	44	HOBS, HENRY G.	57
. LOU	92	SALLIE CALDWELL	44	HODGE, JAMES W.	9
. NANNY LAZELL	142	HILL, ALFRED	13	. JOHN H.	61
HERRON, ADDIE	61	. ANNA J.	36	. MARY J. SHULTZ	61
. ALPHONSO P.	74	. BETTY ALLSUP	39	. ROBERT G.	2
. KATE SCOTT	74	. ELIZABETH ROSS	13	. SARAH	72
. SALLIE	61	. FRANK H.	22	. SARAH BARNHART	9
HESS, BELL	142	. HODA MAINORD	117	. SARAH E. STRONG	2
. GEORGE EDWIN	20	. IDA HENRY	136	HODGES, LAURA	50
. MOLLIE E. REEDER	20	. JAMES H.	39	HOEFMAN, ANNIE	88
HESSLING, JOHN	81	. JAMES M.	81,117,136	SARAH	88
LEE W. BAEHR	81	. LAURA B.	38	HOEHN, JENNIE	148
HICK, DELLA O. BRINE	49	. LELA PARKER	22	. PETER	43-44,48,116-117
THOMAS	49	. LEVY	41	.	122,125-126,131
HICKS, ALECK	83	. LEWIS SAMUEL	143	HOEN, PETER	45
. AMELIA PHELABAR	128	. LOUISE	22	HOGAN, AMANDA	41
. ANNA SISK	135	. MARGARET RAINWATER	41	. BRADFORD	136
. ELIJAH	83	. MARY A. VAUGHN	26	. JENNY	62
. HARRIET	122	. PAULINE ROSS	81	. LIDA NICHOLAS	138
. LOTTIE DAVIS	83	. SALLIE	113	. LOGAN	87
. LOU DAVIS	81	. SALLIE KEITH	104	. LOTTA RITTENHOUSE	136
. MATT	128	. SIAH D.	26	. ROBERT	138
. RICHARD	135	. WILLIAM H.	104	. TEDFORD	97
. SAMUEL	81	HILLIS,		. TELFORD T.	60
. THOMAS	122	. HARRIETT HAMPTON	7	. TILFORD	41
HIGGERSON, ANDREW J.	65	. THOMAS	7	. TILFORD T.	6
. DORA LAPLANT	65	HILLSMAN, GEORGE A.	96	. ZILFORD	31
. JAMES A.	152	RUTH E. POWELL	96	HOGLAN, CHARLES	101
. KATHIE	147	HIND, AMANDA	112	MATTIE McKINEY	101

INDEX
(New Madrid, Co., MO. Marriages Vol #2)

HOGUE, ANNE	111	TONIE	116	. ANNIE	5		
HOGUIS, JOHN W.	97	HONOT, BETTIE	113	. BECKY CORNWELL	121		
MALINDA RIGGS	97	HOOD, NANCY A.	27	. DAVID	121		
HOGWOOD, S.C.	32	HOOPER, SAMUEL	8	. J.H.	8,146		
HOLCLEN, F.M.	37	HOPEL, CHARLES	70,86,126	. JAMES H.	3		
HOLCOMB, EURA	142	. MOLLIE	126	. JENNIE	13		
HOLDEN, A.M.	58	. MOLLIE WATERS	86	. JOHN	30,57		
. ELVALINE	42	HOPKINS, D.E.	9	. JONAH	25		
. F.M.	37-39,41-42,46,48	DAVID	44	. JOSEPH	59		
.	55,58,131	HOPPER, JANIE	117	. LENA DAWSON	1		
. FRANCES	100	HORN, MARY E.	28	. LOTTY PORTER	59		
. J.M.	64	HORNBECK, NANCY	77	. LUKE BYRNE	1		
. JOHN D.	95-96	HORNBERGER,		. MARIAH	32		
. MATILDA	100	. CATHARINE JONES	45	. MARY	153		
. WILLIAM	42	. HOZA	45	. MARY WESLEY	57		
HOLDNEARY, FIDELLA	148	. S.A.	79	. MAY R.	30		
HOLE, FANNY	149	HORNBURGER, HENRY	117	. PATTIE	129		
HOLINSWORTH, LOUISA	93	. HOSEA	124	. TEARESA	58		
HOLLAND, ALICE	125	. IDA DEMPSEY	117	. WILLIAM	57		
. ELIZABETH	13	. MARTHA SHIRKEY	124	HOWE, SALLIE ANN	2		
. W.M.	91	HORNEBURGER, HOSEY	57	HOWELL, W.R.	122		
HOLLINGSWORTH,		NANCY FURLONG	57	HUBBARD, LOUIS	70		
WILLIAM S.	99	HORNER, AMANDA	147	. MAGGIE YOUNG	145		
HOLLOWAY, ALSA POWELL	58	HORNES, CALONY F.	83	. MARY MARTIN	70		
. JAMES	58	WILLIAM	83	. WALTER M.	145		
. SARAH	87	HORTON, A.G.	70,78,80	HUDGENS, J.A.	32		
HOLMAN, HENRY	41,45	. ALBERT G.	67	. LUCY RILEY	32		
HOLMES, AGNES	121	. H.G.	65	. MARGARET C. JONES	17		
. ASA V.	125	. JAMES L.	14	. STEPHEN	17		
. CHARLES W.	29	. SALLIE CABLES	14	HUDGINS,			
. ELLA M. YATES	29	. VINA	12	. JOSEPHINE OAKES	62		
. MAGGY	123	HOTT, HAMILTON	56	. WILLIAM J.	62		
. MATTIE	63	HOUBEN, JENNIE	128	HUDSON, JANIE	128		
. MURY	41	HOUSELE, REBECCA	3	THEO.	109		
. VISEY WELLS	125	HOUSTON, GEORGE W.	10	HUDSPETH, BASE	148		
HOLT, JAMES	138	. LOUISA	12	. C.C.	20,29,33,36,38-40		
MARTHA THOMPSON	138	. LOUISA PARKER	10	.	47,50-52,60,90,97		
HONARD, LIZZIE JONES	116	HOWARD, ALICE CAMPBELL	25	. IDA THOMPSON	148		

INDEX
(New Madrid, Co., MO. Marriages Vol #2)

. JAMES C.	88	. VERRY YOUNG	35	. MARY E. TICKELL	10
. NORA BAYNE	88	HUNTER,ALBERT B.	10,130	. MATTIE	120,128
HUELETT,		. AMANDA McWILLIAMS	81	. NANCY PICKET	118
. LETITIA CRAVENS	66	. ANN	114	. NANNIE	14
. SAMUEL	66	. ANNA BIRD	42	. NEAL	56,79,126
HUFF,MAUD	25	. ANNIE	84	. SALLIE M.	9
HUFFMAN,IDA PHILLIPS	115	. ATLINE JACKSON	126	. SHAPLEY R.	15
. J.C.	138	. CLARRISA	126	. STERLING P.	66
. JOHN	115	. EDA	56	. WASH	126
HUFFORD,		. ELLA H.	1	. WILLIAM	79
. ELIZABETH WEEKS	115	. ELLA PACK	10	. WILLIAM L.	1
. LOUIS	115	. EMMA	134	. ZENIA	80
HUFFSTEDER,JAMES	56	. EULA W.	74	HUNTINGDON,ALEXANDER	115
HUFSTETTER,		. FANNIE FITZPATRICK	74	MARTHA BRANNACK	115
. ELLA GRAHAM	119	. FERG	6	HUNTINGTON,JOHN	146
. JAMES C.	34	. GEORGE T.	42	MANDY HARRIS	146
. NANCY HURLEY	34	. GEORGE Y.	81	HUNTSINGER,ELIZABETH	2
. SAMUEL	119	. H.	24,54-55	HURLEY,	
HUFSTUDLER,		. HENRY	18,23,25,29,31	. METILDA BALDWIN	70
. LINDA LAMB	144	. 35,37-38,42-46,48-49		. NANCY	34
. WILLIAM S.	144	. 50-51,56-57,59-61,63		. WILLIAM H.	70
HUFSTUTTER,LEE	82	. 65-67,70-72,74-75,77		HURLY,AMANDA PIPPEN	149
HUGGINS,MAGGIE	122	. 86,92-94,98,100-101		ROY	149
HUGHES,HENRIETTA	37	. 104-105,109,113,115		HUSK,LULESHER	82
HUMBURGER,		. 123-124,127,131,136		HUSTON,KATIE	115
. ELVALINE HOLDEN	42	. 143,147,151,153		MINTA	29
. WILLIAM D.	42	. HENRY M.	118	HUTCHENS,AMANDA	65
HUMMEL,BELL SHERWOOD	55	. IRENE C. COKER	1	HUTCHENSON,	
JOHN A.	55	. JOHN	114	. CYNTHA VOWELL	51
HUNOT,HAMPTON	92	. JOHN CLAY	10	. JOHN A.	51
. LOUIS	119	. JOHN N.	118	HUTCHINS,LOUISA	141
. REBECCA SEARS	92	. JOHN W.	74	HUTTON,CHARLES C.	146
. SALLIE BROWN	119	. JOSEPH	13,55	MARY JANE JONES	146
HUNOTT,MARY A.	74	. KITTY HAMPTON	79	HYDE,R.T.	105
HUNT,ELLA BARRNETT	116	. L.F.	5,14	HYLES,BULAH	152
. JAMES	116	. LIBBIE BROUGHTON	15	JUNE	152
. LAWSON	35	. LILLY GIBONY	66	IMBODEN,ELIZABETH	1
. MARY	146	. MARY	19,62,79	INGOLD,ADRIAN DEES	73

INDEX
(New Madrid, Co., MO. Marriages Vol #2)

NATHANIEL	73	. JAMES	17	LAURA K. DAVIS	35
INGRAM, EMMA	34	. JANE BRYANT	25	JASPER, H. LEE	87
. JOHN K.	30	. JEWETT	129	. MARY	133
. NELLIE SANDFORD	30	. JOHN	124	. MARY H. BOYCE	87
. NELLIE STANDFORD	30	. JOHN WATT	10	JAYNES,	
INMAN, A.M.	67	. JOSEY	112	. BETTIE J. MALONE	113
. ANES	141	. LAURA	54,81	. JESSIE	113
. JAMES C.	154	. LAURA CASTLEBERRY	153	JEFFREYS, EDWARD	103
. KATIE McCOLUM	154	. LOU	78	JEFFRYS,	
IRBY, IRA P.	148	. MARTHA MORRIS	12	. AMANDA ENGLAND	68
IRVIN, ANNA J.	91	. MARY HARRELL	29	. CHARLES	68
. JAMES	35	. MARY L. DAWSON	10	JENKINS, ANNIE HUNTER	84
. SARAH LIE FLORE	35	. MARY LAFORGE	51	. ELLA WILLIAMS	127
ISABEL, PRESULLA	56	. MATTIE	141	. JOHN	84
ISBELL, CATHERINE	148	. MATTIE BROWN	52	. LILBOURN	113
JACKSON, ALTHIA	84	. NANNIE	41	. MAGGIE DUNN	113
. AMANDA	91,98	. NANNY ADAMS	51	. ROBERT	127
. AMERICA WILLIAMS	17	. NED	93	JEWELL, JAMES F.	54,145
. ANDREW	127	. PATSY HARRIS	93	LAURA JACKSON	54
. ANNA LEWIS	131	. SARAH	54,88	JINEN, BELL CONNOR	60
. ATLINE	126	. SARAH R.	70	MILLARD F.	60
. BEULAH B.	20	. SAUL	67	JOHNSON,	25
. C.B.	44-45,51-53-54	. THOMAS	51	. ALBERT	29
. C.P.	49	. THOMAS L.	153	. ALICE	32,134
. CAROLINA	71	. W.T.	128	. ALSEY	27
. CAROLINE	63	. WILLIAM	52,131	. ALSY	41
. ELLA WILLIAMS	127	JACOBS, ALLEY	72	. AMANDA BUNCH	10
. ELLEN	77	. AMANDA U. BEAVERS	12	. ANN RANELS	1
. ELLEN JACKSON	77	. ELLA	140	. ANN REYNOLDS	1
. EMERSON D.	51	. WALTER G.	12	. CANDY LEWIS	116
. EMMA	151	JAMES, CATHARINE	51	. CAROLINE	80
. F.	77	. JENNIE MAYES	6	. CAROLINE MOORE	131
. FANNIE	149	. WILLIAM S.	6	. CARRY HARRISON	46
. GEORGE	29,77	JARDIN, JOHN	57	. CATHERINE	33
. GEORGE W.	12	ROZETTA TAPP	57	. CHARLES A.	143
. HENRY	25	JARVIS, CHARLES T.	37	. DAISY POTTS	98
. IDA	124	MATTIE MAYS	37	. DANIEL	19,46
. IDA JACKSON	124	JASPAR, JOHN B.H.	35	. DORA	76

INDEX
(New Madrid, Co., MO. Marriages Vol #2)

Name	Page
. EMMA	71,109
. FLORENCE GRAY	36
. GEORGE	150
. H.E.	64
. HENRY	7,148
. HOLLY ROSS	148
. IDA	152
. J.	77
. J.J.	98
. JAMES	16
. JAMES H.	98
. JANE	44
. JOHN	132
. JOHN R.	10
. JOHN W.	144
. JOSEPH	32,59
. JULIA WATERS	98
. LAURA	134
. LOUIS	137
. LULA	152
. LULA MOORE	150
. MAGGIE MORROW	150
. MAGGIE NORTON	144
. MARTY	136
. MARY E. TONEY	16
. MARY WEBSTER	143
. MINTA HUSTON	29
. MOLLIE CLEMONS	32
. MOLLY	59
. NOLAND	150
. OLIVE	49
. SALLIE	2
. SALLY	24
. SARAH FARMER	137
. SARAH KENWORTHY	111
. SARAH WILSON	7
. SERENA	77
. SHEP	116
. THOMAS	13-14,17,24,64
.	68,70,72,75,79-80,97
. TOM	131
. W.F.	112,122
. W.J.	127
. W.T.	88-89,92,96
.	112-113,128-129,134
.	140,142-143,150-151
.	153
. W.W.	132
. WILLIAM	1,36
. WILLIAM E.	98
. WILLIE N.	111
JOHNSTON, CHARLES W.	10
MOLLIE KLEIN	10
JONES, ALBERT A.	132
. ALEXANDER	10
. ALICE JOHNSON	32
. ALICE MONAHAM	130
. ANNER	104
. ANNY P. MAHAR	50
. BEULA A. COLE	132
. CATHARINE	45
. CHARLES	105
. CHRISTINE	116
. DAVID E.	60
. DAVID W.	99
. DORA ARKADE	122
. E.	21
. ELBY	147
. ELI	56
. ELIZABETH	4
. ELIZABETH C.	95
. ELIZABETH CARTER	43
. ELIZABETH DAVIS	10
. ELLEN ROSE	120
. EMMA LUCY	90
. ETTA ELLIS	105
. FRANK	90
. G.S.	132,138,152
. GEORGE S.	43
. HENRIETTA GILBERT	59
. HENRY H.	12
. HESTER TESOY	143
. HESTER TROY	143
. IDA M. CARTER	99
. JAMES A.	95-96,143
. JAMES B.	59
. JOHANNAH	33
. JOHN	43
. JOSEPH	130
. JOSEPHINE	116
. L.R.	15
. LAURA	77
. LAURA A.	12
. LAURA McCREERY	97
. LAURA PAUL	43
. LENA	148
. LIZZIE	116
. MARGARET	31
. MARGARET C.	17
. MARGARET WARD	95-96
. MARTHA E.	139
. MARTHA LAWSON	69
. MARY	68,139
. MARY A.	107
. MARY CARAL	44
. MARY E.	21
. MARY JANE	146
. MARY WRIGHT	12
. MELIE	88
. MISSOURA	104
. PARIELEE	67
. RACHEL NANNEY	123
. RENE	81
. RICHARD	44

INDEX
(New Madrid, Co., MO. Marriages Vol #2)

. SALLIE RANSBURGH	60	. JAMES	107	. FRANK D.	34,141
. SAM C.	69	. MARY WILLIAMS	125	. LUELLA MUKUM	141
. SAMUEL C.	50	KELLY,ALMEDA	96	. WILLIAM F.	141
. SARAH E.	2	. AMANDA	95	KING,DICY	86
. SYLVA GUY	56	. ANDREW J.M.	29	. FRANCES	120
. WILLIAM	32,120,122	. CAROLINE CURLEY	29	. JOHN	5
. WILLIAM E.	123	. CAROLINE WORLEY	29	. LANA BELL DUNN	104
. WILLIE E.	97	. CORNELIA	59	. MARMGARET CARPENTER	5
JONT,SARAH E.	152	. JAMES G.	24	. MARY	44
JONTE,MARY	144	. MARY E.	127	. MARY BELL	61
JORDIN,JENNY	89	. MARY McGREW	24	. MATT	104
WARREN	89	. MATTY	135	. SISSIE	127
JOUT,NORMA C.	51	KEMEROTHY,MARY	40	. W.	85
JUDY,HENRY	5	KENDALL,		. WILLIAM	93,118
. MARY	124	. MARGRETT COPELAND	87	KINKADE,DAVID C.	117
. MOLLIE WEST	5	. WILSON	87	SARAH McGITHERS	117
JULIEN,MARY A.	7	KENNEDY,ROBERT D.	132	KIRBY,	
JUSTIN,OSCAR K.	29		133,138,141	. ADALINE MORRELL	150
KANE,MARY	2	KENWORTHY,MATTY	148	. JOHN	150
KASINGER,JOHN R.	90	SARAH	111	KITCHENS,FLORA	125
MARY PEEPERS	90	KERR,AMERICA POTTER	11	KITTERMAN,	
KAYSINGER,JESSEY	84	WILLIAM	11	. BENJAMIN O.	150
KEASTER,JULIA	12	KETTERMAN,DAVID	50	. SARAH DRIVALL	150
KEELER,ANNA	36	EMELINE	50	KLEIN,ANN	79
KEESTER,MARTHA	47	KEW,ELIZABETH C.	2	. EMERY	145
KEGER,JEFF D.	31	KEY,ADDY	111	. LENA	79
MATTIE COOLEY	31	. ANNIE RHODES	118	. MOLLIE	10
KEINGHAW,JOHN	39	. FRANKLIN J.	118	KLINE,MOLLIE	33
ROSA MELECK	39	. LOU	114	KNIGHT,BETTIE	97
KEITH,A.	2,4-5	. NANCY RANDOLPH	92	. J.J.	97,113-114
. AMBROSE	2,4	. SALLIE	93	. 117-120,122,132-133	
. LECRETIA	75	. TABITHA CHAPMAN	110	. 138,142,148,150,152	
. MINNIE	113	. THEAD T.	110	. J.L.	110
. SALLIE	104	. THOMAS	92	. LISSIE	137
KELLER,ADENE E. COOK	82	KEYS,ANDY	112	. MARY CARNEY	2
. D.J.	70,82	JOSEY JACKSON	112	. THOMAS	2
. ELIZABETH COOK	70	KILGON,LADUSKY	118	KNOTGRASS,JENNIE	125
KELLEY,C.Q.	125,153	KIMES,ELLA	133	KNOTT,ELIZA J. MASSEY	37

INDEX
(New Madrid, Co., MO. Marriages Vol #2)

Name	Page	Name	Page	Name	Page
. GEORGE	69	. ALBERT W.	56,145	LAIR, AMELIA FORSYTHE	91
. GEORGE W.	37	. AUGUSTUS	13	. FANNY HANY	34
. SARAH	114	. BAUSLL	72	. JONATHAN	34
. SARAH L.	114	. CARRIE WATERS	56	. THOMAS J.	91
KNOX, DRUZILLA	12	. IDA	48	LAMAR, ANNA	78
. POLLY ROUNGEE	4	. JENNY	69	LAMB, CLARA	101
. SARAH E.	16	. JOHN	120	. DELISLE	21
. SILAS	4	. JOHN B.	56,72	. ELIZA LOUIS	3
. WILLIAM	18	. L.F.	118-119,124-125	. JENNIE	13
KNUCKLES, AMANDA	22	.	127,129,133-135,140	. LINDA	144
KOCHTITZKY, MARY	15	.	143,145,149-151	. RUDOLF	3
KOPP, F.	26	. L.G.	133	. SIDNEY GODAIR	21
. FRANZ	14	. L.O.C.	117	LANDERS, A.	33
. SALLIE MORRISON	14	. LAFAYETTE	21	. ABRAHAM	37,85
KOUNER, EMILY	64	. LUCY BUTTS	120	. ELLEN	37
KULUMIS, MARY	68	. LULA BELL	72	. JENNETT	52
KUNCKELS, AMANDA E.	23	. MARY E. LONG	21	. MARY I.	33
KURNEY, LUCY J.	14	. MASITITE LESIEUR	145	. SARAH WESTERMAN	85
LABOW, IDA L. PIGGOTT	30	. MATILDA	151	LANE, ALICE SHAW	12
WILLIAM B.	30	. MATTIE	41	. ANDREW J.	116
LAFAVENS,		. PARALEE DELISLE	16	. HATTIE HIX	116
. ELMIRE GADDIE	126	. R.L.	76,102,119	. JOHN T.	12
. ROBERT	126	. RENA	144	. SARAH E.	32
LAFERNEY,		. ROBERT	2-3-6,8-10,13	LANG, J.H.	33
. AMELIA BERTHOLISON	67	. 15-16,19-21,29-30,36		. JOHN	118
. DICK	87	. 39,48,55,59		. MOLLIE KLINE	33
. JULIA SIMEOR	65	. ROBERT L.	91,103-104	. MOLLIE LUCY	118
. JULIA SINKO	65	. TEREASY GODAIR	13	LANGDON, E.J.	102
. L.	60	LAFORGE, A.A.	14	LANIN, HENRY M.	115
. LAURA PIKEY	87	. ALPHONSE C.	126	KATIE HUSTON	115
. LOUIS	65	. HATTIE	14	LANY, POLLY	52
. WILLIAM	67	. HETTIE	10	LAPLANT,	
LAFOE, JOHN W.	8	. LETITIA LEWIS	126	. ANNIE M. PORTER	65
. LENA	85	. LIZZIE	6	. DORA	65
. MAGGIE	86	. MARIE	128	. JOHN	74
. NANCY A. ALFORD	8	. MARY	51,98	. MARY	137
LAFOND, L.F.	117,121-122	. ROBERT	14	. ROBERT LEE	65
LAFONT, A.J.	16	LAFORT, ROBERT	23	LASSLER, ADELE	64

INDEX
(New Madrid, Co., MO. Marriages Vol #2)

Name	Page	Name	Page	Name	Page
LASTER, AARON	58	LAWSON, ANDREW	70,77,98	. MINNIE STOREY	102
. ADELE BOON	58	. ANNA WOODS	77	. PHILLESER MAULSBY	88
. ADELL BROWN	58	. MARTHA	69	. ROBERT	45
. HARON	58	. MATILDA PATTERSON	98	. STEPHEN	109,118-119
. JULIA	71	LAY, MARIAH	138	.	123
. JULIA H. EARLES	48	. MARTHA	131	. WILLIAM	45,134
. LOTTY	107	. MELINDA	13	LEEK, JASPER	64
. OLIVE JOHNSON	49	. RANSOM	13	LEEKE, AMANDA	64
. RICHARD	48	. TOLIVER	13	ELIZABETH	48
. WILLIAM	107	LAYGRANE, NANCY MASON	5	LEESHER, CONRAD	84
. WILLIAM HARMON	49	WILLIAM	5	LEFERNEY, MARY	3
LATHAM, H.C.	6,14	LAZELL, ELIAS	98	LEFTMUEH, JOHN A.	40
IDA	10,87	. FRANKIE WATERS	98	JOSEPHINE BROWN	40
LATIMORE, MARY	6	. NANCY	22	LEFTURCH, JOHN A.	51
LATTREMON, ALEXANDER	26	. NANNIE	22	KATY YARBER	51
ELIZA O. COBB	26	. NANNY	142	LEGATE, IDA JOHNSON	152
LAURY, ELIZA	66	LEADBETTER,		THOMAS	152
LAVALLEE,		. GEORGIA RAY	60	LEGETT, ETTA	15
. CORNELIA NEWSUM	22	. RILEY	60	LEGRAND, ELIZABETH	39,92
. LILLEY	81	LEAKE, JOSEPH F.	48	. MARTHA	59
. ROBERT L.	22	LEDBETTER, C.M.	121	. ROSA	92
LAVALLEY, ISAAC	7	LEE, ALBERT	31	. TERASE	39
SILVIA GAY	7	. ANNA	40	LEGRANDE, EDIE	59
LAW, ANNIE M.	125	. CHARLES	88	LEGRANDS, EDWARD	36
J.S.	151	. DAISEY L.	138	LEISSLER, CONRAD	78-79
LAWFIELD, GEROGE	152	. ELLA DAWSON	134	.	81-82,84,97,103
. JUNE HYLES	152	. ELLEN	62	. NANCY E. BROWN	79
. LENA	13,107	. GEORGE	7	LEMM, ALLEN	38
. THOMAS	13	. IDA	93	. JERRY	38
LAWGHLIN, JAMES	17	. J.M.	111	. MARY BANKS	38
MARY SECOY	17	. JAMES R.	24	LEMONS, AMANDA OGDEN	119
LAWRENCE, MARY	3	. JOHN P.	102	. JOSEPHINE	11
LAWS,		. LAURA E.	149	. LIZZIE	112
. CATHERINE ESSARY	129	. LELIA P. CRAWFORD	24	. WILLIAM	119
. ELZA DAVIS	146	. LOUIS	57	LENIER, EQUILEE	49
. NEWTON C.	129	. MARY	13	LENON,	
. SALLIE	119	. MARY THOMAS	7	. ALICE FARRENBURG	34
. WILLIAM W.	146	. MATTIE	131	. JAMES R.	34

INDEX
(New Madrid, Co., MO. Marriages Vol #2)

. NANCY		34	LEVY,CLARA B. RIFFLE	19	. ZENUS G.		15
LERALE,DANIEL		115	. LUCY	102	LIGON,JAMES F.		74
LESIEUR,ADAM L.		133	. SOLOMON	19	. JENNY		51
. ADOLPH		42	LEWIS,ANNA	131	. SARAH WEST		74
. AUGUSTUS		46	. ANNIE	100	LIKINS,ANNIE		132
. CINDA		84	. CANDY	116	LINCKE,KATY		56
. CLARA WATERS		16	. D.E. HOPKINS	9	LINDLEY,JANE SHULTZ		104
. ELLA DAVIS		46	. DANIE	8	. JOSEPH		101
. ELLA KIMES		133	. ELIZA DAVIDSON	115	. KATIE UPTON		101
. EMMA		70	. ELIZABETH	34	. SAMUEL		104
. FELIX N.		16,60	. ELIZABETH EARINGTON	52	LING,ELIZABETH SWILLEY		5
. FRANCIS		124	. FANNIE WYNE	20	. JOHN		5
. FRANK		100	. FANY	31	. SARAH		4
. GODFREY ALBERT		16	. H.C.	18	LINSEY,J.S.		151
. LAURA		120	. HENRY S.	21	NOLA MARNING		151
. LAURA WILLIAMS		100	. J.W.	9	LINSON,MARY		75
. LUE NICHOLUS		97	. JESSIE	52	LISLER,CONRAD		91
. MASITITE		145	. JOHN W.	20,61	LISSLER,CONRAD		76
. NANNIE MILLER		60	. JULIA A.	30	LITTLE,FANNIE PALMER		119
. NAPOLEON		27	. L.	13	MANUEL		119
. RAPHAEL		48	. LEMUND	92	LIVINGSTON,JAMES		15
. RAPHEL		97	. LETITIA	126	LEONA DEPRO		15
. SALLY E. STONE		27	. LILBOURNE	14	LLEWALLYN,		
. SUSAN		7	. MAGGIE	133	. AMANDA CATHERAN		2
. TEARCE ADAMS		48	. MALISSA	128	. FRANKLIN		2
. TERASE PHILLIPS		42	. MARY BELL KING	61	LOGAN,AMANDA HORNER		147
. WILL		100	. MARY HUNT	146	. ELIZA		151
LESSIEUR,CHRISTINE		5	. MELISSA BROWN	21	. JERRY		127
. CLAIREMOUR MEATTE		5	. MORLEY COLEMAN	8	. JULIUS		147
. RAPHAEL		5	. N.	31	. KATY		68
LESSLER,CONRAD		85	. REUBEN	115	. RACHEAL BROWN		127
LESTER,CONRAD		66	. ROBERT L.	128	LONG,ADDIE		58
. J.C.		124	. ROSA McDONALD	128	. BIRDIE		73
. MOLLIE C.		66	. SARAH E. WILLIS	92	. DELIA BROWN		110
. PAULINE ROSS		124	. THOMAS	146	. ELLEN		73
LETT,MATILDA		3	. W.H.	34	. EMILY KOUNER		64
LEUN,ARSULA CRAMON		94	. W.L.	128	. FANNY		58
THOMAS J.		94	. W.W.	25,28	. HARRISON		110

INDEX
(New Madrid, Co., MO. Marriages Vol #2)

Name	Page	Name	Page	Name	Page
. IDA	136	LUMMI, AMBROSE	56	MAINORD, ADA A.	141
. JOHN	7,21,58	PRESULLA ISABEL	56	. CHARLES N.	23
. LAURA	73	LUMPKIN, MISSOURI	118	. HODA	117
. MARY E.	21	NANCY ANN	118	. J.F.	22
. SIMON	64	LUMSDEM, MATTIE	134	. JOHN F.	66
. VINA A. DAVIS	7	LUMSDEN, GREEN	134,136	. KATIE	91
LONYOU, CHARLES W.	58	MARY	136	. MARY	83,94
FANNY LONG	58	LUNYOW, CHARLES	23	. MARY E. MIZE	23
LOOMIS, ADALINE DEES	146	MARTHA MARTIN	23	. MILAS	60
. HENRY	146	LUSLER, CONRAD	90	. MOLLIE MAGEE	98
. SUSIE BIRDWELL	135	LYNCH, ELLEN LEE	62	. PERLIE STONE	57
. THOMAS	135	. MARTHA	53	. SAMUEL	57
LOUDERMUCH, W.L.	131	. MARY	118	. W.W.	141
LOUIS, DALSEY	4	. MINNIE	136	. WILLIAM	98
ELIZA	3	. SAMUEL	62	MAJORS, CORA	145
LOVE, CATHERINE	26	LYONS, SUSIE	101	MALODY, J.D.	92
. LOUISE	57	MABERRY, JAMES W.	112	MARY C. RUSSELL	92
. MINERVA	3	MARTHA J. RAY	112	MALONE, BETTIE J.	113
LOVENGOOD,		MACFARLAN, ALLEN	130	. DRURY WILLIAMS	143
. ADELIA MIFLEN	50	MACFARTAN, ALLEN	125	. FANNY	123
. NEWTON	50	MACKE, CELA	138	. GEORGE W.	143
LOVING, GEORGE	136	MADRAY, ELIZABETH	14	. J.H.	139
MAY DUKE	136	MAERLEY, ISAAC	93	. MOLLIE	141
LOVINGOOD,		LOUISA HOLINSWORTH	93	. NANCY	139
. FLONNA ALLEN	28	MAGEE, MOLLIE	98	MANESS, G.T.	133
. NEWT	28	MAGENTLY,		. HENRY A.	119
. RICHARD	90	. LULESHER HUSK	82	. W.A. CONNER	119
. ROXANA HERNDON	90	. RILEY	82	MANGUM, J.I.	99
LOW, ADA	109	MAHAN, CAROLINE	78	MATTIE L.	99
LOUISE	56	MAHAR, ANNY P.	50	MANION, CEINDA	113
LOWRY, IKE	53	. NELLIE G.	111	MANN, DAVID	115
MARTHA LYNCH	53	. WILLIAM T.	50	. LELIA OBANNON	115
LUCAS, JENNIE HALL	14	MAHONE, EUGENE F.	3	. MAGGIE	139
JOHN H.	14	MARTHA J. WILLIAMS	3	MANNING, JOHN	65
LUCY, EMMA	90	MAINARD, ALLEN WINSTON	38	MARY E. MURPHY	65
MOLLIE	118	. LAURA B. HILL	38	MANUEL, ADALE SMITH	109
LUKE, CHARLES	116	. MARY PATTERSON	39	. BILLI McLEAN	11
ELSIE BURTON	116	. MILAS	39	. ELIZABETH	36

INDEX
(New Madrid, Co., MO. Marriages Vol #2)

. EQUILEE LENIER	49	. AMANDA J. STEWART	142	. JOHN E.	3
. GEORGE W.	49	. DAVID L.	102	. LOUISE BUCKER	127
. HENRIETTA ROSS	11	. ELLA WESTERMAN	44	. MARY P.	91
. ISIE	109	. ELLE	74	. MINERVA LOVE	3
. ISRAEL	11	. EMELINE	74	. NANCY	5
. JOE GRAY	109	. EMMA	60	. SAMUEL A.	6
. JOHN	11	. GEORGE	19,142	MASONVILLE,	
. WILLIAM	109	. HESTER GREER	142	. ELIZABETH BARNES	118
MANUS, L. ANGELINE	133	. HILL	77	. ELLEN GOSSETT	21
MARCUS, MOLLIE S.	29	. JAMES	101,142	. JOSEPH	21,118
MARION, CLUMBIA	130	. JOHN	3,23	. MARY	13
MARKHAM, A.E. HANCOCK	16	. JOHN J.	4	. MODEST	66
. R.H.	16	. JOHN S.	109	MASS, GEORGE	84
. SARAH CAMMEL	133	. LUCY NEAL	102	JESSEY KAYSINGER	84
. WILLIAM	133	. MAGGIE	116	MASSEY, ELIZA J.	37
MARKS, CHARLES	120	. MALINDA	77	. EMELINE RODIS	24
DORA COLBURN	120	. MARTHA	23	. JAMES	24,141
MARNEY, BELL F.	97	. MARTHA A. STEWART	109	. JAMES C.	52
. TERRY A. WALLS	84	. MARTHA KEESTER	47	. MARGARET	144
. WILLIAM A.	84	. MARY	4,70,99	. MOLLIE	141
MARNING, NOLA	151	. MARY HUNTER	19	. POLLEY WESTERMAN	52
MARQUE, MARY S. STILL	18	. MATILDA	99	MASSIE, CHARLES	129
VALENTINE	10	. MATILDA LETT	3	MASTERSON, MARY E.	38
MARR, LIZZIE	107,151	. PID	101	. REANIE FORD	111
MARRE, W.H.	141	. SAMUEL H.	47	. WILLIAM	111
MARRS, FANNY McELHANEY	21	. SARAH J.	56	MATHENEY, JAMES C.	102
HUGH	21	. SCOTT	19	MARGARET BUCKMAN	102
MARS, LIZZIE	31	. SOPHIA	69	MATHERSON, ARTHUR	8
MARSDEN, EMALINE	60	. STELLA FOUNTAIN	19	ELIZABETH ROTH	8
MARSH, MARY J.	19	. THOMAS	44	MATSINGER, ELLA DOOD	102
MARSHAL, LIZZIE BROOKS	82	MARYWETHER, WILLIS	1	MATTHEW J.	102
R.G.	82	MASEL, MAHALEY	121	MATTHEWS, CHARLES	123
MARSHALL, EMMA	6	MASENVILLE,		. DANIEL	109
. HUME H.	37	. EDITH REESE	66	. DAVID	83
. THEODORE MAXEY	37	. FRANK	66	. ELLA	109
MARTENS, JOSEPH	68	MASON, AMANDA NANSON	4	. ELLEN TAYLOR	83
MARY KULUMIS	68	. FREEMAN L.	4	. FANNY MALONE	123
MARTIN, ALLY PHILLIPS	101	. GEORGE	127	. GEORGE	107

INDEX
(New Madrid, Co., MO. Marriages Vol #2)

. GEORGE A.	15	. JOHN	137	MICHAEL, J.H.	93,107
. IDA BARNES	107	. JOSEPH	18	MICHAELS, J.H.	107
. MAGGIE BRYANT	15	. LUKE	112	MICHELL,	
. MINNIE RICHARDSON	109	. SAM	82	. ANNIE RANDOLS	107
MAUCHMAN, C.P.	108	. VELMA GODARD	137	. DORA	7
MAULSBY, CORA	106	MEATTE, CINDA LESIEUR	84	. JERRY	107
. JOHN	106	. CLAIREMOUR	5	MIDGET, CORA SWAN	136
. KATY E.	29	. CLARA CRABTREE	18	JAMES	136
. PHILLESER	88	. EDWARD	5,71	MIDGETT, ANGELINE	8
. SAM	31	. ELIZABETH	6	MIFLEN, ADELIA	50
MAWDY, ELLA	40	. ELLEN WELCHANCE	16	MILHORN, ELLEN THORPE	128
MAXEY,		. IDA GUNN	93	JOHN A.	128
. HUME H. MARSHALL	37	. LOUIS	93	MILIKIN, ELLA SIMON	148
. RENY	88	. LUKE	18	MONROE	148
. TENNESSEE	68	. MARY	71	MILL, JOHN N.	39,44
. THEODORE	37	. MITCHELL	16,84	MILLAN, R.	31
MAXWELL, MARY	129	. MODEST	15	MILLARD, ADDIE LONG	58
MAY, NORMA C. JOUT	51	. MOLLIE	150	GEORGE E.	58
WILLIAM	51	. SAMUEL	93	MILLER, ALBERT	62
MAYES, JENNIE	6	MECKLEM, SAMUEL	114,116	. ALLIE	132
PENESE	54	. 119-120,123-127,130		. AMANDA PRICE	31
MAYNAR, MARY E.	140	. 132,143-144,150		. ANDREW	31
MAYS, LAURA HODGES	50	MEDDERS, NANCY	107	. ANN COLEMAN	31
. LOUISA EARLY	103	MELECK, ROSA	39	. ANNY	110
. MARY	114	MELRUN, COLA DAVIS	78	. GEORGE	31
. MATTIE	37	JAMES	78	. J.N.	31
. PERRY J.	103	MELTS, J.N.	136	. JANE OGDEN	46
. ROBERT	50	MERLEN, LIZZIE	31	. JOHN N.	138
MAYWEATHER, ALFRED	15	MERRELL, JAMES	42	. LENA SHELBY	62
JOSAPHINE SEWELL	15	JANE CASTLEBERRY	42	. MARY	49,119
MEADORS, NANCY J.	45	MERRETT, ELIZA	41	. MATTIE WILLIAMS	78
MEARS, HENRY	93	MARTHA	91	. NANNIE	60
NELLIE BOZARK	93	MERRILL, A.C.	77	. PETER	46
MEATT, ADALINE	112	. AMANDA	77	. SARAH ANN	119
. AMELIA	82	. EFFA L. SAMUELS	103	. V.J.	78
. ANNA WELCHANCE	18	. JAMES W.	77,103	MILLIGAN,	
. FLORA	82	. NANCY HORNBECK	77	. ADALE DUNKLIN	60
. FRANK	48	MERSHALL, SARAH	131	. JOHN	60

INDEX
(New Madrid, Co., MO. Marriages Vol #2)

MILLIS,BEN	98	. MARY	69	MONTGOMERY,JASPER	132
. LIZZIE ROSS	98	. MARY HUNTER	62	. LUKE	132
. V.J.	71-72,86	MINS,CATHARINE HARRIS	95	. MARY DAVIS	132
MILLS,C.S.	142	GEORGE	95	. SUSAN	70
. ELAM B.	. 13	MIPPLETON,ALVA	104	MOODY,MARTHA E.	21
. J.A.	40-41	MIREHAND,CARRIE TONY	122	. MARY	52
. J.N.	40-41,44,53,61	EDWARD L.	122	. MINERVA	12
.	131,133,136,139-140	MISSOURI,NANCY	120	. R.C.	35
.	146,153	MITCHEL,SARAH	7	MOORE,ALVIN	26
. J.W.	33	MITCHELL,CATHARINE	5	. AMANDA E.	31
. JOHN	44-45,54	. CEOLA OBANNON	101	. CAROLINE	131
. JOHN A.	33,117-118	. CHARLES	73	. CELESTE	105
. JOHN B.	36	. CHARLES L.	65	. CHARLES	139
. JOHN L.	118	. ELLE MARTIN	74	. ED GARTNEY	34
. JOHN M.	30	. EMMA	98	. ELLA M.	102,108
. JOHN N.	33,35,37-38	. FANNY ORSIC	92	. EM C.	34
.	46-52,55-58,63-65,111	. FRANK	92	. EMMA CHANNEY	150
.	112,116,120-122,128	. J.W.	99-100	. EMMA O. EWING	99
.	134,139-140,145	. JENNY WATSON	65	. FLORNE E. MORTE	40
. V.J.	65	. JULIA DENSORY	73	. ISIAH	5
MINER,NALLIE	1	. LAURA	153	. J.W.	143
MINEWEATHER,HARISON	35	. LOUISA	90	. JENNY	69
MARY ENGLISH	35	. MATTIE GRIMES	30	. JESSIE L.	99
MINNER,		. ROBERT	30,74	. JOSEPH S.	22
. CATHERINE BEAVERS	57	. ROSA	67	. JOSEPHINE	69
. DORA GRAVES	39	. SREPTY BUCKMAN	115	. LAURA	96
. JAMES	41,94,126	. THOMAS	115	. LIZZIE BROWN	139
. KATY	37	. WILLIAM	101	. LOUIS	114,130
. LEMUEL	39	MIZE,LIZZIE BROWN	95	. LOUISE HILL	22
. LENNY BURGESS	126	. MARY E.	23	. LUCINDA RICE	130
. MAKINZY	57	. THOMAS	95	. LULA	129,150
. MARTHA SEWELL	41	MIZELL,NANCY	85	. M.L. STONE	26
. MARY MAINORD	94	MOHAN,LEVI	92	. MATTHEW A.	147
. WILLIAM	39	PURLY McCOY	92	. MAUDY	141
MINNEWEATHER,		MOHLER,S.S.	72	. MILES	150
. CAROLINE WADE	70	MONAHAM,ALICE	130	. PURCILLA SLAWS	5
. HARRISON	70	MONTAGUE,GEORGE V.	99	. SALLIE SPENCER	122
. ISAAC	62	LILLY DUROCHER	99	. SAMUEL F.	40

INDEX
(New Madrid, Co., MO. Marriages Vol #2)

Name	Page(s)
. SAMUEL J.	41
. SARAH KNOTT	114
. WILLIAM	122
MOOREHEAD, LEWANDA	93
MOORING,	
. CHRISTOPHER B.	137
. MARY LAPLANT	137
MOREHEAD,	
. FANNIE OVERFIELD	107
. JOSEPH	107
MORGAN, ANNE HOGUE	111
. ANNIE REDIN	111
. BETTY	24
. FANNY BLACKMAN	143
. GEORGE	113
. HIRAM	111
. J.M.	109,125,130,137
. JAMES	111
. JOHN M.	123
. MAGGIE LAFOE	86
. MEDIA BANKS	113
. NETTY	145
. POLLY	94
. R.M.	146
. RICHARD	86,143
. THOMAS W.	111
. W.H.	65
MORLAND, EMMA	16
MORRA, ANDREW	110
LULA WOODS	110
MORRELL, ADALINE	150
MORRIS,	
. ALLEY WILLIAMS	140
. ASALEE	58
. CORRINEY	94
. J.A.	110
. J.R.	90,93,99-100,103,111-112
. J.W.	153
. JENETTE	146
. JORDON	11
. M.M.	94
. MARTHA	12
. MELVINA CATHRELL	11
. R.	94
. ROBERT	58,140
. ROBERT M.	146
. RUTH B. WEST	153
. SUSAN A.	1
. W.H.	153
MORRISON, ADALINE	82
. ANNIE	119
. FLORENCE	82
. FRANS W.	49
. JAMES	82
. MARY MILLER	49
. SALLIE	14
. T.J.O.	5-6,8,14,16,26,62,66,68,72,74,76-77,81,83-86,88,95-96,98,99-101,103-107
. T.J.P.	65
. THOMAS J.O.	14-15
MORROS, JOSEPH	38
MARGARET SMITH	38
MORROW, MAGGIE	150
MORTE, FLORNE E.	40
MORTON, A.G.	79
MOSELEY, JAMES	19
PAULINA AUSTIN	19
MOSS, HENRY F.	20
. JESSIE	110
. SARAH W. DENHART	20
MOTE, ALSIE	46
. CHARLES	40
. EMMA	23
. SARAH A.	46
MOTT, ARLIE	119
. CLARA	16,57
. HANNAH	66
. JOHN	26,53,119,140
. JOHN A.	1,23,37,52
. LOUIS W.	100
. OLIVE	119
. SAMUEL	119
. WILLIAM F.	75
MOTTE, AMANDA RENION	124
OLIVER	124
MOUNDS, HENDERSON	31
MUDD, CALLY	72
HARRIET	24,54
MUKE, DINAH	120
MUKES, DICY KING	86
. MELLER	86
. MILLER	44
. SARAH HALL	44
MUKUM, LUELLA	141
MULLIGAN,	
. FLORENCE A. SAY	38
. MARY BRUNSON	28
. MATTISON	38
. T.L.	148
. THOMAS	28,151
MUNSON, GEORGIA	84
MURMED, WILLIAM	37
MURPHY, ADDY	131
. CHARLES T.	84
. ELIZABETH LEEKE	48
. ELLEN	61
. FANNIE RILEY	25
. HENRY	48
. IDA BOGARD	106
. JOHN	25
. LUCY HARDON	121

INDEX
(New Madrid, Co., MO. Marriages Vol #2)

Name	Page	Name	Page	Name	Page
. MARY E.	65	. RACHEL AKINSON	122	McDANIELS, L.B.	1,8
. MARY E. RAY	84	. WILLIAM	122	McDENOUGH, WALTON	51
. MINNIE BURNES	151	McCLISTER, FRANK	91	McDONALD, ROSA	128
. MOLLIE	8	RACHEL THOMPSON	91	SALLIE	125
. WILLIAM H.	106	McCLOUD, LAVADA	46	McDONOUGH, MARY	11
. WILLIAM HENRY	151	MARY J.	19	McDOWELL, M.L.	89
. WILLIAM T.	121	McCLUER, U.	6,8-9	. MARY	6
MYATT, A.C.	70	McCOLUM, KATIE	154	. MATHEW	8
MYERS, ALICE CALDWELL	30	McCONNEL, BETTIE	49	. MOLLIE J. SUMMERS	8
. ELLA DELISLE	114	McCONNELL, DAVID	27	McELANEY, SARAH	75
. EMMA	118	. JAMES A.	110	McELAVY, JOSEPHINE	73
. JAMES O.	70	. JESSIE MOSS	110	McELHANEY, CHARLES W.	33
. JOSEPH	30	. MARY	91	. FANNY	21
. LOUISA E. FRY	70	. MARY PINLEY	27	. JOHANNAH JONES	33
. MARY JANE	6	McCORMAC,		McELHANY,	
. WILLIAM R.	114	. FRANCIS VANOVER	9	. JOSEPHINE COSBY	75
McADOO, BELL	135	. RIVERS	9	. MOLLIE	37
. CHARLES	91	McCORMIC, NANCY	86	. WILLIAM	75
. KATIE MAINORD	91	McCORMICK, MARY	101	McELMURRAY, JOHN W.	65
McALISTER, MARTHA	2	. NORA E. BOWEN	146	MATTY CLEMENS	65
McCANNON, JOHN	95	. R.V. BRANHAM	153	McFADDEN, ALFRED F.	100
MEDITA TEMPA	95	. RACHEL BOLINGER	111	MINNIE DAVIS	100
McCARMACK, MARY	129	. ROBERT	111	McFADEN, ANDREW I.	116
McCARRIE, ELLEN	86	. W.H.	153	IDA BYERS	116
McCARTY, WILLIAM	1	. WILLIAM H.	146	McFARLAN, ALLEN	129
McCARY, COLUMBIS	69	McCOY, ANNA	1	PATTIE HOWARD	129
. MARTHA STEWART	4	. CARRY DOW	50	McFARLAND, ALLEN	124-125
. RICHARD	68	. JAMES	50,120	. HARRY	2
. ROBERT S.	4	. JOSEPH	1	. HENRY	48
. SALLY OBRYAN	68	. MANURVEY	33	. IDA LAFONT	48
McCLANE,		. PURLY	92	. LULA	43
. ELIZABETH DAVIS	50	. SAMUEL	38	. SALLIE JOHNSON	2
. JAIKE M.	50	McCREERY, LAURA	97	McGARAY, MARY HAMPTON	77
McCLARD, NANCY	103	McDANIEL, JANUS	12	THOMAS	77
McCLELLAN,		. JOSIAH	94	McGARIN, RUTH	36
. EMMA TOMPKINS	32	. LULA STEPHENS	94	McGARTH, GEORGE	104
. G.W.	32	. ROSALEE	88	IDA JANE TAYLOR	104
McCLELLANDE,		. SARAH C. BARNS	12	McGEE, ANNIE E.	106

INDEX
(New Madrid, Co., MO. Marriages Vol #2)

. BETTIE HONOT	113	. ALICE HOLLAND	125	. NANCY		81
. BETTIE KNIGHT	97	. AMANDA DAVIS	46	. ROSETTA		76
. CHARLES R.	97	. E.A.	7,47,52,63,69,72	. Y.V.		81
. LAURA	88	.	77,151	NALLY, FRANCIS A.J.	16
. WILLIAM	113	. E.H.	22	NANNEY, RACHEL	123
McGENTHY, ELIZABETH	84	. E.P.	84,87,90-91,94	NANNY, JAMES	123
McGEORGE, ELLA	104	.	104,107,109,118	NANSON, AMANDA	4
McGEUGH, JOHN	70	. ELIZABETH TRAMMELL	124	NASH, CHARLES	57,60
McGILL, LOU JACKSON	78	. ELLA JACOBS	140	. EMALINE MARSDEN	60
. SARAH BRADLEY	129	. EPHRAIM	56	. LENA V. FORE	57
. WILLIAM	78,129	. EPHRAIM A.	55,61-62,73	. LOU	47
McGINTRY,		.	84	NEAL, ALICE	40
. JENNY ALEXANDER	59	. JOHN	46	. ARTHUR	40
. WILLIAM	59	. JOHN F.	124	. BENJAMIN	131
McGINTY, JAMES	63	. R.M.	140	. DAVID	2
SARAH JANE DUFFY	63	. ROBERT W.	125	. EDDIE	149
McGITHERS, SARAH	117	McLEAN, BILLI	11	. LUCY	102
McGLASSION,		McLEMON, A.J.	136	. MARTHA ADAMS	131
. ELIZA FRAZIER	125	McLEMORE, BELL	136	NEEL, LULA	144
. JAY	125	. EMILY	79	NEELY, JAMES KELLEY	107
McGLOFLIN, SARAH	81	. EMMA WELSHANS	130	MONROE	107
McGLOTHEN, ERION BUSHY	48	. JAMES	130	NEIL, GRANT	140
WILLIAM	48	. SUSAN	38	STELLER PIERCE	140
McGLOTHLIN,		McLENNON, MELA	71	NEILL, ALBERT T.	1
. ERIVN BUSBY	43	McMANN, HELENA	88	. AMANDA J.	7
. WILLIAM	43	McMILLAN, MARTHA	45	. ANNA GRAHAM	1
McGOWAN, JULIA	24	McNAMEE, P.J.	31,41	. DANIEL N.	2
McGREW, MARY	24	R.J.	35	. DAVID N.	3
McGROW, LIZZIE BROWN	139	McNAURMAN, J.	32	. IDA	37
ROBERT	139	McQUAQUE,		. JAMES	9
McINTIRE, JESSIE F.	49	. FRANCES SMRUING	123	. SUSAN F. GULION	9
NANCY E. DOWDY	49	. WILLIAM	123	. WILLIAM R.	3
McKENNEY, E.A.	1,37,85	McTOUCH, HANNIE	121	NELSON, CHARLES	4
McKENNY, E.A.	146	McWILLIAMS, AMANDA	81	. FRANCIS	25
McKINEY, MATTIE	101	. EMILY	142	. HENRIETTA	8
McKINNAN, DANIEL	6	. G.W.	76	. LETHA	25
EMMA MARSHALL	6	. GEORGE W.	142	. LUCY Q.	100
McKINNEY,		. MARY	58	. MAGGIE GODWIN	100

INDEX
(New Madrid, Co., MO. Marriages Vol #2)

Name	Page	Name	Page	Name	Page
. MARY MARTIN	4	. LIDA	138	. WILLIAM R.	12
. POLINA SAINT AUBIN	16	. LUCINDA	145	NORTON, MAGGIE	144
. POLINA STAUBIN	16	. MARY E.	3	. MATTIE HUNTER	128
. SIMON	16	. MARY PHILLIPS	109	. WILLIAM	128
NEVILS, BOB	63	. MOLLIE S. MARCUS	29	NOWELL, W.R.	128-129
MAUDE BOOKER	63	. NANCY	87	NUNLEY, WILLIAM	22
NEWBAUER,		. ROBERT H.	29	NUNN, FANNIE SETTLES	121
. BARBARA RAIDT	41	. SALLIE	149	JAMES	121
. GUSTA	70	. W.	87	NUNNELLY, NANCY GLOVER	9
. LOUIS	41	. WILLIE	93	W.W.	9
. MARY	72	NICHOLIS, DAN	77	OAITAIN, LENA	61
NEWBERRY,		MALINDA MARTIN	77	OAKES, JOSEPHINE	62
. ELLA MATTHEWS	109	NICHOLSON,		OBANNON, ALONZO	17,45,48
. SAM	109	. EURA HOLCOMB	142	.	71
NEWMAN, CYNTHA	113	. MORTON	142	. CEOLA	101
. HESTER BRANHAM	53	NICHOLUS, LUE	97	. ELLA	144
. HESTER BROWN	53	NICKLES,		. FLORENCE	118
. JOANN	116	. JANE ROBERSON	105	. J.	93
. THOMAS	53	. TOM	105	. JAMES	45,64,66-67,71
. WILLIAM HENRY	53	NIGHT, JOSAPHINE	16	.	73,75,78,83,85,87,92
NEWSUM, CORNELIA	22	NIPPEN, MARGARIT	125	.	98-99,106,108-109
. CORRIE BROWNELL	76	NIPPER, GRUEN	91	. JENNY	65
. ELIZABETH IMBODEN	1	MARTHA ROBERTSON	91	. JOHN	61
. LOUISA	109	NOBLE, ADALINE	53	. JOSEPH	30-31,35,38,49
. MARTHA V.	27	MARY J.	53	.	54,56,60,65,76-77,125
. W.C.	76	NOEL, CATHERINE LOVE	26	. LELIA	115
. WILSON CARY	1	WILLIAM	26	. MELISSA WALKER	45
NEWTON, BELL	48	NOELL, PARETHENA	95	. NANNIE BROWN	125
. IDA	108	PAULINE	96	OBANON, JAMES	96
. MARY	48	NOLAN, ANNIE	137	OBRYAN, BENJAMIN	139
. MARY A.	46	NOLEN, JOHN F.	93	. SALLY	68
NICHOLAS, CHARLES	109	SUSAN CRAIG	93	. TEDA SULLIVAN	139
. DAVID	149	NOLLNER, G.W.	126	OGDEN, AMANDA	119,145
. EDWARD	38	NORMAN, BENJAMIN	86	. DANIEL	99
. ELIZA WILLIAMS	38	. SARAH	86	. JANE	46-47
. HENRY	29	. SARAH E.	83	. JOSEPHINE BROOKS	121
. IDA LEE	93	NORRIS,		. PHEBE	11
. JULIA HENDERSON	29	. MARY A. PERMINTER	12	. VINA WOODS	99

INDEX
(New Madrid, Co., MO. Marriages Vol #2)

Name	Page	Name	Page	Name	Page
. WASHINGTON	121	JOSEPH B.	23	. MINNIE	130
OGDON, MARY PLEAS	112	PACK, ELLA	10	. NANNIE	144
MELLICI	112	. EMMA MITCHELL	98	. P.C.	149
OGLIN, JAMES	75-76	. JOHN C.	98	. REBECCA SMITH	78
. MATTIE TERREL	75	PACKETT, MARY	12	. SARAH	53
. MATTY FERREL	76	PACQUETT, ELLEN	61	. SARAH ROLAN	148
OICEMAN, AUGUSTUS	107	JENNETH	61	. SARAH S.	57
LENA LAWFIELD	107	PAIN, JOHN	102	. SISSIE KING	127
OLIVER, J.W.	115,130	MATILDA YOUNG	102	. THEODOCIN	20
. JENETTE MORRIS	146	PAINE, JOHN	152	. W.C.	78
. MARY	2	PALHANUS, CORNEALIUS	80	. W.T.	143
. PERMELIA	2	MARY POPE	80	. WILLIAM	98
. SAMUEL	146	PALMER, CARRIE	143	PARKERSON, CHARLES M.	59
OLNEY, MARY L.	11	. FANNIE	119	. EMMA	56
OLSBY, NANNY	59	. FRED	75	. MARY WOODS	59
ONEAL, LAURA	95	. LENA	75	PARKISON, C.M.	32
OQUIN, A.M.	141	PALMIER, JENNY MOORE	69	NANCY TALLEY	32
OQUINN, A.M.	111,135,153	JOSEPH	69	PARKS, J.R.	36,60-61
ORR, BUFORD	113	PANELL, ANGELINE	136	ROBERT	5
. MALISA	113	PANKEY, ANDREW	139	PARROT, ALTHA	154
. MARY E.	75	MAGGIE MANN	139	PARROTT, ADA YOUNG	109
. REBECCA	113	PARIS, JOHN	135	. GABRELLA	71
. REFORD	75	PARKER, A.F.	150	. NELLY	111
ORRALL, JOHN	38	. ALFORD	31	. WILLIAM	109,111
MARY	38	. AMANDA JACKSON	98	PARSON, NANCY	124
ORSIC, FANNY	92	. BELL	53	PASQUIN, BENJAMIN	-59
OSBURN, EMMA	152	. CORA	149	. FLORINDA	3
FLORENCE	70	. EMMA	123	. FRANK	26
OSBY, NELLY PARROTT	111	. FLORENCE SMITH	143	. MARGARET	26
THOMAS	111	. FRANK	127	. MARGARET PASQUIN	26
OUSLEY, J.V.	143	. JENNIE	54	. MARTHA LEGRAND	59
J.W.	135,144	. JOHN	31	. MARTIN	39
OVERFIELD, FANNIE	107	. JOHN D.	148	. TERASE LEGRAND	39
OWENS, NANIE DAVIS	133	. LELA	22	PASS, BENJAMINE	85
RIVERS D.	133	. LOUISA	10	CINDY WOODS	85
OWESLEY, H.W.	134	. LOUISA TERRY	31	PATERSON, MINNIE	138
OWSBY, J.W.	142	. LUE	49	PATRICK, MARY	8
PACE, JENNY BOHANNON	23	. MARY	31	PATTEN, EMMA	131

INDEX
(New Madrid, Co., MO. Marriages Vol #2)

Name	Page	Name	Page	Name	Page
PATTERSON, A.M.	69	. NANCY A.	4	PEEVYHOUSE, ANDREW	4
. ANNA LAMAR	78	. THOMAS A.	129	SARAH LING	4
. ANNIE	96	PAYTON, P.P.	141, 149	PEGERS, JOSEPH	109
. DAVID	18, 69	PEACE, EPHRAIM	120	PEGGES, JOSEPH	109
. DAVID A.	107	JULIA EVANS	120	PEGGUS, JOSEPH	134, 137
. FANNY TODD	78	PEARCE, GAINES	47	PEGUES, JOSEPH	109
. JEFFERSON	24	THERESA FULLER	47	PEGUS, JOSEPH	109, 127
. JOHN	78	PEARIE, RILLIE	63	PEILER, W.T.	40
. JOSIAH	60	PEARMAN, R.P.	153	PEINE, ALSEY JOHNSON	27
. LOTTY LASTER	107	PEARSONAN, R.G.	135	JACOB	27
. MARY	39	PEARY, MARY E. FRY	118	PENDERS, AFT	50
. MARY E. BURNS	60	NUTE	118	EMELINE KETTERMAN	50
. MATILDA	98	PEBYHOUSE, DANIEL	147	PENIX, JOHN L.	113
. O.A.	138	ELBY JONES	147	PENROD, HENRY T.	125
. SALLY JOHNSON	24	PEELE, W.T.	147-148	. JENNIE	140
. SARAH	18	PEELER, DORA	153	. JENNIE KNOTGRASS	125
. THOMAS	78	. SARAH	79	PEPLES, BENSON W.	53
. ZELIA	112	. T.O.	70	ELIAZA WHITWORTH	53
PATTON, P.O.	154	. W.	94	PEQUES, JOSEPH	121
. SARAH A.	101	. W.C.	117	PERCELL, HENRY	13
. W.H.	149	. W.G.	38, 74	MARTHA BRAVOIS	13
PAUL, LAURA	43	. W.P.	73	PERCHY, ELIZABETH	110
PAXTON, AMOS	23, 35, 126	. W.T.	40, 42-43, 53, 57	PERMINTER, MARY A.	12
. BOWMAN	4, 18	.	59-60, 80, 88, 90, 95, 98	PETTIE, IDA	74
. ELIZA	97	.	99, 101, 104, 108, 113	PETTY, ALFRED	89
. F.M.	28	.	114, 122, 124-127, 131	. B.F.	15
. FRANCIS	28	.	135, 137-138, 145, 152	. EMMA HAMPTON	89
. FRANCIS E.	75	. W.Z.	46	. JOSAPHINE BARNETT	15
. HELLEN B. STEWART	4	. WILLIAM	79	. LASLY POPE	104
. IDA CURFORD	126	PEELERS, JESS	81	. LUCY A.	105
. IDA M.	129	MALESSA CUNNINGHAM	81	. MAGER	89
. ISAAC	129	PEEPERS, MARY	90	. MARY M.	33
. JANE PINKLEY	28	PEEPLES, BENJAMIN W.	131	. NELLIE	89
. JOSEPH	35	. BENSON Q.	107	. WILLIAM A.	104
. MARGARET	9	. EMMA PATTEN	131	PEURMAN, R.P.	141
. MARY	35	. JANE WEST	130	PFOFF, LOUISA HOUSTON	12
. MARY A. STUART	18	. LAURA	107	MATHEW H.	12
. MARY McCARMACK	129	. SAMUEL F.	130	PHARRIS, WILLIAM	74

INDEX
(New Madrid, Co., MO. Marriages Vol #2)

Name	Page	Name	Page	Name	Page
PHELABAR, AMELIA	128	. MELINDA POWELL	6	PIGGUS, JOSEPH	54,62
PHELON, LAURA	103	. MOLLIE	80	PIGUS, JOSEPH	50
PHERRIS, J.H.	50	. MOLLIE PHILLIPS	80	PIKE, CHARLES	40
PHESCH, JENNY	95	. MURRAY	5	PIKEY, AUGUSTUS G.	101
PHILABAR, ADA	150	. MURRAY WEBSTER	53	. BENJAMIN F.	110
PHILIBOW, ADA	140	. NEELIE WATERS	68	. C.	76
PHILLIPS,		. PAUL	130	. ETTA BABB	36
. ADA F. BARNES	35	. PAUL H.	130	. GIRARD	87
. ALLY	101	. PLASELDIN GAINGNE	8	. LAURA	87
. AMANDA J.	139	. RICHARD	34	. LEODER	101
. AMELIA MEATT	82	. RICHARD A.	20	. LIZZIE SINKS	112
. ANN DELIA	6	. RICHARD J.	6,13,15	. LUCY HENSON	110
. ANNA	6	. SAMUEL A.	17	. MARTHA SHEPARD	14
. ANNIE HOWARD	5	. SHAP G.	83	. MARTIN	112
. CHARLES P.	151	. SUSIE L.	25	. P.	35
. CORDA M. GANT	151	. TERASE	42	. PETER	14
. D.C.	137	. W.B.	70,73-74,78,85,89	. SAMUEL	36
. DEWITT C.	27	. WILLIAM	82	. SUSAN McLEMORE	38
. DURUTHA THOMPSON	123	. WILLIAM B.	67,71,80,84	. WILLIAM A.	38
. E.A.	80	PHILLIPS.D.C.	139	PILLOW,	71
. ELIZABETH LEWIS	34	PICKET,		. A.J.	49
. ELLA	6	. AMANDA L. SHEPPARD	6	. MARY SHAFER	49
. FANNIE	144	. JOSEPH C.	6	PINKLEY, JANE	28
. FRED	123	. NANCY	118	PINLEY, MARY	27
. HENRY M.	35	PICKETT, MOLLIE	50	PINNELL,	
. IDA	115	. NANCY ABBOTT	73	. GUSTA NEWBAUER	70
. J.W.	8	. OMA B.	73	. HATTIE LAFORGE	14
. JOSEPHINE	57	PIERCE, STELLER	140	. WILLIAM	10
. LEANA A. STEWART	20	WILLIAM	140	. WILLIAM W.	14,70
. LEE	68	PIGG, J.P.	47	PIPPEN, AMANDA	149
. LILBOURN	66,80	JOSEPH	59	PLEAS, MARY	112
. LINDA	83	PIGGEE, JOSEPH	89,93	PLEASANT, GEORGE W.	71
. LINDA PHILLIPS	83	PIGGERS, JOSEPH	51	MARY SHOCKONAY	71
. LULA POWELL	130	PIGGIE, JOSEPH	90	POE, ADA VEST	20
. MARTHA V. NEWSUM	27	PIGGOT, ANNIE WATSON	138	. DELLA LOU ALLEN	23
. MARY	109	FREDERICK T.	138	. DESHEY WELLS	39
. MARY E. WATSON	17	PIGGOTT, IDA L.	30	. J.F.	150
. MARY HARDIN	53	PIGGS, JOSEPH	43	. JOHN E.	23,69

INDEX
(New Madrid, Co., MO. Marriages Vol #2)

. LAURA LESIEUR	120	POSTSTON,		. BETTIE	87		
. MARY E. EDWARDS	69	. CAROLINE GRUN	126	. GEORGE T.	15		
. MARY F.	67	. DANIEL W.	126	. JAMES C.	52,131		
. MATTIE SUTHERLAND	150	POTTER, AMERICA	11	. MARY DAVIS	131		
. ROSA BASSET	76	ELLEN	76	. NAOMIA DILLARD	52		
. TILLIE	10	POTTS, DAISY	98	. SALLIE BROUGHTON	15		
. W.R.	67	POWELL, ALSA	58	. SARAH	2		
. WILLIAM R.	39,76,120	. ANGELINE COLEMAN	62	PRICHETT, LOUIS	105		
. WILLIAM T.	20	. DIXIE	63	MARY PRESTON	105		
POLLACK, BETTY GILMORE	34	. ELVINIA	15	PRIDDY, ELIZA BROWN	55		
DAVID C.	34	. JOHN M.	62	JOHN L.	55		
POLLICKE,		. LULA	130	PRIEST, C.	10		
. BETTIE GILMORE	27	. MELINDA	6	R.C.	10,13-14,16		
. DAN C.	27	. RUTH E.	96	PRISSON, DAILEY O.	148		
POPE, JOHN	120	POWERS, DAVID	1	. JOHN M.	102		
. LASLY	104	. GEORGE N.	21	. MARY L. WELLS	148		
. MARY	80	. NANCY ANN DORSON	21	PRITCHETT, EDWARD	30		
. ROSE	120	. SARAH F. RAY	1	HARRIET L. DAZAN	30		
PORTEL, SUSAN	24	PRAT, CHARLIE	86	PROE, FLORENCE	114		
PORTER, ANNIE M.	65	ISA COOPER	86	PRUDY, ZULA A.	95		
. CYRUS	95,138	PRESLEY, ETTA BRATTEN	123	PRUETT, JERRY L.	74		
. ELIAS	50	. JOSEPH	123	PRUITT, ANNA SPEAKMAN	135		
. ELVATINE	13	. MARGARET	45	SETH	135		
. EMMETT G.	91	PRESSON, DANIEL	140	PUCKETT,	19		
. GEORGE W.	96	. HENRY T.	139	PULER, W.T.	37		
. ISAAC	38	. J.J.	5,16,91,141	PURCELL,			
. LEVERNA	38	. J.M.	91,98,105,139,148	. ATLANTA STEWART	44		
. LOTTY	59,67	. JOHN M.	94	. BISHOP	44		
. LYMUS	144	. MARY E. MAYNAR	140	PURDY, WILLIAM B.	32		
. MELINDA FRANCIS	96	. MINNIE WATSON	151	ZULA RANDSBURG	32		
. MINNIE PATERSON	138	. S.A.	91	RACKLEY,			
. NEELY	127	. TABITHA	139	. CATHERINE ISBELL	148		
. NORA EICEMAN	95	. WILLIAM H.	151	. DAVID V.	148		
. RENA LAFONT	144	PRESTON, JAMES	45	RAGLON, ELIZABETH	143		
. ROSALEE GASPETH	104	. MARY	105	JOHN	143		
. S.A. PRESSON	91	. NANCY GIBSON	45	RAGSDALE,			
. SYLVIA DAUGHTERY	50	PREWITT, LIZZIE	72	. CLARA BLACKWELL	106		
. THOMAS B.	104	PRICE, AMANDA	31	. JAMES T.	106		

INDEX
(New Madrid, Co., MO. Marriages Vol #2)

. LETHA	19	RANSON, ELIZABETH	23	.	53-54,66-67,69,72,76		
RAIDT, BARBARA	41	RASSON, CALEB R.	23	.	81,86-87,100,121,129		
. BASIL	10	ELIZABETH RANSON	23	.		146	
. DANIEL W.	91	RATCLIFF, ANNA	148	. CHSEL.	29		
. KATHY	112	RATLIFF,		. EVERETT	55		
. LENA	10	. ELVATINE PORTER	13	. FRANCIS M.	52		
. LENA A.	63	. MARGARET	91	. INA B.	16		
. MARY P. MASON	91	. MARGAT	81	. JOHN H.	54		
. PHILLIP	14	. RICHARD	13	. JULIA GUTDRIDGE	55		
RAINWATER, CLEMENTINE	124	RATTLIFFE, NARCISSUS	70	. LUERITIA WEAVER	54		
. FLORENCE	99	RAY, ARSENIA VETETOE	72	. MALINDA J.	1		
. IDA LONG	136	. CATHERINE EVANS	78	. MOLLIE	20		
. JOHN F.	136	. CRIS	78	. POLLY LANY	52		
. MARGARET	41	. ELIZABETH	133	. SUSAN FLETCHER	54		
. T.M.	99	. EUGENE	114	. SYLVESTER F.	94		
RALSTON, JENNIE	24	. FRANCIS A.J. NALLY	16	REEDE, JAMES	107		
RAMATTER, CLEMENTINE	84	. GEORGE W.	52	NANCY MEDDERS	107		
RAMSEY, BENJAMIN	25	. GEORGIA	60	REEDER, CHARLES	137		
MELINDA GRAY	25	. HENRY	16	. HATTY	42		
RANDOLPH, ADDY KEY	111	. JOHN	98	. JOHN	20,42		
. AMANDA	97	. LIZZIE BURNUM	98	. LELIA	55		
. CARRIE	90	. MARTHA J.	84,112	. MOLLIE E.	20		
. GEORGE E.	114	. MARY E.	84	REESE, EDITH	66		
. JOHN	1,90,93	. POLK	60	REEVES, GEORGE A.	4		
. JOHN W.	111	. RICHARD E.	72	. JOHN	4		
. LOU KEY	114	. ROSA DUNN	114	. MARY C. CARSON	4		
. MARY	90	. SARAH F.	1	. MARY FRY	116		
. NANCY	92	RAYBURN, MARY	80	. SARAH COATS	4		
. SALLIE KEY	93	READE, MAMIE	54	. WILLIAM	116		
RANDOLS, ANNIE	107	REAVES, JOHN	16	REID, CHARLES	92,103,143		
RANDSBURG, ZULA	32	JOSAPHINE NIGHT	16	REILLY, H.H.	45		
RANELS, ANN	1	RED, THOMAS	119	REIS, MARY E.	107		
RANKIN, JERUSHA	26	REDDICK, DECILLA	26	RENES, HATTIE FOLEY	76		
RANSBURGH, ANNA	108	REDIN, ANNIE	111	IRENIUS	76		
. JOHN L.	73	REED,	105-106	RENFOE, MISSIE	86		
. MAMIE	106	. ADOLPH	35	RENFRO, AMANDY WRIGHT	149		
. MOLLIE RODGERS	73	. ANNIE DOW	94	. HAMILTON	86		
. SALLIE	60	. CHARLES	32,43,46-47	. LOUIS	149		

INDEX
(New Madrid, Co., MO. Marriages Vol #2)

Name	Page
. LUCY BROWN	86
RENION, AMANDA	124
RENO, NELLY	147
REVELLE, ROSA	147
REYNOLDS, ANN	1
OLIVIA	8
RHOADS,	
. ELLEN WILLIAMS	143
. THOMAS	143
RHODES, ANNIE	118
. EDWARD	55
. ELLA BISHOP	130
. ELLA HAMPTON	67
. HENRY	67, 130
. LAURA	55
. ROBERT P.	16
. SARAH E. KNOX	16
RIACH, MARY JANE	36
RICE, BETTIE McCONNEL	49
. CHARLES	38
. JIMMY DEAN	74
. JOHN G.	74
. LUCINDA	130
. MARY	150
. MARY E. MASTERSON	38
. NORA J.	67
. WILLIAM A.	49
RICHARD, DANIEL T.	112
FLORENCE BROWN	112
RICHARDS, BIUS	145
. CHARLES	59
. CORDELIA	110
. DAVID	24, 29
. KATY	121
. LUCY DAVIS	29
. MARY ASHBY	59
. NETTY MORGAN	145
. RUFUS	110

Name	Page
. SUSY DAVIS	24
RICHARDSON,	
. AMANDA HAMPTON	3
. AMSON	109
. ANSON	7
. DOUGLAS	30
. ELIZA SAWYERS	30
. GEORGIA	140
. HATTIE	146
. LUCY ARBUCKLE	19
. MAGGIE	99
. MINNIE	109
. SUSAN LESIEUR	7
. UNION	3
. W.B.	21
. WILLIAM	19
RICHEY, H.	2
MARY KANE	2
RICHY, EMMA	48
RIDDLE, ASA	6
. ELLEN M. TAYLOR	6
. JOSEPH A.	33
. JOSEPHINE	40
. JOSEPHINE BAILEY	33
. LERRSA	142
RIDLEY, CHARLEY	141
MARGARET ROBINSON	141
RIELLY, H.H.	46
RIFFLE, CLARA B.	19
L. JOSEY	42
RIGGS,	69
. CARLIN	97
. JOHN	11, 18
. MALINDA	97
. NANCY D. STEWART	11
. SARAH	142
. SARAH PATTERSON	18
RIKARD, ALIE SOUTHARD	83

Name	Page
W.H.	83
RILEFORD, ROSANA	23
RILEY, C.H.	144-145
. CHILION	10
. DAVIS B.	42
. E.T.	24
. ELIZA DAWSON	31
. EMMUND T.	31
. FANNIE	25
. H.H.	43, 48-49
. HATTY REEDER	42
. HENRY C.	1, 5, 13
. JENNIE HOWARD	13
. LAURA JACKSON	81
. LUCY	32
. SARAH	65
. SUSIE	149
. WILLIAM	1
. WILLIE	81
RINEY, LAFAYETTE T.	66
MOLLIE C. LESTER	66
RINKEL, E.J.	93-94
RINKLE, E.J.	86, 91
RITTENHOUSE, A.A.	26
. ELIZABETH MEATTE	6
. LOTTA	136
. THOMAS F.	6
RITTERHOUSE, A.A.	21
ROACH, ELLEN	21
ROAN, MAGGIE	91
ROBERTS, ISABEL	66
ROBBINS, BARBARA	28
. ELLEN	25, 75, 111
. JOSEPH	25, 28
. MARTHA	75
. MARY	134
. MELENY	25
. WILLIAM	36

INDEX
(New Madrid, Co., MO. Marriages Vol #2)

ROBERSON, JANE	105	. HENRY	147	. THOMAS	15	
SAMANTHA	7	. SARA	145	ROTH, ELIZABETH	8	
ROBERTS,		ROLENDS, R.C. MOODY	35	WILLIAM	23	
. ANNA CARPENTER	62	R.W.	35	ROUNDS, JAMES	132	
. JOSEPH F.	62	RONY, MARY GLASS	123	NELLIE FROST	132	
. MARTHA	130	ROSS	123	ROUNGEE, POLLY	4	
. MOLLIE TIBBS	36	ROOTS, MAGGIE	152	ROYERS, AGNES	79	
. P.H.	152	ROPER, JOHN H.	4	RUBLE, CORA MAJORS	145	
. W.A.	36	. JOHN LOGAN	44	PETER	145	
ROBERTSON, MARTHA	2,91	. MANDA	138	RUCKER, ALENN	18	
ROBINS, CAMELIA	65	. MELISSA J. BARNES	4	RUCKETTS, MARY	81	
ELLEN	65	. NANCY C. BURKHART	44	RUDDER, ROBERT R.	128	
ROBINSON, ALLIE	80	ROSE, ELIZA M.	16	RUDDLES, ANNY MILLER	110	
. AMELIA SMITH	44	. ELLEN	120	JAMES P.	110	
. CHARLES	60	. JOHN ROBERT	120	RUDE, CHARLES	37,39	
. CINDA	80	. JOSIE STUART	120	RUGGLES, KATY FRENSO	149	
. ELIZAH GODAIRD	60	. MAY	139	. RODY TUCKER	89	
. JAMES	44	ROSEBERRY, GEORGE	134	. SIDNEY	89,149	
. JANE	87	MATTIE LUMSDEM	134	RUHEY, ALICE WISEMAN	68	
. JOHN F.	79	ROSS, AMANDA	45	GEORGE W.	68	
. MARGARET	141	. CARELINE	89	RUMMELS,		
. MARY F.A. THORN	79	. CORA L.	53	. DECILLA REDDICK	26	
ROBISON, EARNEST	44	. ELIZABETH	13	. HENRY C.	26	
JANE JOHNSON	44	. EMMA PARKER	123	RUPLES, M.J.	153	
ROCHELL, ALBERT	76	. HENRIETTA	11,64	RUSHING, MINNIE	149	
. ANNIE SECOY	76	. HESTER	24	RUSSELL, ANSELEM	26	
. ELLA TONEY	104	. HOLLY	148	. EMMA FOUST	26	
. HENRY	104	. JANE WITHERSPOON	138	. MARY C.	92	
RODES, EDWARD	151	. JOHN	64,89,138	RUST, JAMES M.	22	
MATILDA LAFONT	151	. JOSEPH	123	MARTHA BLACKEN	22	
RODGERS, JAMES	133	. LIZZIE	98	RUTHERFORD, JAMES	2	
. JOHN M.	132	. LYDIA	72	PERMELIA OLIVER	2	
. MARTHA HALE	132	. MARIAH	72,140	RYAN, JAMES	115	
. MOLLIE	73	. MAUDE GOODIN	15	. JOSIE	115	
RODIS, EMELINE	24	. MOLLY	63	. MICHAEL	11	
ROGERS, SUSAN	99	. PAULINE	81,124	. PERNELIA J. HADEN	11	
ROLAN, SARAH	148	. T.	24	SACKETT,		
ROLAND, AMANDA WHITT	147	. TALBOT	29	. POLLY A.C. BRADEN	23	

INDEX
(New Madrid, Co., MO. Marriages Vol #2)

. WILLIAM D.	23	. ELIZA	30	MINERVA COOPER	64
SALES, JOHN	92	. JAMES M.	91	SEARS, REBECCA	92
SALT, MARIE E. EARLES	8	. JAMES W.	19,30,129	SEAS, AMANDA CARR	42
MARTIN A.	8	. JULIA A. LEWIS	30	ANDY	42
SAMUELS, EFFA L.	103	. LETHA RAGSDALE	19	SEATON, MARY	135
SANDEFUR,		. M.M.	30	SEBY, SALONEY	79
. LEE HUFSTUTTER	82	. MARTHA MERRETT	91	SECOY, ANNIE	76
. LOUIS W.	82	SAY, FLORENCE A.	38	. EDWARD	103
SANDER,		SCHINK, MATTIE	133	. LINDA	114
. AMANDA TOWNSEND	35	SCHNEIDER, ADAM	13	. MAMIE WILLIS	103
. JAMES	35	. ANN	13	. MARY	17
SANDERS, ABRAHAM	20	. ANN SCHNEIDER	13	SEIPLER, CONRAD	97
. ABRAM	20	SCHULTZ, NELLY RENO	147	SENDER, E.F.	75
. D.Q.	50	WILLIAM D.	147	SENTER, E. FRANKLIN	80
. FANNY	20	SCIMMONES, A.J.	107	. E.F.	75,77,79,81
. JOHN	8	SCIMMONS, A.J.	140	. ELOIS F.	78
. MARY J. EWING	8	O.J.	139	SETTLE, MARY E.	65
. MARY M. TILL	137	SCIMS, ELLEN	100	SETTLES, ELIZA	46
. ROBERT C.	137	SCOTT, ALBERT	62	. FANNIE	121
SANDFORD, NELLIE	30	. D.P.	83	. GEORGE	65
WILLIAM	30	. ELIZA HARRIS	62	. M.G.	46
SANDS, ALICE	22	. ELIZABETH HUNTSINGER	2	. SALLIE	88
. ALVEY COX	117	. EPHRAIN	2	. SAM	3
. BELL McLEMORE	136	. KATE	74	. SAMUEL	108
. CATHERINE COATS	127	. KATIE BEACLLES	83	. SUSAN	3,108
. JOHN	117	. MAGGIE DUW	92	. WESLEY F.	2
. JOHN N.	136	. MARY E. HARRIS	68	SEVER,	
. MONROE	127	. MISSOURI	76	. EASTER CROWNSHAW	86
SANVILLE, MARY	24	. MISSOURI SUGS	42	. JOHN	86
SATTERWHITE, JOHN D.	152	. RANSOM	92	SEWARD, ELLEN ROACH	21
SAULS, ABRAHAM	112	. RANSON	42	. JOHN	21
. ELLA GRAY	63	. SHIRLEY	68	. JOSEPH	65
. ELLEN PACQUETT	61	SCUMMONS, A.J.	109	. ROSA BELL GASSETT	147
. FRANCIS O. BAKER	28	SEAL, GEORGE H.	24	. SARAH RILEY	65
. JOHN W.	28,61	SEALS,		. WILLIAM HENRY	147
. JOSAY	112	. CELINDA WHITESTORE	93	SEWELL, JOSAPHINE	15
. THOMAS W.	63	. RICHARD J.	93	MARTHA	41
SAWYERS, CHARLES M.	30	SEAR, BEN F.	64	SEXTON, ADA	144

INDEX
(New Madrid, Co., MO. Marriages Vol #2)

SHAFER, MARY	49	SHEEKS,		SHIDLER, LOTTA	133		
SHAFFER, MARY SULIVAN	12	. FRANCIS K. ELLIS	40	SHIELDS, ALBERT	125		
THOMAS	12	. SHELBY	40	. ANNA B.	54		
SHANK, GEORGE H.	56	SHELBY, ALBERT	90, 126	. ANNIE M. LAW	125		
. GEORGE W.	56	. BEATRICE HERNDON	90	. EMMA MOTE	23		
. MARTHA E. SIMMONS	56	. C.A.	37	. GEORGE	81		
. MARTHA SIMMONS	56	. CAROLINE	58	. GEORGE W.	23		
SHANKS,		. CAROLINE HENDRIX	5	. JAMES B.	9		
. ALVA MIPPLETON	104	. G.A.	123	. JOSEPH	54		
. JAMES	63	. J.E.	5, 21, 113, 146	. LILLEY LAVALLEE	81		
. JAMES M.	1	. J.L.	74-75, 87, 89, 91	. LOUISA YOUNG	9		
. MARY F. GRAY	1	.	95-96, 106-107, 132	SHIMEFUT, ALBERT	94		
. MOLLY ROSS	63	. JACOB L.	46	SUSAN CARRS	94		
. MONROE	104	. JOSEPH	58	SHIRKEY, BENJAMIN L.	5		
. VINA GRAY	4	. KATIE	21	. ELIZABETH WATSON	5		
. WILLIAM F.	4	. LENA	62	. FANNIE BARRON	46		
SHARP, CHARLES D.	87	. MARTHA	74	. MARTHA	124		
. ELLEN BANDY	9	. MARY	124	. WESTON	46		
. MARY C. DEAN	87	. MOLLIE GRIFFEY	126	SHIRLEY, J.L.	115		
. STEPHEN H.	9	. N.E. STRINGER	37	JOSIE	124		
SHAVER, CHRISTOPHER C.	71	. SARAH CERNE	46	SHOAT, MARY	107		
. JULIA LASTER	71	SHELFER, EMMA	104	SHOCKONAY, MARY	71		
. MAGGIE ACORD	136	. M.E.	104	SHRADER, HENRY	70		
. OTIS	136	. T.E.	104	SUSAN MONTGOMERY	70		
SHAVERS,		SHELSON, ALICE	106	SHUBIT, JOHN W.	92		
. AMANDA DRIVER	108	SHELTON,		SHULTZ, ALBERT C.	11		
. COLUMBUS	108	. BETTY CHILDERS	133	. ANTONETTE GRAY	11		
SHAW, ALICE	12	. LENA	33	. JANE	104		
. WILLIAM	80	. MARY E.	12	. KATIE	126		
. ZENIA HUNTER	80	. WILLIAM	133	. MARY J.	61		
SHAY, MARGARET	117	SHEPARD, MARTHA	14	. MARY J. SNEED	1		
SHEAD, JAMES ALCOTT	98	SHEPPARD, AMANDA L.	6	. ROBERT	147		
MARY LAFORGE	98	SHERBUT, LULA	92	. SARAH	3		
SHEAPPARD,		SHERKEY, MARY	85	. TOMPY AILES	147		
. ALLIE BLIZZARD	96	WASH	85	. WILLIAM W.	1		
. WILLIAM	96	SHERWOOD, BELL	55	SHUMAKER, ELIZABETH	47		
SHEEFER, EMMA	130	W.E.	2	. LIZZIE MARS	31		
SHEEHY, J.L.	116	SHIDETER, PEAL E.	135	. MARCUS	31, 47		

INDEX
(New Madrid, Co., MO. Marriages Vol #2)

Name	Page	Name	Page	Name	Page
. PAUSHY BEARDE	47	. J.	34	. NANCY E.	130
SHY, JESSE	40	. JAMES B.	16, 75	SISK, ANNA	135
. LAURA L. WATHEN	146	. MANAH	114	SKAGGS, ALFORD H.	12
. MARY KEMEROTHY	40	. MARTHA	56	LAURA A. JONES	12
. SAMUEL R.	146	. MARTHA E.	56	SKANKS, BETTIE HENRY	100
SIBLEY, L.D.	44	. MARY CRASHARD	110	ED	100
SIGARS, JOHN	2	. PERMINCE J.	71	SLAUGHTER, ADA	127
MARTHA McALISTER	2	. R.J.	89	SLAWS, PURCILLA	5
SIGGERS, JOHN W.	153	SIMMS, AUGUSTUS J.	113	SLAYTON, ELLA	34
LILLIE	153	. CHINNEY CULAT	113	SLOAS, DANIEL	16
SIKES,	98	. MARY E.	1	. ELLIOT	34
. ABRAHAM	81	SIMON, ELLA	148	. ETTA WILLIS	34
. ANNA	5	SIMPSON, CHARLES A.	27	. LAURA WILLIS	16
. ANTHONY	24	. GEORGE W.	67	. MINERVA	53
. BETTY MORGAN	24	. LUVENE	93	SMALL, ANN	50
. CYNTHA A.	18	. NANCY A. HOOD	27	SMITH, ADA LOW	109
. EDWARD	33	. NORA J. RICE	67	. ADALE	109
. FLORENCE OBANNON	118	. SARAH	116	. ADOLPH M.	85
. FRANCIS	118	SIMS, ANNIE MORRISON	119	. ALICE GOSSETT	19
. JOHN	79	. DAVID	109	. AMANDA MERRILL	77
. JULY ANN	94	. ED	108	. AMELIA	44
. MANURVEY McCOY	33	. EMMA JOHNSON	109	. ANIE WOODS	105
. MARY HUNTER	79	. HENRY	103	. ANN HUNTER	114
. NEEDHAM	10, 14	. JOHN	119	. ANNIE	33
. SALLIE WYATT	14	. LELA E. DOYLE	108	. BENJAMIN	61
. SARAH McGLOFLIN	81	. PAMELA WINCHESTER	50	. CAROLINE MAHAN	78
. WILLARD	81	. THOMAS K.	50	. CATHERINE	96
SIMEOR, JULIA	65	SINE, BETTY	49	. CHARLES M.	34
SIMES, IDA CONRAD	62	SINGLETON, ANNIE SWAN	41	. CHARLEY	14
J.W.	62	WILLIAM	41	. EDWARD	81
SIMIS, FANNIE	103	SINKO, CHARLES A.	65	. ELVINIA POWELL	15
SIMMON, MARY E.	51	JULIA	65	. EMELINE MARTIN	74
SIMMONS, A.J.	66, 90	SINKS, LIZZIE	112	. ETTA LEGETT	15
. 105-106,108,110-111		SINNERILL, MARGARET	39	. EUGENE	143
.	120	SIONS, MARY PACKETT	12	. FLORENCE	143
. BEUREGARD	110	PLEASANT B.	12	. FRANK	40
. ELIZA M. ROSE	16	SISCO, DANIEL B.	130	. GEORGE	19, 83
. FRANCIS E. PAXTON	75	. JULIA	130	. H.	14

INDEX
(New Madrid, Co., MO. Marriages Vol #2)

Name	Page	Name	Page	Name	Page
. H.A.	5,10	. JENNIE PARKER	54	LUCINDA FORD	120
. J.D.	40	. WILLIAM	54	SPENCER,	
. JAMES	94	SMITTEN,		. LAVADA McCLOUD	46
. JAMES A.	143	. L. JOSEY RIFFLE	42	. MINNIE RUSHING	149
. JAMES D.	19	. WILLIAM T.	42	. SALLIE	122
. JESSIE	105	SMOTHERS,		. SOPHIA MARTIN	69
. JESSIE L.	114	. MARY McCORMICK	101	. THOMAS D.	149
. JOHN	74,78	. NEWTON	101	. WILLIAM	46,69,79
. JULY ANN SIKES	94	SMRUING, FRANCES	123	SPIVA, E.A. PHILLIPS	80
. LUCY J. KURNEY	14	SMULLINS, ROENA	3	HOMAR	80
. MARGARET	38	SMULLON, ANDREW J.	4	STACK, ANNIE FARMER	132
. MARGIE HATCHEL	34	CAROLINE GROSS	4	HORAN	132
. MARTHA BEASLEY	106	SNEAB, ALLIE MILLER	132	STACY, DICEY BURKS	5
. MARY	112	WILLIAM H.	132	JOHN M.P.	5
. MARY CANTRAL	105	SNEED, MARY J.	1	STAFFORD, C. WILLIAMS	82
. MARY ELLIS	39	SNIDER, CAROLINE	41	. MARY	94,130
. MARY SEATON	135	. EDWARD	147	. T.	82
. MELISSA	135	. KATHIE HIGGERSON	147	STALLCUP, ELIZABETH	1
. MELISSA ADKINS	61	. SARAH	45	. MARK	46
. MOLLY HARRIS	143	SNIFFER, A.	116	. MARK H.	5
. NELLY	49	SNOW, J.T.	119	. SUSAN GREGORY	5
. OSEAL	109	PETTIE	70	STALLCUPS, M.H.	65
. REBECCA	78	SOLOMAN, BARBARA	134	STALLINGS, MARY E.	32
. ROSA GOODMAN	83	SOUERS,		STAN, PAULINE NOELL	96
. SALLY HENDERSON	72	. COLUMBIS McCARY	69	THOMAS	96
. SAMUEL	72	. WILLIAM H.	69	STANDFORD, NELLIE	30
. SARAH H. STEWART	143	SOUTH, M.E.	80,135	STANLEY, RUTHLY	154
. TENA VAUGHN	85	SOUTHARD, ALIE	83	STARKS,	80
. THEODORE	15	SOUTHERN, JENNIE LAMB	13	STARR, H.C. LEWIS	18
. THOMAS	49	JOHN A.	13	. JOHN THOMAS	18
. THOMAS T.	77	SOWDERS, SARAH WINTZ	55	. PARETHENA NOELL	95
. W.L.	38	WILLIAM H.	55	. THOMAS	95
. WASHINGTON D.	39	SPARKS, C.A.	133	STAUBIN, MARY ANN	20
. WILLIAM	15,25,35,106	MINERVA J.	7	POLINA	16
. WILLIAM J.	135	SPAULDING, MARSHALL	51	STEIMAN, AMERICA	2
. WILLIAM L.	36,38-39,42	MARY TOMPKINS	51	STEIN, J.D.	141
. WILLIAM S.	32	SPEAKMAN, ANNA	135	STEPHENS, JAMES H.	70
SMITHMAN,		SPELLER, ALLEN	120	. JOHN Q.	25

INDEX
(New Madrid, Co., MO. Marriages Vol #2)

. LULA	94	.	124,129,142,148,150	. M.L.	26
. MAUD HUFF	25	.	152-154	. PERLIE	57
. SARAH R. JACKSON	70	. JAMES T.	141	. SALLY E.	27
STEPP,ALBERT A.	152	. JOHN	87	STONEBRACKER,MILKEY	25
. CORA L. ROSS	53	. JOHN C.	20	ROBERT	25
. GRACE BERRYMAN	126	. JOHN M.	142	STONEBRAKER,ELIZA	61
. IDA C. HART	152	. LAURA BRANHAM	77	STONEBREAKER,	
. J.D.	12,18,20-23-28,31	. LEANA A.	20	. ELIZA EUGRAM	21
.	34-35,51,79,119,126	. LOUISA HUTCHINS	141	. ROBERT C.	21
. J.T.	115	. MARTHA	4	STOREY,MINNIE	102
. JAMES	52,56,84,92,131	. MARTHA A.	109	STORY,JOSEPH H.	29
. JAMES D.	64,67,69,73	. NANCY D.	11	NANCY HAMPTON	29
	78,83,88	. SALLIE	68	STOUT,J.H.	102
. JAMES E.	126	. SARAH H.	143	MARY STILES	102
. JEFF D.	118	. SARAH PRICE	2	STOVAL,CASSEY	101
. JEFFERSON D.	53	STILES,MARY	102	STOWE,FRANCIS WATSON	147
STEVENS,S.R.	84	STILL,E.D.	18	POPE	147
STEWARD,JAMES	24	. M.J.	18	STRAIN,JAMES	95
. JOHN L.	77	. MARY S.	18	LAURA ONEAL	95
. SERENA JOHNSON	77	STINE,J.D.	112,114	STRATTON,JOHN	87-88
. SUSIE	132	. JAMES D.	91,94,99,124	. MAHALEY	87
STEWART,AMANDA J.	142	.	132,136	. MARY	61
. ATLANTA	44	. JOSEPH D.	133,149,152	. SARAH JACKSON	88
. BELL HESS	142	. ROSA	133	STREETS,MARY	100
. BURRELL W.	74	STLIGER,STELLA	78	STRINGER,N.E.	37
. CARRIE	86	STMARY,JOSEPH	94	STRINGFIELD,MARY	25
. D.Y.	77	. JOSEPH G.	94	WILLIAM	1,8-9
. ELLA MAWDY	40	. NONA EWING	111	STRONG,B.M.	75
. EULA W. HUNTER	74	. OLA R. AKIN	94	. BENJAMIN R.	111
. FERNAND	92	. STEPHEN	111	. DEBY E.	52
. FERNANDO C.	40	. STEPHEN W.	111	. ELLEN ROBBINS	111
. GEORGE	2	STOCKARD,		. JAMES G.	75
. HELLEN B.	4	. MARY STREETS	100	. MARTHA ROBBINS	75
. JAMES	13,23-24,28-30	. WILLIAM	100	. MARY	75
	35,39,41,43,49,61,67	STOKES,MARY A.	117	. SARAH E.	2
	69-70,72-76,80,84,86	STOLDER,MARY	54	STUART,JAMES	30
	87-89,92,97,99-100	STONE,JAMES D.	121	. JOSIE	120
	103,113,119-120,122	. LIZZIE	64	. MARY A.	18

INDEX
(New Madrid, Co., MO. Marriages Vol #2)

Name	Page
STUBBLEFIELD,	
. CLEM. RAINWATER	124
. JAMES	62,68,71,124
. JAMES F.	124
. MARY JONES	68
. MINNIE	71
STUBBS, ALICE SHELSON	106
DALLAS	106
STUCKEY, J.C.	26
MARY VICKERS	26
STULL, GEORGE W.	101
. M.J.	101
. SARAH A. PATTON	101
STURGEON, HENDERSON	108
. MARY	64
. SUSAN FORD	108
STURGILL,	
. S.F. BLACKBURN	33
. W.B.	33
SUDBERRY, BETTY	129
SUGS, MISSOURI	42
SULIVAN, MARY	12
SULLIVAN,	
. ANNIE ADCOCK	122
. LUCY	79
. SAMUEL W.	122
. TEDA	139
SUMMERS, A.J.	102
. EMMA	93
. JAMES	90,149
. MARY	149
. MOLLIE J.	8
SUMNER, ANDREW	25
. HARRIETE	14
. SEPTIMA WARD	25
SURARD, JOSEPH	65
SARAH RILEY	65
SUTHERLAND,	
. ADDIE HERRON	61
. J.H.	61
. MATTIE	150
SUTTLES,	
. MARGARET JONES	31
. SAMUEL	31
SUTTON,	
. BETTIE WILLIAMS	28
. ELIZA	11
. EMMA ADAMS	15
. HENRY	27
. JACOB	109
. JAMES	28
. JAMES C.	23
. JENNY TOMY	23
. MARY RAYBURN	80
. ROBERT	80
. SALLIE DEWITT	109
. SAMANTHA	9
. WILLIAM H.	15
SWAN, ANNIE	41
. CORA	136
. ELIZABETH McGENTHY	84
. J.T.	52
. THOMAS	41
. WILLIAM F.	84
SWANK, BENJAMIN M.	121
MAHALEY MASEL	121
SWEAT, ALLEN	139
. CORDELIA BANHAM	154
. CORDELIA COX	139
. WILLIAM	154
SWIFT, F.S.P.	16
THERESA CHAMBERLAIN	16
SWILLEY, ELIZABETH	5
SWING, EDWARD	85
FRANCES DAWSON	85
SYKES,	24
TALBOT, ADALINE NOBLE	53
GEORGE M.	53
TALLEY, NANCY	32
W.T.	133
TANKSLEY, SARAH PEELER	79
WILLIAM	79
TANNER, W.S.	139
TAPP, ROZETTA	57
TARTETON,	
. MARGARET GITTON	42
. ROBERT	42
TARVEN, LEVENA FURLONG	29
NATHAN	29
TATE, FRANCES	82
THOMAS	82
TAYLOR, ANNA	139
. BENJAMIN	8
. ELLEN	83
. ELLEN M.	6
. HENRIETTA HUGHES	37
. IDA JANE	104
. ISAAC	88
. JOHN	8
. LANCY	94
. LAURA PEEPLES	107
. LILY WILLIAMS	8
. LIZZIE A.	151
. MATTIE FOWLER	88
. OLIVIA REYNOLDS	8
. WALLARD	107
. WALT	37
TEGUE, EVA	115
TELLEFRO, JESSIE A.	63
LENA A. RAIDT	63
TEMPA, MEDITA	95
TERREL, MATTIE	75
TERRY, ELIZABETH	18
. JOSEPH E.	146

INDEX
(New Madrid, Co., MO. Marriages Vol #2)

Name	Page	Name	Page	Name	Page
. LOUISA	31	. CHARLES	78	. MARY E.	10
. LYIA	141	. DURUTHA	123	TIDWELL, DORA JOHNSON	76
. MARGARET	126	. ELIZABETH	32	. JASPER N.	76
. MARY A. BROWER	146	. EMMA	110	. LOUIS R.	70
TESOY, HESTER	143	. EMMA RICHY	48	. NARCISSUS RATTLIFFE	70
MAINY	143	. F.F.	91	TILBERT, HENRY	147
THARP, MINNIE	137	. FLORA KITCHENS	125	ROSA REVELLE	147
THOM, AGNESS CARLISLE	145	. GEORGE	55, 125	TILL,	
JOHN M.	145	. GEORGE A.	65	. DIXEY WILLOUGHBY	134
THOMAS, AMANDA WATSON	47	. IDA	106, 127, 148	. ELLEN BULLOCK	56
. AMOS J.	135	. JESSE	82	. MARY M.	137
. C.C.	20	. JOHN	55, 125	. POMPY	134
. CALLY MUDD	72	. JOSEPH	63	. WILLIAM	137
. CAROLINE SNIDER	41	. JOSIE RYAN	115	. WILLIAM H.	56
. CENE CRAIG	102	. M.A.	82	TILLMAN, ALSE BUCKER	119
. EUGENE P.	148	. MARIAH DAVIS	63	WILLIAM	119
. HENRY	89	. MARTHA	138	TIMBERMAN, EMMA BISHOP	4
. JAMES M.	102	. MARY CRABTREE	82	JOHN D.	4
. JENNIE HOEHN	148	. MARY MEATTE	71	TINKER, PHILLIP	120
. JOHN A.	12	. MARY STRONG	75	ROSE POPE	120
. MACK	72	. MAY WATSON	125	TINNIN, CHARLES	106
. MAHALA UPTON	12	. RACHEL	91	NANCY J. GRANT	106
. MARSHALL	41	. S.S.	82	TINSLEY, ANNA EVANS	32, 36
. MARY	7	. SAMUEL E.	115	JOHN	32, 36
. MARY J. GRIFFY	89	THORN, LOU WHEAT	51	TIPPET,	
. MOLLIE	20	. MARY F.A.	79	. ELIZABETH PERCHY	110
. SAMUEL	47	. NATTIE YOUNG	123	. JAMES	110
. SARAH GILLBRITH	135	. WILLIAM	51, 79, 123	TISON, EXER BLOT	82
THOMPKINS, BETSY	134	THORP, BIRDIE LONG	73	WILLIAM	82
. LAURA CLIMMONS	105	MOSES	73	TODD, FANNY	78
. NATT	105	THORPE, ELLEN	128	TOLBETT, LIZZIE ELLIS	46
. PEARL	134	THURMON, MARY E.	7	WARREN R.	46
THOMPKON, EMELINE	98	THURSTON, DAVID J.	128	TOMISOON, ANNA	60
THOMPSON, A.J.	75	JENNIE HOUBEN	128	TOMPKINS, CHARLES	65
. ALBERT	48	TIBBS, MOLLIE	36	. EMMA	32
. BETTIE	91	TICKELL, L.A.	10	. JENNY OBANNON	65
. CAMELIA ROBINS	65	. LOUIS A.	1	. MARY	51
. CAVE	71	. M.J.	10	. SARAH	10

INDEX
(New Madrid, Co., MO. Marriages Vol #2)

TOMY, JENNY	23	. ELIZABETH	124	. GREEN	35		
TONEY, AMELIA	85	. GEORGE	139	. ROBERT	137		
. BETTIE	11	. JARSITE	103	. RODY	89		
. CHARLES P.	101	. JEWETT	124	. ROSA	137		
. CLARA	129	. LAURA CRISEL	139	TULL, J. WEBSTER	53		
. CLARA LAMB	101	. LAURA McGEE	88	. WEBSTER	22, 42-43, 46-49		
. DORA BUTLER	62	. MARY	103	.	54-55, 59-60		
. ELIZABETH HOLLAND	13	. MARY PAXTON	35	TURNER, ED	108		
. ELLA	104	TREADWELL, ADALINE	24	. LOUIS	95		
. EMERY KLEIN	145	. ALBERT	135, 144, 153	. MAMIE	95		
. HATTIE	39	. GOODWIN	24	. SUSAN SETTLES	108		
. JESSIE	43	. MARTHA	30	TYRART, MARY OLIVER	2		
. JOSEPH	62	. SUSAN PORTEL	24	WILLIAM A.	2		
. MARY E.	16	TRIGNED, MARTHA	26	ULOTT, R.L.	15		
. SUMMERS	145	TRIPP, JOSEPH	124	UMPHRIES,			
. W.H.	104	NANCY PARSON	124	. MAY BLANKENSHIP	101		
. WILLIAM H.	13	TROGDEN,		. WILLIAM T.	101		
TONY, CARRIE	122	. ALICE BREVARD	140	UNDERWOOD, BETTY	26		
. MAY YOUNG	135	. JOHN	140	. ELIZABETH ALEXANDER	7		
. WASHINGTON	135	TROLLENGED, J.H.	58	. EMILY McLEMORE	79		
TOWNSEND, AMANDA	35	TROLLINGER,		. JAMES	7, 108		
. EMILY	4	. HANNAH CLAYTON	15	. JAMES T.	79		
. JOHN	40	. JOHN H.	15	. SARAH	10		
. MARY BEASY	40	TROTER,		. V. ADMER	108		
. MARY BRACY	40	. MARGARET SINNERILL	39	UPTON, JAMES	99		
TOWNSON, JOHN	124	. RUBIN	39	. KATIE	101		
MARGARET CAVELENON	124	TROTTER, ANNER JONES	104	. LUCY DOSS	99		
TRAMMEL, DANIA COCHRAN	30	. REUBEN	104	. MAHALA	12		
. DOUGLAS	87	. REUBON	149	VAIDEN, HENRY	119		
. EDWARD J.	104	. SALLIE NICHOLAS	149	MAME CRAWFORD	119		
. EDWARD JARRETT	83	TROY, HESTER	143	VAIL, GEORGE E.	6		
. EMMA SHELFER	104	TRUMAN, JOHN	124	LENA DEROCHER	6		
. ISABEL HEROLDE	24	JOSIE SHIRLEY	124	VAMPETH, JOHN	97		
. JOHN	30	TRUMPER, JOSAY SAULS	112	NANCY ARBUCKLE	97		
. MAHALEY STRATTON	87	WILLIAM D.	112	VANAMBURGH,			
. PHILLIP M.	24	TUCKER, ANNIE	84	. MATTIE LEE	131		
. SARAH E. NORMAN	83	. DINAH BOOKER	35	. ROBERT W.	131		
TRAMMELL, CHESTER	35, 88	. DORA BARNES	137	VANBIBBER,			

INDEX
(New Madrid, Co., MO. Marriages Vol #2)

. MARY LUMSDEN	136	. LOUIS W.	56	. CYNTHA NEWMAN	113
. THOMAS	136	. PATSEY	13	. D.W.	60
VANFELT,		. WILLIAM	64	. DAVID W.	18
. MARY A. STOKES	117	WAGGONER, BALCET	130	. DRUZILA	44
. WILLIAM	117	EMMA SHEEFER	130	. DRUZILLA KNOX	12
VANOVER, CHARITY	4	WAIDE, NETTIE	128	. ELLEN CREVOISIER	89
FRANCIS	9	WALDROP, DANIEL	107	. EMMA	60
VAUDRIE, AMY	117	. ELIZA	83	. FRANK	12
VAUGHEN, KATY LINCKE	56	. MARY SHOAT	107	. GEORGE W.	89
MATHEW	56	WALKER, ANNA CARROLL	105	. GEORGIA WIMP	40
VAUGHN, BETTIE PRICE	87	. BEN F.C.	116	. J.H.	141
. JOHN R.	8	. CHRISTINE JONES	116	. JACOB	141
. MARY A.	26	. DAVID	102,130	. JAMES	113
. MATTHEW	87	. DORA	104	. JANIEVE GODAIR	18
. SARAH DEMINT	8	. ELIZA	135	. JOHN THOMAS A.	40
. TENA	85	. EMELINE	53	. JUDY	43
VEDETAE,		. JACKSON	117	. MARGARET	95-96
. ADA BELL BALDER	153	. LAURA	151	. MARY E. FORD	12
. WILLIAM M.	153	. MARY J.	28	. MAUDY MOORE	141
VEST, ADA	20	. MARY STAFFORD	130	. SEPTIMA	25
VESTAL, ANN AUGUSTINE	97	. MOLLIE	67	. THOMAS	3
VETETOE, ARSENIA	72	. NANCY	28	. WILLIAM B.	12
WILLIAM	72	. PEARL ANGELO	117	WARE, GABRELLA PARROTT	71
VETILE, ALICIA	103	. SAMUEL	105	WILLIAM	71
VIA, GEORGIA WILLIS	77	WALLACE, C.F.	92	WARING, ROGER D.	143
JAMES J.	77	. LULA SHERBUT	92	TISHY EULETT	143
VICKERS, MARY	26	. MAGGIE	92	WARREN, EMMA MARTIN	60
VINSON, BELL	145	. SARAH E.	92	. JOHN	112
. ERRION	145	WALLS, ADA PHILIBOW	140	. MARTHA WOODS	112
. HENRYETTA	145	. AMELIA	13	. WILLIAM	60
. R.C.	50	. LYDIA ROSS	72	WARRINGTON,	
VOUDIN, AMY	117	. SISSY	13	. ELIZABETH EDMONDSON	6
CHARLES T.	117	. TERRY A.	84	. GUSTAVUS	6
VOWELL, CYNTHA	51	. WILLIAM	72,140	WATER, ANNIE BELL	108
WADDELL, MARY	137	WALTRIP,		LOUIS	108
WADE, CAROLINE	70	. AMELIA WHITSON	134	WATERS, ALBERT	56
. EDA HUNTER	56	. JAMES M.	134	. ANDY	35
. HENRIETTA ROSS	64	WARD, COLUMBIA	123	. ARMSTRONG	145

INDEX
(New Madrid, Co., MO. Marriages Vol #2)

. CARRIE	56	. NANNIE	86	WAYDE, CAROLINE		13,143	
. CLARA	16,113	. NELLIE G. MAHAR	111	LOUIS		143	
. CLARENCE	134	. WILLIAM R.	111	WAYETT,			
. ELIZABETH WILLIAMS	32	WATKINS, D.A.	115	. CRISTINE BLACKMAN		18	
. ELIZAH	56	WATSHINS, JAMES	26	. GEORGE		18	
. ELLA PHILLIPS	6	WATSON, A.J.	130	WEAKS, BETTY SUDBERRY		129	
. EVERLINER	80	. AMANDA	47,66	WILLIAM		129	
. FANNIE PHILLIPS	144	. AMANDA FOX	115	WEATHERSPOON, DANIEL		47	
. FRANCES J.	48	. ANNIE	138	JANE OGDEN		47	
. FRANKIE	98	. BEULAH B. JACKSON	20	WEAVER, LUERITIA		54	
. HENRYETTA VINSON	145	. BURNEY M.	76	MARY ANN		66	
. JOHN S.	32	. C.J. AUCTINE	82	WEBB, ANNIE L.		144	
. JULIA	98	. DELELAH	89	. EMILY McWILLIAMS		142	
. LENA	63	. ELIZABETH	5	. JAMES D.		142	
. LOU	105	. FRANCIS	147	. WILLIAM		139	
. LOUIS	16	. HATTIE	145	WEBSTER, MARY		143	
. LOUIS A.	1,6	. HATTIE DAY	76	WEED, KATE ELLIS		94	
. LUCINDA	96	. JAMES	20,78	LEE		94	
. MARY ANN	47	. JENNY	65	WEEK, HERBERT		23	
. MARY H.	1	. JOHN	138	WEEKS, ELIZABETH		115	
. MATTIE JACKSON	141	. JULY ANN	43	. MANERARY CARLISLE		131	
. MAY WATSONAT	6	. MANDA ROPER	138	. THOMAS		115	
. MOLLIE	86	. MARY E.	17	. WILLIAM		131	
. MOLLIE GIBSON	35	. MATTIE E.	63	WEIGEL, JOSEPH		6	
. NEELIE	68	. MAY	125	WEIGLE, JOSEPH		2,14	
. PEARL THOMPKINS	134	. MINNIE	151	PRUDE BUTLER		2	
. R.J.	1	. RANDOLPH	72,80,115	WELCHANCE, ANNA		18	
. RACHEL	118	. RILLA	143	. ELIZA SUTTON		11	
. SALLIE	47,129	. SALLIE	91	. ELLEN		16	
. SAMUEL	141	. SAMUEL S.	6,8	. JOHN D.		11	
. SAMUEL A.	6	. SYLVIA	75	. TAYLOR		18	
. THOMAS	47	. W.P.	82	WELL, DELLA WILES		83	
. V.V.	48	WATSONAT, MAY	6	WILEY J.		83	
. VICK	22	WATT, HENRY N.	14	WELLENBRINK, HY		4	
. WASH	96	WATTS, HENRY N.	10	WELLES, ROBERT W.		139	
. WILLIAM	144	WAUGH, CYNTHA A. SIKES	18	TABITHA PRESSON		139	
. WILLIAM W.	1	. JAMES E.	18	WELLMAN, JOSEPH		45	
WATHEN, LAURA L.	146	. KATIE	16	MARY WITT		45	

INDEX
(New Madrid, Co., MO. Marriages Vol #2)

WELLS, DESHEY	39	. JOHN D.	27	WHITLEY, L.P.	103
. MARY L.	148	. POLLEY	52	. LUCINDA GODAIR	133
. VISEY	125	. SARAH	85	. MARQUS S.	133
. Z.T.	148	WESTLEY, JAMES	88,108	. NANCY McCLARD	103
WELSEY, JAMES	115	WESTMAN, JAMES A.	138	WHITSON, AMELIA	134
WELSHANS, EMMA	130	MARY A. CAGLE	138	. AMELIA DELISLE	10
WESLEY, ANNA	121	WHALEY, ALBERT N.	128	. IDA M.	132
. DIXIE DAVIS	140	JANIE HUDSON	128	. WILLIAM J.	10
. GEORGE	129	WHAT, ISAAC	28	WHITT, AMANDA	147
. JAMES	59,71,85-86,90	SAUNDRA BURKINSON	28	WHITWORTH, ELIAZA	53
	93,100,103,112,116	WHEAT, CYNTHIA	126	WILBOURN, ELMER	106
	122,131,138,149	. ELIZABETH TERRY	18	WILBURN, BENJAMIN F.	95
. JOHN	140	. LOU	51	. DEEK ASHBY	69
. MARY	57	. LUCY ANN	140	. EMMA WINTERS	58
. MARY RANDOLPH	90	. MATHAME	131	. JAMES	87
. NANNIE	136	. MOTT	140	. JOSEPH RICHARD	58
. NANNY OLSBY	59	. NATHANIEL	18	. MAMIE TURNER	95
. SALLIE WATERS	129	. SARAH MERSHALL	131	. SARAH	58
WESLY, RITTA	57	. THANUSE	126	. WASHINGTON	69
WEST, ELLEN LANDERS	37	WHEELER,		. WILLIE	90
. FANNY SANDERS	20	. FANNIE BLACKWELL	114	WILES, BEATRICE	118
. JAMES L.	37	. MARY E.	153	. DELLA	83
. JANE	130	. SILAS	114	. ELIZABETH	83,118-119
. JOSAPHINE ALLISON	22	WHITAKER, M.J.	10	WILEY, CAREY M.	142
. MAGGIE A. FORD	64	WHITE, ANN SMALL	50	. FRANKY	143
. MARY J. McCLOUD	19	. BELL	52	. HENDISON	70
. MOLLIE	5	. ELLA McGEORGE	104	. JOHN G.	74
. RICHARD G.	19	. J.P.	135	. MARTHA SHELBY	74
. RUFUS	33	. JAMES D.	104	WILKERSON,	
. RUFUS B.	20	. JO	14	. AZALEE ALLEN	67
. RUTH B.	153	. KITTEY	11	. DAVID	126
. SARAH	74	. NATHANIEL	50	. EMMA WOODS	19
. WILLIAM C.	22	WHITEHEAD, ADA BOYER	100	. JERRY	19
. WILLIAM H.	64	. SUSSANA	137	. JOHN	67
WESTERMAN,		. WILLIAM	100	. MARY BROWN	126
. AGNES ROYERS	79	WHITELOW, JEFF	128	WILLENBRINK, HY	2
. CHARLES	79	KATIE AUGDEN	128	WILLET, SUSAN J.	11
. ELLA	44	WHITESTORE, CELINDA	93	WILLETT, EDDIE NEAL	149

INDEX
(New Madrid, Co., MO. Marriages Vol #2)

J.A.P.	149	. J.W.	80	. SUSIE LYONS	101
WILLIAMLS,		. JAMES	24,47	. T.W.	9
. FRANCIS BROWN	15	. JAMES A.	22	. THODIUS	148
. WINFIELD S.	15	. JAMES C.	25	. THOMAS	22
WILLIAMS,ALLEN	9	. JAMES E.	11	. THOMAS B.	101
. ALLEY	140	. JAMES M.	149	WILLIS,ARLEE	37
. ALLIE ROBINSON	80	. JIM	89	. ARLIE MOTT	119
. AMANDA DUNKLIN	49	. JOHN	101,143,152	. BELL CHANNY	100
. AMERICA	17	. JOHN J.	80	. CERERO	37
. ANDREW J.	19	. KING	103	. ELI SAMUEL	119
. ANGELINE WILSON	71	. LACKEY J. BARKER	19	. ELIZABETH	12
. BELL CHANEY	84	. LADUSKY KILGON	118	. GEORGE	106
. BEN	85	. LAURA	100	. GEORGIA	77
. BENJAMIN	49	. LAURA CURR	103	. HENRY	100
. BETTIE	28	. LAURA HAMPTON	101	. JOHN H.	8
. BILL	22,24	. LENA JONES	148	. JOSEPHINE LEMONS	11
. C.	82	. LILY	8	. LAURA	16
. C.L.	37	. LOU NASH	47	. MADARY	81
. CAROLINE WAYDE	13	. LULA BELL LAFONT	72	. MAMIE	103
. CLARRISSA	28	. LULA JOHNSON	152	. MARY J. BELCHER	8
. DON	84	. MAGGIE J. CARROL	34	. MARY JANE MYERS	6
. DRURY	143	. MAGGIE J. CARROLL	35	. MATTIE	140
. ED J.	118	. MANUEL	13-14,72	. PAMELA	53
. ELIZA	38	. MARTHA J.	3	. S.T.	103
. ELIZABETH	32	. MARY	125	. SALLIE	142
. ELIZABETH RAGLON	143	. MARY A. JONES	107	. SARAH E.	92
. ELLA	127	. MARY L. OLNEY	11	. SUSAN ROGERS	99
. ELLEN	143	. MARY SHERKEY	85	. TANNER	103
. ELMINA CULBERTSON	22	. MATTIE	33,36,78	. TEXANA	34
. EMILY BRADSHAW	44-45	. MATTIE HAMILTON	22,24	. TEXANNA	119
. FANNIE JACKSON	149	. MILKEY STONEBRACKER	25	. V.J.	73,76
. FERMAN	107	. N.	88	. W.C.	77
. FRED	71	. NAPOLEON	54	. WESLEY A.	99
. G.W.	15	. NELLIE PETTY	89	. WILLIAM A.	6,8,11
. GEORGE W.	44-45	. OLLY B.	80	WILLOUGHBY,DIXEY	134
. HATTY BRISTOL	80	. REBECCA CUNNINGHAM	9	WILLSON,GEORGE W.	32
. HENRY	34-35	. SALLIE SETTLES	88	SARAH E. LANE	32
. HESTER ROSS	24	. SARAH BLAIR	54	WILSON,A.G.	137

INDEX
(New Madrid, Co., MO. Marriages Vol #2)

. A.J.	94,107,111	. MOLLIE	98	WOODS,ANIE	105		
.	130-133,135-136,139	. MOLLY HAYES	41	. ANNA	77		
.	140,146,150	. W.L.	73	. BETTIE BEVINS	5		
. ALBERT	119,148	WINBRY,A.J.	36	. CINDY	85		
. AMANDA LEEKE	64	WINCHESTER,ALBERT	142	. EMMA	19		
. ANGELINE	71	. AMELIA	74	. ESTHER	25		
. CHARLES	53,80	. CORDELIA CONSTANT	142	. JEFFERSON	5		
. CINDA ROBINSON	80	. PAMELA	50	. LULA	110		
. CORNELIA	47	WINDER,JAMES	39,121	. MARTHA	40,68,112		
. DORA	31	WINDERS,FRANCIS FOX	152	. MARY	59		
. ELIZABETH WILLIS	12	. JAMES	30-31,36,40	. MELISSA SMITH	135		
. ELLA CONLEY	55	.	45-46,49,51,54,62,65	. NAT	40		
. FRANK	109	.	131,151-152	. NETTIE WAIDE	128		
. GEORGE	64	WINTERS,EMMA	58	. PENN	77		
. HARRIET	109	WINTZ,ANNA J. IRVIN	91	. THOMAS	46,85,135		
. HARRIET WILSON	109	. SARAH	55	. TISHY CHERRY	46		
. HENRY P.	55	. WILLIAM	91	. TONY	128		
. HESTER GOINS	53	WISE,LUCILLE	70	. VINA	99		
. JASPAR	118	WISEMAN,ALICE	68	WORKMAN,CYNTHIA	55		
. JENNIE	81	. F.B.	78	. CYNTHIA WORKMAN	55		
. JOHN A.	148	. LAFAYETTE	132	. EMMA	88		
. JOHN W.	28	. STELLA STLIGER	78	. J.A.	33,36,112,137		
. JORDAN	55	. SUSIE STEWARD	132	. JAMES	60,66		
. LAURA RHODES	55	WITHERSPOON,JANE	138	. JAMES A.	23,48,62,64		
. MARY J. WALKER	28	WITT,MARY	45	.	76,78,80,92		
. MARY LYNCH	118	WITTER,MAGGIE	69	. JOHN	55		
. MATTY KENWORTHY	148	WLLIS,W.W.	88	. JOHN H.	56		
. ROBERT	47	WOOD,BETTIE ALSUP	122	WORLEY,CAROLINE	29		
. SARAH	7	. IDA	16	WORSHAM,JAMES V.	15		
. SARAH ANN MILLER	119	. IDA M. WHITSON	132	MARY KOCHTITZKY	15		
. WILLIAM	12,23	. JOSEPH	3	WORTH,DEBY E. STRONG	52		
WIMP,ALPHONSE	38	. MARTHA BENNETT	55	. FRANK	99		
. ARCHY	90	. MARY JANE	64	. JEROME	52		
. GEORGIA	40	. MATT	25	. LIZZIE ADCOCK	111		
. JERRY BAINES	38	. MOTT	25	. MAGGIE RICHARDSON	99		
. JOSEPH	41	. NATT	55	. MORGAN	111		
. MARY DOSS	90	. WILLIAM	132	WORTHAM,J.A.	111		
. MAY	136	. WILLIAM A.	122	WRAY,GEORGE W.	47		

INDEX
(New Madrid, Co., MO. Marriages Vol #2)

. SARAH E. CHOAT	47	. ELLA M.	29	. MATILDA	102
WREN,J.D.	107	. JOHN M.	20	. MAY	135
WRIGHT,AMANDY	149	. MALBERRY DILLARD	20	. NATHAN	132
. B.F.	32	. MARY KING	44	. NATTIE	123
. BENJAMIN F.	22	. NALLIE MINER	1	. PATSEY	99
. CORA GROVES	46	. SAMUEL	29,44	. PLES	45
. EDWARD A.	46	YELLEMAN,APELLES C.	51	. SARAH	75
. EMMA SUMMERS	93	MARY E. SIMMON	51	. SARAH CARSON	46
. JACOB	1-2	YORK,J.L.	25	. VERRY	35
. JENNETT LANDERS	52	. JOHN L.	28	. YOUNG	5
. MARY	12	. MARGARET CANOY	21		
. MARY E. SIMMS	1	. WILLIAM T.	21		
. MARY S.Q. COMBS	2	YORK.J.L.	21		
. NANNIE LAZELL	22	YOUEM,J.F.	110		
. ROBERT	93	YOUNG,ADA	109		
. SARAH TOMPKINS	10	. ALBERT	53		
. THOMAS G.	10	. AMANDA WATSON	66		
. WILLIAM A.	52	. CLARA TONEY	129		
WYATT,A.C.	48	. ELLEN	73		
. E.Z.	70	. EMELINE	146		
. JAMES	71	. EMELINE WALKER	53		
. LUCILLE WISE	70	. FRED	129,135		
. MARY PARKER	31	. IDA MARY	123		
. MINNIE STUBBLEFIELD	71	. JAMES	46,73		
. SALLIE	14	. JOHN	5,7,15-16,19,21		
. SARAH O.	55	.	34,41-43,52,58-59,62		
. WILLIAM	31	.	68,73,81-82,86,89,91		
WYNE,FANNIE	20	.	93,95,97,105,108,110		
WYNN,DORA MICHELL	7	.	112-113,120,123-124		
. J.A.	49,60,64	.	130,150		
. JACOB	7	. LAURA	91		
. JACOB A.	15	. LAURA LONG	73		
. MARY CHANDLER	15	. LING	66		
WYNNE,MAY R. HOWARD	30	. LOUISA	9		
ROBERT W.	30	. LULA BOWENS	45		
YARBER,KATY	51	. LULA BROWN	132		
YARBROUGH,WESLEY	26	. MAGGIE	145		
YATES,ALFRED	1	. MARY	129		

www.ingramcontent.com/pod-product-compliance
Lightning Source LLC
LaVergne TN
LVHW091542060526
838200LV00036B/677